Pier Groups

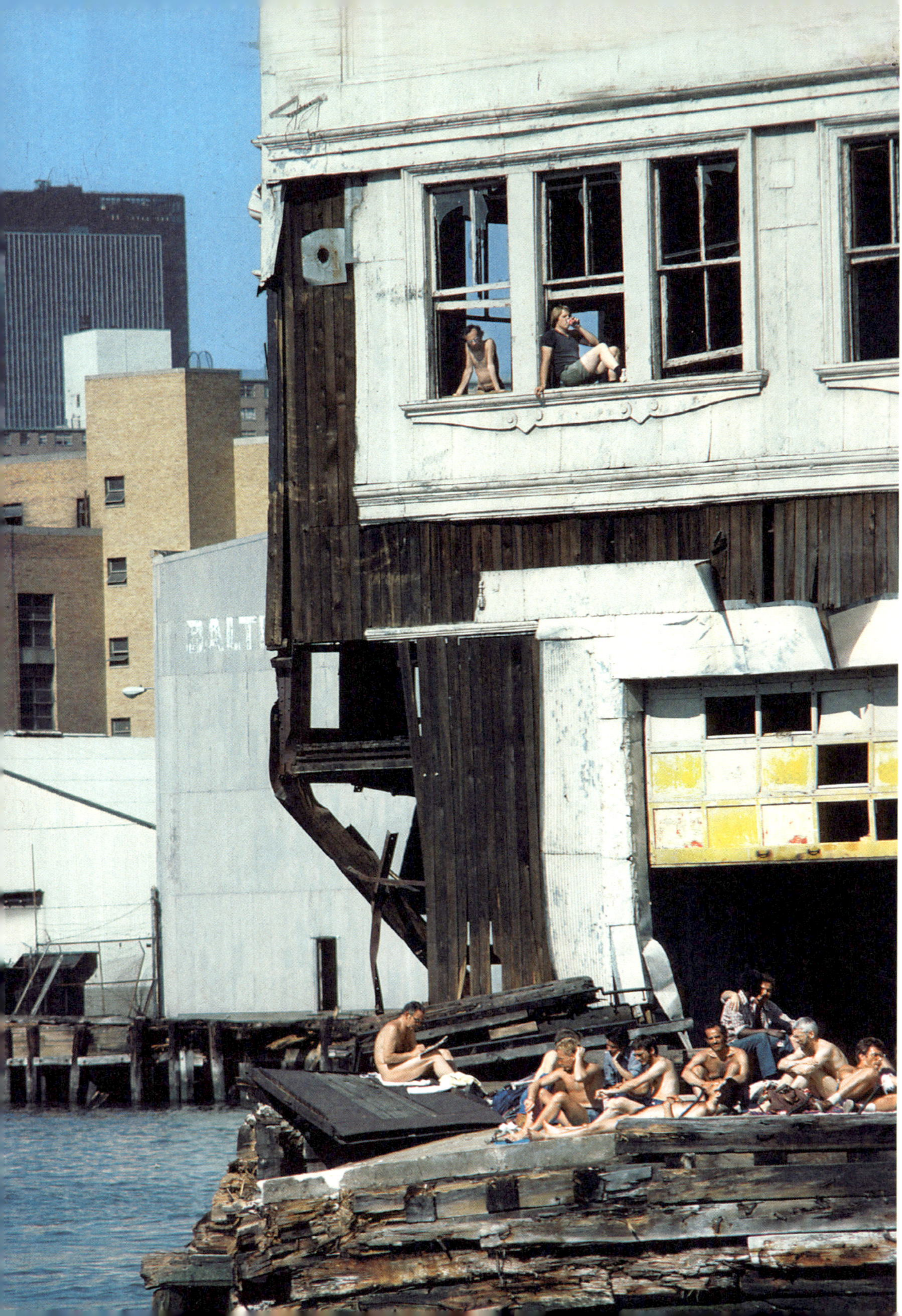

Pier Groups

Art and Sex Along the New York Waterfront

Jonathan Weinberg

The Pennsylvania State University Press

University Park, Pennsylvania

This book was published with the assistance of the Frederick W. Hilles Publication Fund of Yale University and the Yale Fund for Lesbian and Gay Studies.

Additional Credits

Fig. 1 (p. ii): Shelley Seccombe, *Sunbathers, Pier 51, Vertical, with Onlookers Above*, 1977, © Shelley Seccombe; fig. 2 (pp. vi–vii): Frank Hallam, *En Masse, Sunners Seen from Pier 45*, 1982, private collection; figs. 3, 4 (pp. viii, x): *N.Y. City's Waterfront*, 1947, full image and detail, Lionel Pincus and Princess Firyal Map Division, The New York Public Library. Photo from The New York Public Library, https://digitalcollections.nypl.org.

Library of Congress Cataloging-in-Publication Data

Names: Weinberg, Jonathan, 1957– author.
Title: Pier groups : art and sex along the New York waterfront / Jonathan Weinberg.
Description: University Park, Pennsylvania : The Pennsylvania State University Press, [2019] | Includes bibliographical references and index.
Summary: "Explores the uses of the abandoned Hudson River docks in New York City by artists and a newly emerging gay subculture between 1971 and 1983"—Provided by publisher.
Identifiers: LCCN 2018035900 | ISBN 9780271082172 (cloth : alk. paper)
Subjects: LCSH: Art, American—New York (State)—New York—20th century. | Waterfronts—Social aspects—New York (State)—New York—History—20th century. | Artists—New York (State)—New York—Social conditions—20th century. | Gay culture—New York (State)—New York—History—20th century. | Homosexuality and art—New York (State)—New York—History—20th century.
Classification: LCC N6535.N5 W45 2019 | DDC 709.73/0904—dc23
LC record available at https://lccn.loc.gov/2018035900

Printed in Slovenia
Published by The Pennsylvania State University Press,
University Park, PA 16802–1003

The Pennsylvania State University Press is a member of the Association of University Presses.

It is the policy of The Pennsylvania State University Press to use acid-free paper. Publications on uncoated stock satisfy the minimum requirements of American National Standard for Information Sciences—Permanence of Paper for Printed Library Material, ANSI Z39.48–1992.

For Nick

The ruin is not in front of us; it is neither a spectacle nor a love object.

It is experience itself.

—Jacques Derrida, *Memoirs of the Blind*

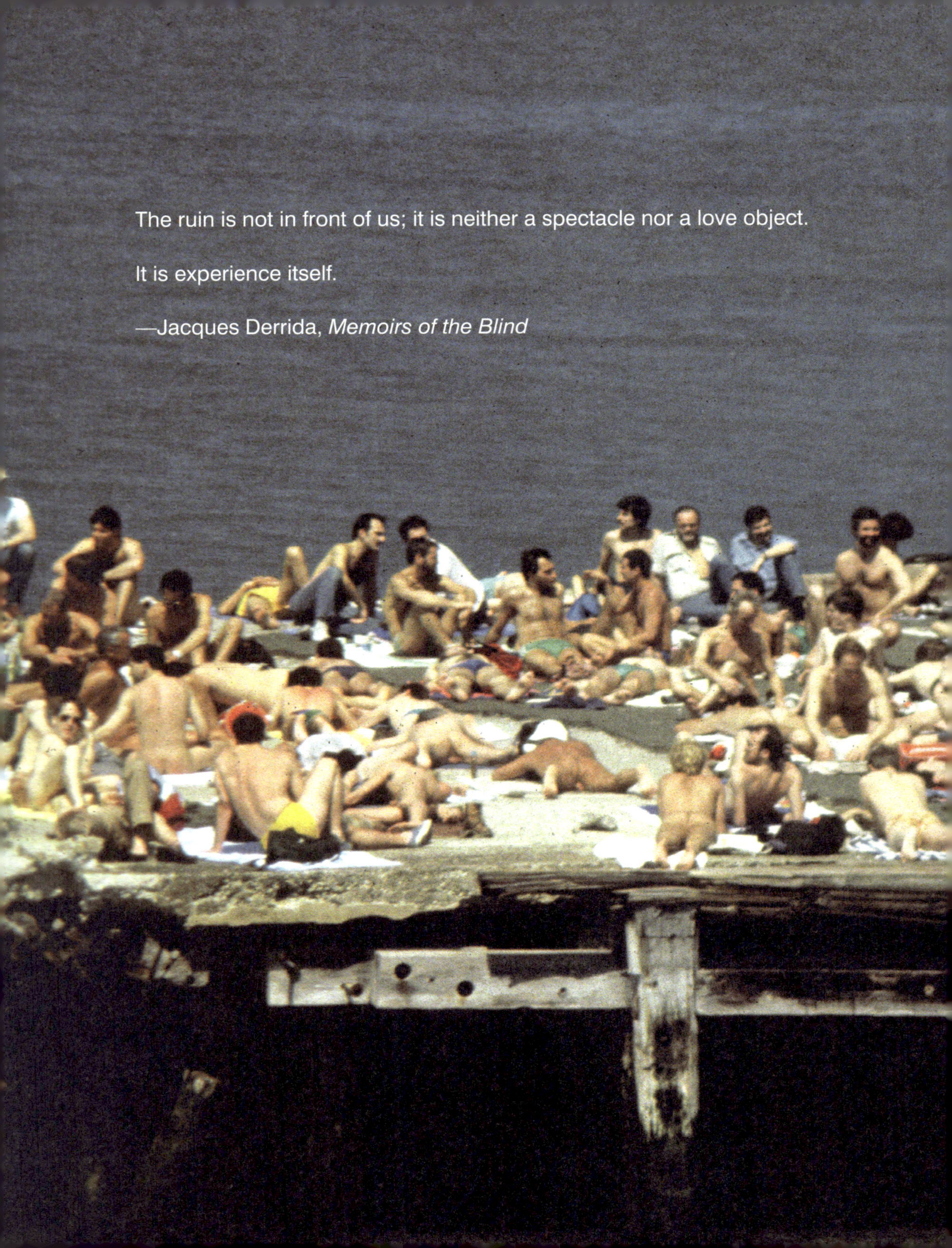

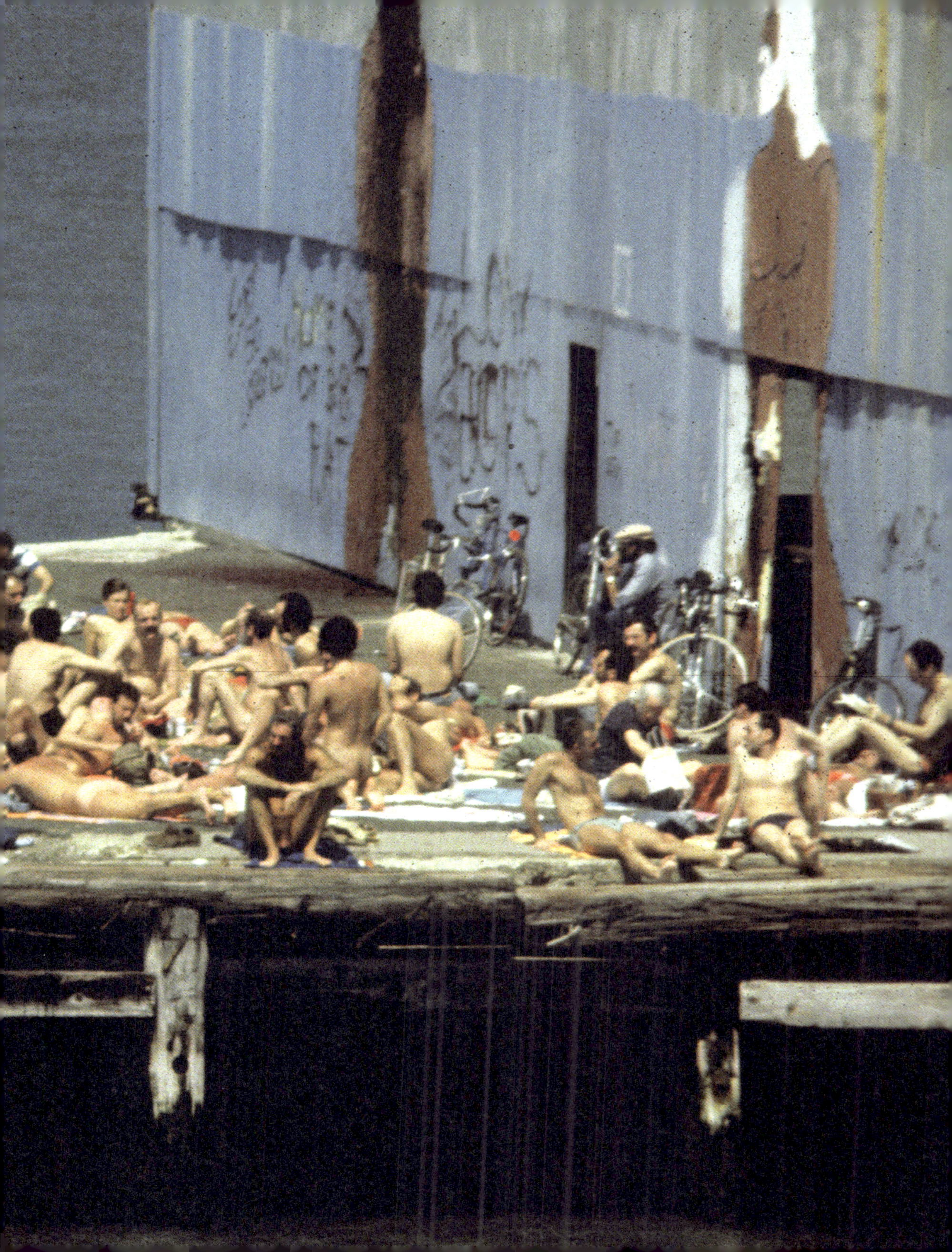

N. Y. City's WATERFRONT

NEW JERSEY

WEST NEW YORK

Pier	Company	Location
	HARBOR TANK STORAGE CO.	Ferry Rd.
2.1	N.Y., ONTARIO & WESTERN RY.	67th-66th Sts.
16	JAGELS FUEL CORP.	65th St.
13.12.11A.11.9.7-5	N.Y.C.R.R.	64th-51st Sts.

WEEHAWKEN

Pier	Company	Location
4.2.1.K	N.Y.C.R.R.	51st St.-Highwood Ter.
	SHAMROCK TOWING CO.	Baldwin Ave.
	CLEARY BROS.	Baldwin Ave.
A-G.F.H	ERIE R.R.	Shippen-19th Sts.
	TODD SHIPYARDS CORP.	19th-17th Sts.

HOBOKEN

Pier	Company	Location
	TODD SHIPYARDS CORP.	17th-15th Sts.
16	LAMPORT & HOLT LINE	15th St.
15.14.4-1	BETHLEHEM STEEL CO.	15th-12th Sts.
	GENERAL FOODS CORP.	12th St.
S-P	PENNSYLVANIA R.R.	10th-8th Sts.
	EAST ASIATIC CO.	8th St.
	YARKA CORP.	6th St.
	HOLLAND-AMERICA LINES	5th-4th Sts.
	MARRA BROS.	3d St.
	JAMES HEALING CO.	2d St.
1.2	LACKAWANNA R.R.	Ferry St.

JERSEY CITY

Pier	Company	Location
3-10	LACKAWANNA R.R.	18th-12th Sts.
9	AMERICAN PRESIDENT LINES	11th St.
9.8	ERIE R.R.	11th St.
4	RAILWAY EXPRESS AGENCY	Pavonia Ave.
2.1	ERIE R.R.	8th St.
M	BERWIND WHITE COAL MINING CO.	6th St.
L-J.H	PENNSYLVANIA R.R.	4th-Bay Sts.
F.D.C	AMERICAN EXPORT LINES	Bay St.-Exchange Pl.
B	MOORE-McCORMACK LINES	Grand St.
A	COLGATE-PALMOLIVE-PEET CO.	Sussex St.
	PENNSYLVANIA R.R.	Morris St.
	INTERNATIONAL ELEVATING CO.	Morris St.
	INTERNATIONAL ELEVATING CO.	Essex St.
	OPEN WHARFAGE	Essex St.
B-E.G-I.L	LEHIGH VALLEY R.R.	Johnston Ave.
5-7.10-16.18.19	C.R.R. OF N.J.	Communipaw
7-4	LEHIGH VALLEY R.R.	Black Tom
	U. S. ARMY	Caven Point
	LEHIGH VALLEY R.R.	Claremont Terminal
B-D	PENNSYLVANIA R.R.	Greenville Terminal

BAYONNE

Pier	Company	Location
	U. S. NAVY	Bayonne Terminal
7-4.6	STANDARD OIL OF N.J.	Constable Hook
	ASIATIC OIL CO.	Constable Hook
	CONSTABLE HOOK SHIPYARDS	Constable Hook
	STAUFFER CHEMICAL CO.	Constable Hook
3-1	STANDARD OIL OF N.J.	Constable Hook

STATEN ISLAND

Pier	Company	Location
2.8.6.4	BALTIMORE & OHIO R.R.	St. George
	U.S. COAST GUARD	Borough Pl., St. George
1.2	ROBIN LINE	Tompkinsville
3	SOTTNEK TERMINAL CORP.	Tompkinsville
4.5	ISTHMIAN S.S. LINES	Tompkinsville
6	CITY OF NEW YORK	Tompkinsville
7	BRISTOL CITY LINE	Tompkinsville
8	OPEN WHARFAGE	Stapleton
9	ISTHMIAN S.S. LINES	Stapleton
10	AMERICAN PRESIDENT LINES	Stapleton
11-14	N.Y. PORT OF EMBARKATION	Stapleton
15.16	N.Y. FOREIGN TRADE ZONE	Stapleton
17	UNITED STATES LINES	Stapleton
18	U.S. COAST GUARD	Stapleton
19	BANK LINE	Clifton
20	AMERICAN EXPORT LINES	Clifton
21	BOOTH AMERICAN SHIPPING CORP.	Clifton
22	MERRITT CHAPMAN & SCOTT CORP.	Rosebank
	RICHMOND ICE CO.	Rosebank
23	L.A. DREYFUS CO.	Rosebank
24.25	O'BRIEN BROS.	Rosebank

MANHATTAN

NORTH RIVER

Pier	Company	Location
A	DEPT. OF MARINE & AVIATION	Battery Pl.
1	OPEN WHARFAGE	Battery Pl.
2.3.7	UNITED FRUIT CO.	Battery Pl.-Morris St.
8	LEHIGH VALLEY R.R.	Rector St.
9	UNITED FRUIT CO.	Carlisle St.
10.11	CENTRAL R.R. OF N.J.	Albany-Cedar Sts.
11	COLONIAL NAVIGATION CO.	Cedar St.
13	LACKAWANNA R.R.	Dey St.
14.15	AMER. HAWAIIAN S.S. CO.	Fulton-Vesey Sts.
16.17	N.Y.C.R.R.	Barclay St.-Park Pl.
18	EASTERN S.S. LINES	Murray St.
19-21	ERIE R.R.	Warren-Duane Sts.
22.23	BALT. & OHIO R.R.	Harrison-Franklin Sts.
23	INTERNATIONAL FORWARDING CO.	Franklin St.
25	BALTIMORE & OHIO R.R.	N. Moore St.
25	OLD DOMINION LINE	N. Moore St.
25	EASTERN S.S. LINES	N. Moore St.
26	U. S. NAVY	Beach St.
27-30	PENNSYLVANIA R.R.	Hubert-Desbrosses Sts.
32	MOORE-McCORMACK LINES	Canal St.
34.36	N.Y. & CUBA MAIL S.S. CO.	Canal St.
37	BELGIAN LINE	Canal St.
38	LEHIGH VALLEY R.R.	King St.
38	INTERNATIONAL FORWARDING CO.	King St.
39	BALTIMORE & OHIO R.R.	Houston St.
40	PENNSYLVANIA R.R.	Clarkson St.
40	NATIONAL CARLOADING CORP.	Clarkson St.
41	LACKAWANNA R.R.	LeRoy St.
41	ACME FAST FREIGHT CO.	LeRoy St.
42	TEXAS LINE	Morton St.
43	OPEN WHARFAGE	Barrow St.
45	ALCOA STEAMSHIP CO.	10th St.
46	MOORE-McCORMACK LINES	Charles St.
48	ERIE R.R.	11th St.
48	NATIONAL CARLOADING CORP.	11th St.
49.50	PENNSYLVANIA R.R.	Bank-Bethune Sts.
51	STATES MARINE CORP.	Jane St.
52	PENNSYLVANIA R.R.	Horatio St.
52	NATIONAL CARLOADING CORP.	Horatio St.
53	GARCIA & DIAZ	Little West 12th St.
54.56	CUNARD WHITE STAR LINE	13th-14th Sts.
57.58	GRACE LINE	15th-16th Sts.
59-62	UNITED STATES LINES	18th-22d Sts.
64	PANAMA LINE	24th St.
65	GRACE LINE	25th St.
66	LEHIGH VALLEY R.R.	26th St.
66	ACME FAST FREIGHT	26th St.
67	ERIE R.R.	27th St.
67	NATIONAL CARLOADING CORP.	27th St.
68	LACKAWANNA R.R.	28th St.
68	ACME FAST FREIGHT	28th St.
72	OPEN WHARFAGE	32d St.
73.74	UNITED STATES LINES	33d-34th Sts.
75.76	OPEN WHARFAGE	35th-36th Sts.
77	PENNSYLVANIA R.R.	37th St.
77	ACME FAST FREIGHT	37th St.
78	PENNSYLVANIA R.R.	38th St.
80	OPEN WHARFAGE	40th St.
81	HUDSON RIVER DAY LINE	41st St.
83	OPEN WHARFAGE	43d St.
84	AMERICAN EXPORT LINES	44th St.
86	FURNESS, WITHY & CO.	46th St.
88	FRENCH LINE	48th St.
90	CUNARD WHITE STAR LINE	50th St.
92	PORTO RICO LINE	52d St.

CONTINUED IN COLUMN ON RIGHT

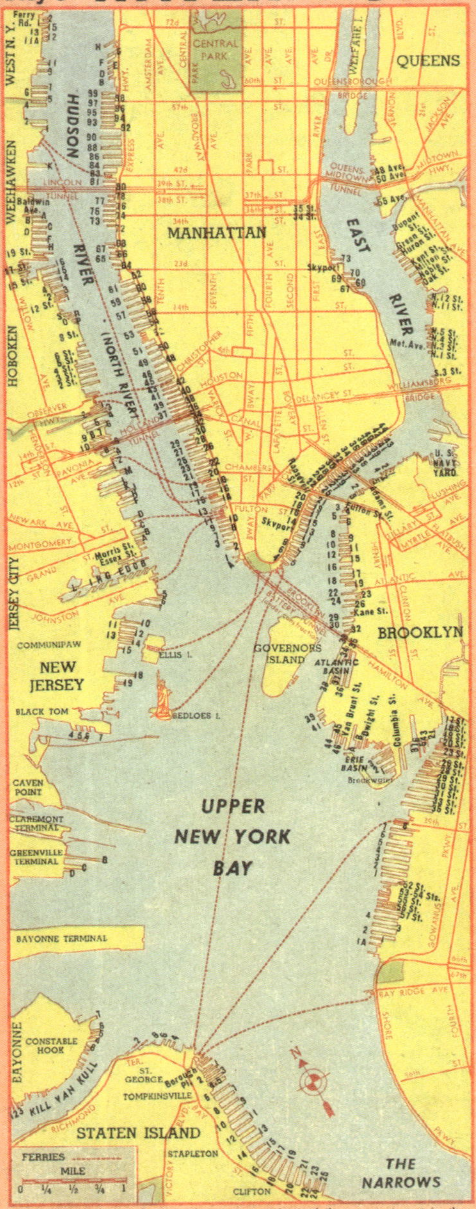

THIS MAP, covering the most important sections of the greatest port in the world, is the result of weeks of research, undertaken at the request of many readers. It is as up-to-date and authoritative as possible in view of frequent changes. Manhattan piers are listed from south to north; others north to south.

Pier	Company	Location
93.94	OPEN WHARFAGE	53d-54th Sts.
95	FURNESS-BERMUDA LINE	55th St.
96	FURNESS-RED CROSS LINE	56th St.
97	FURNESS, WITHY & CO.	57th St.
97	SWEDISH AMERICAN LINE	57th St.
98	OPEN WHARFAGE	58th St.
99	DEPT. OF SANITATION	59th St.
B.D-H	N.Y.C.R.R.	60th St. Station

MANHATTAN

EAST RIVER

Pier	Company	Location
4	METROPOLITAN VOCATIONAL H.S.	Broad St.
5	OPEN WHARFAGE	Coenties Slip
6	NEPTUNE SHIPPING	Coenties Slip
7	ERIE R.R.	Coenties Slip
8	NEPTUNE SHIPPING	Cuylers Alley
9	U.S. COAST GUARD	Old Slip
11	OPEN WHARFAGE	Gouverneur Lane
	DOWNTOWN SKYPORT	Wall St.
13	STEVENSON LINE	Wall St.
14	ISBRANDTSEN CO.	Depeyster St.
15	ISBRANDTSEN CO.	Fletcher St.
16	STOCKARD & CO.	John St.
17	FULTON MARKET FISH ASSN.	Fulton St.
18	N.Y. FISH DEALERS ASSN.	Beekman St.
19	FLOMARCY CO.	Peck Slip
20	NORTH ATLANTIC & GULF S.S. CO.	Peck Slip
21	BALTIMORE & OHIO R.R.	Dover St.
21	CARLOADER CORP.	Dover St.
21	PENNSYLVANIA R.R.	Dover St.
21	CENTRAL STATES FREIGHT SERVICE	Dover St.
	DEPT. OF SANITATION	Roosevelt St.
22	QUEBEC PAPER SALES CO.	James St.
25	QUEBEC PAPER SALES CO.	Oliver St.
26	LACKAWANNA R.R.	Catherine Slip
27.28	J. W. ELWELL & CO.	Catherine-Market Slips
28	FABRE LINE	Market Slip
29	CENTRAL VERMONT TERMINAL	Market Slip
30	OPEN WHARFAGE	Market Slip
31	AQUA SHIPPING CO.	Pike Slip
32	G.M. STILL	Pike Slip
33	FERN LINE	Rutgers Slip
34	U.S. TRUCKING CORP.	Rutgers Slip
34	N.Y.C.R.R.	Rutgers Slip
35	N.Y.C.R.R.	Jefferson St.
36	OPEN WHARFAGE	Jefferson St.
37	ICELAND S.S. CO.	Clinton St.
38	OPEN WHARFAGE	Clinton St.
39	N.Y., N.H. & H.R.R.	Montgomery St.
40	OPEN WHARFAGE	Montgomery St.
41	OPEN WHARFAGE	Gouverneur St.
42	OPEN WHARFAGE	Gouverneur St.
43	O'BRIEN BROS.	Jackson St.
44	LEHIGH VALLEY R.R.	Jackson St.
67	OPEN WHARFAGE	19th St.
68	U.S. TRUCKING CORP.	20th St.
69	OPEN WHARFAGE	21st St.
70	DEPT. OF SANITATION	22d St.
	MIDTOWN SKYPORT	23d St.
73	FLOMARCY CO.	25th St.
	LEHIGH VALLEY R.R.	34th St.
	CONSOLIDATED EDISON CO.	35th St.

QUEENS

Pier	Company	Location
	LONG ISLAND R.R.	48th-50th Aves.
	NATIONAL SUGAR REFINING CO.	55th Ave.

BROOKLYN

Pier	Company	Location
	OPEN WHARFAGE	Dupont St.
	LUMBER EXCHANGE TERMINAL CO.	Green St.
	SEALAND DOCK & TERM. CORP.	Huron-Kent Sts.
	CARTER & WEEKES ST'V'G CO.	Milton St.
	CITY OF NEW YORK	Noble St.
	CARTER & WEEKES ST'V'G CO.	Oak St.
	SOCONY-VACUUM OIL CO.	N.12th-11th Sts.
	BROOKLYN EAST. DIST. TERM.	N.11th-5th Sts.
	PENNSYLVANIA R.R.	N.4th St.
	BROOKLYN EASTERN DIST. TERM.	N.4th St.
	AUSTIN, NICHOLS & CO.	N.3d St.
	CITY OF NEW YORK	Metropolitan Ave.
	CHAS. PFIZER & CO.	N.1st St.
	AMERICAN SUGAR REFINING CO.	S.3d St.
1.2	JAY ST. CONNECTING R.R.	Bridge St.
3-5	FAMOUS REALTY INC.	Jay-Pearl Sts.
	SINRAM BROS. COAL CO.	Adams St.
2.3	FAMOUS REALTY INC.	Main St.
	CITY OF NEW YORK	Fulton St.
3	ARUNDEL CORPORATION	Fulton St.
4	ARTHUR TICKLE ENGIN. WORKS	Doughty St.
5	UNIVERSAL TERM. & ST'V'G CO.	Middagh St.
6	BARBER S.S. LINES	Cranberry St.
8.9	ARGENTINE STATE LINE	Orange-Clark Sts.
10-12	ROYAL NETH'L'DS S.S. CO.	Clark-Montague Sts.
15.16	MOORE-McCOR'K LINES	Montague-Remsen Sts.
17	ISTHMIAN S.S. LINES	Joralemon St.
18.19	AMER. SO. AFRICAN LINES	Joralemon-State Sts.
22.23	BULL INSULAR LINE	Atlantic Ave.-Pacific St.
24	SCANDINAVIAN-AMERICAN LINE	Amity St.
26	PORT LINE	Warren St.
	N.Y. DOCK CO. RY.	Kane St.
29.30.32	SOTTNEK TERM. CORP.	Kane-DeGraw Sts.
33	BOOTH AMERICAN SHIPPING CORP.	Hamilton Ave.
34	COSMOPOLITAN SHIPPING CO.	Hamilton Ave.
35	KERR S.S. CO.	Hamilton Ave.
36-38	BARBER S.S. LINES	Pioneer St.
39	AMERICAN EXPORT LINES	Coffey St.
41	N.Y. DOCK CO.	Ferris St.
44.45	ATLANTIC BASIN IRON WORKS	Conover St.
46	WEST COAST LINE	Van Brunt St.
	BEARD'S ERIE BASIN WAREHOUSE	Van Brunt St.
A.B	BANK LINE	Richards St.
	TODD SHIPYARDS CORP.	Dwight-Columbia Sts.
3	ROBIN LINE	Columbia St.
2	INTERNATIONAL FREIGHTING CORP.	Columbia St.
2	DE LA RAMA S.S. CO.	Columbia St.
1	CHILEAN LINE	Columbia St.
	TODD SHIPYARDS CORP.	Columbia St.
	FERN LINE	Columbia St.
	ISTHMIAN S.S. LINES	Columbia St.
8-3	IRA S. BUSHEY & SONS	Clinton-Court Sts.
2.1	MARRA BROS.	Court St.
	HINZMANN & WALDMANN	17th St.
	ARTHUR TICKLE ENGIN. WORKS	18th-19th Sts.
	BROOKLYN WATERFRONT TERM. CORP.	20th St.
	SULLIVAN DRY DOCK & REPR. CORP.	23d St.
	LACKAWANNA R.R.	26th St.
	BETHLEHEM STEEL CO.	26th-28th Sts.
	ISTHMIAN S.S. LINES	29th St.
	LLOYD BRASILEIRO	30th St.
	MOORE-McCORMACK LINES	31st St.
	AMER. SO. AFRICAN LINES	33d St.
	LUCKENBACH LINES	35th St.
8	AMERICAN STEVEDORES INC.	39th St.
7	LLOYD BRASILEIRO	41st St.
6	WATERMAN S.S. CORP.	42d St.
5	UNITED PORT SERVICE CO.	44th St.
4	PRINCE LINE	45th St.
3	JAVA-NEW YORK LINE	47th St.
2	UNITED PORT SERVICE CO.	49th St.
1	FUNCH, EDYE & CO.	50th St.
	DEPT. OF SANITATION	52d St.
	BOARD OF TRANSPORTATION	52d St.
	E.W. BLISS CO.	53d-54th Sts.
	KINGS COUNTY LIGHTING CO.	55th St.
	BETHLEHEM STEEL CO.	55th-56th Sts.
	KERR S.S. CO.	57th St.
4-1.1A	N.Y. PORT OF EMBARKATION	58th-64th St.

Contents

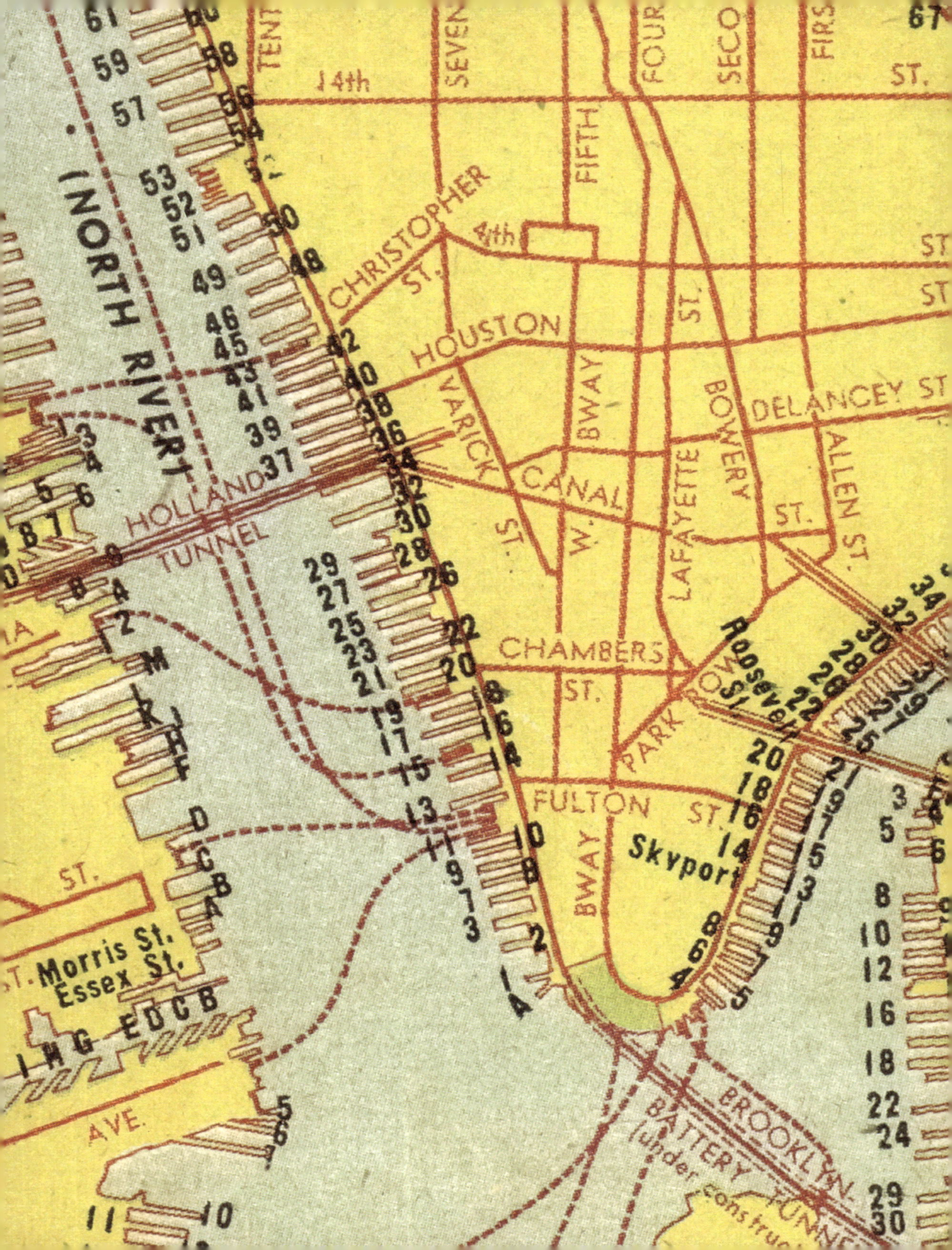

NORTH RIVER
HOLLAND TUNNEL
14th ST.
CHRISTOPHER ST.
4th ST.
FIFTH
HOUSTON
DELANCEY ST
VARICK ST.
CANAL ST.
W. BWAY
BWAY
LAFAYETTE ST.
BOWERY
ALLEN ST.
CHAMBERS ST.
PARK ROW
Roosevelt St.
FULTON ST.
Skyport
Morris St.
Essex St.
AVE.
ST.
BROOKLYN
BATTERY TUNNEL
(under construction)

Illustrations

Acknowledgments

Pier Groups represents the culmination of sixteen years of research, curating, and writing. So many friends and colleagues have helped along the way. I first conceived of this book during a yearlong artist-in-residence stay at the Getty Research Institute in 2002–3. The lectures on the art of Gordon Matta-Clark by Thomas Crow, who was the Institute's director at the time, provided the initial inspiration for the book. I feel so privileged to count Tom and his wife, Catherine Phillips, among my closest friends and counselors. During my residency, Matthew Reynolds was my research assistant, and his hard work helped lay the foundation for this project.

Since 2003 I have been fortunate to have my scholarship supported by fellowships at the Clark Art Institute and the Vera List Center for Arts and Politics at the New School. I have also been the recipient of the J. Clawson Mills Art History Fellowship at the Metropolitan Museum of Art, a John Simon Guggenheim Foundation Fellowship, and a Creative Capital/Andy Warhol Foundation Arts Writers Grant. The publication of this book has been generously supported by the two schools where I teach: through the Professional Development Fund at the Rhode Island School of Design and the Yale Fund for Lesbian and Gay Studies (FLAGS), LGBT Studies, at Yale University, and the Frederick W. Hilles Publication Fund, also at Yale.

In 2012, with the assistance of Darren Jones, I curated an exhibition titled *The Piers: Art and Sex Along the New York Waterfront* at the Leslie-Lohman Museum of Gay and Lesbian Art. Four years later, I curated an exhibition at the Hunter College Art Galleries that focused on Pier 34. These exhibitions were instrumental to the conceptualization of this book, and I want to single out Rob Rosen and the wonderful staff and board of Leslie-Lohman, and Tim Laun, Joachim Pissarro, Howard Singerman, Sarah Watson, and Annie Wischmeyer at Hunter College for all their help and suggestions.

Many archives, museums, and galleries have generously opened their collections to me, including Galerie Buchholz, the Hal Bromm Gallery, the Metro Pictures Gallery, the New York City Municipal Archives, the New-York Historical Society, the New York Public Library, the Peter Hujar Archive, the P.P.O.W. Gallery, and the David Zwirner Gallery. I want particularly to acknowledge the assistance of Marvin Taylor, director of the Fales Library, and Rich Wandel at the LGBT Community Center National History Archive. I want also to thank Leonard Fink's family and David Wojnarowicz's partner, Tom Rauffenbart.

One of the great pleasures of working on this book was the chance it has given me to get to know so many wonderful artists. I want to thank Robert Whitman for answering all my questions about his work with generosity and patience. I could not have completed the chapter on Pier 34, or truly understood that pier's impact, without the help of so many of the Pier 34 artists, and in particular the friendship of Andreas Sterzing, whose magnificent pictures have kept the extraordinary Pier 34 moment alive. Thanks also to Jane Bauman, Mike Bidlo, Paolo Buggiani, Steven Doughton, John Fekner, David Finn, Jean Foos, Judy Glantzman, Kim Jones, Stephen Lack, Marisela La Grave, Liz-N-Val, Bill Mutter, Michael Ottersen, Rick Prol, Dirk Rowntree, Kiki Smith, Betty Tompkins, Peter White, Teres Wydler, Rhonda Zwillinger, and all the other artists in the book who shared their work and their memories.

Sadly, two of the artists whom I got to know through my pier work, Vito Acconci and Frank Hallam, did not live to see it completed. Although I met Vito only once, the long and fascinating interview he granted me was one of the high points of my career. I am also very grateful that I had the chance to get to know Frank Hallam and to work with him in printing some of his most memorable photographs. Although I never met Gordon Matta-Clark, I was privileged to be able to talk with his widow, Jane Crawford, and his collaborator, G. H. Hovagimyan. Lee Jaffe shared his memories of working with Vito Acconci and with the photographic team of Harry Shunk and János Kender (Shunk-Kender).

I am fortunate to have many smart friends and colleagues who were generous with advice, assistance, and information, including Anneliis Beadnell, Mel Bochner, Michelle Brunnick, Cynthia Carr, Anna Conlan, Geoffrey Hendricks, Michael Ann Holly, Jonathan David Katz, Stephen Koch, Marilyn Kushner, Evelyn Lincoln, Diana Linden, Joseph Lovett, Leora Maltz-Leca, Kobena Mercer, Keith Moxey, Molly Nesbit, Wendy Olsoff, Gwendolyn Owens, Leonard Perlson, Flavia Rando, James Romberger, Beatricia Sagar, James Saslow, Sabine Schlosser, Robert Sember, Sally Stein, Sur Rodney (Sur), Marguerite Van Cook, Laura Wexler, Ellie Winberg, Margaret Winslow, and Christopher Wood.

Tirza Latimer read through the manuscript and gave me crucial feedback, encouragement, and criticism. I am eternally grateful to Michelle Piso for her suggestions and her aid in editing the first draft. My research assistant and friend Tyler Fallas helped with proofreading and fact-checking. Suzanne Wolk's expert copyediting and editorial suggestions were invaluable. Above all, I cannot repay the debt of gratitude I owe to Christopher Reed, who acted as a second editor on this project. His advice and prodding made this a better book.

The day I met Ellie Goodman, executive editor at Penn State University Press, I felt I had found someone who truly understood what I was about. She has been a dream to work with, and so has the staff at the Press, including Regina Starace, Brian Beer, and Candace Hyatt.

Finally, there are the people in my extended family who have had to endure my obsession with New York's piers through all these years. They include my brother, Peter Weinberg, and my dear friends Davi Bernstein, Lynn Caponera, Theodore Craig, Joel Handorff, Michael Lobel, Barbara Buhler Lynes, Andrew Raftery, Ellen and Fred Schreiber, and Arthur Yorinks. Above all there is my husband and soul mate, Nicholas Boshnack, who has more than earned the dedication of this book.

Introduction

In a dazzling image in Jacques Derrida's *Memoirs of the Blind*, which provides the epigraph for this book, memory and ruins "open like an eye, or like the hole in a bone socket that lets you see without showing you anything *at all*, anything *of the all*."[1] Derrida's words bring to my mind Gordon Matta-Clark's *Day's End* (fig. 5), a site-specific installation composed of shapes cut into the walls and platforms of the abandoned warehouse of Pier 52 at Gansevoort and West Streets. Like an enormous cat's-eye at the end of the pier, the largest of the cutouts let the viewer look out at the sky. In those moments when the sun aligned with the cut, the spectator standing in the darkened pier building was blinded, as in Derrida's description. When the sun set, and the night sky filled the cutout, it offered a vision of the universe, that is, *the all*. Nevertheless, Matta-Clark's act of creative destruction *ruined* the ruin as a site of mere nostalgia, of romantic reveries of what once was. Day and night, this ruin renewed itself until it too fell into ruins. In *Memoirs of the Blind*, Derrida suggests that all experience is in a potential state of ruin and renewal. The present is already a ruin in our experience of it, as it turns into memory and the past.

I write about Matta-Clark's *Day's End* not from my own experience but from how I imagine it worked on the spectator. I am embarrassed to admit that I was not too young to have seen it. In the 1970s, I used to frequent the waterfront, sketching and cruising for sex, so I am sure that Matta-Clark's cutouts were in my view. But I was blind to *Day's End* as a work of art. So, too, were Frank Hallam, Shelley Seccombe, and Arch Brown, all of whom inadvertently

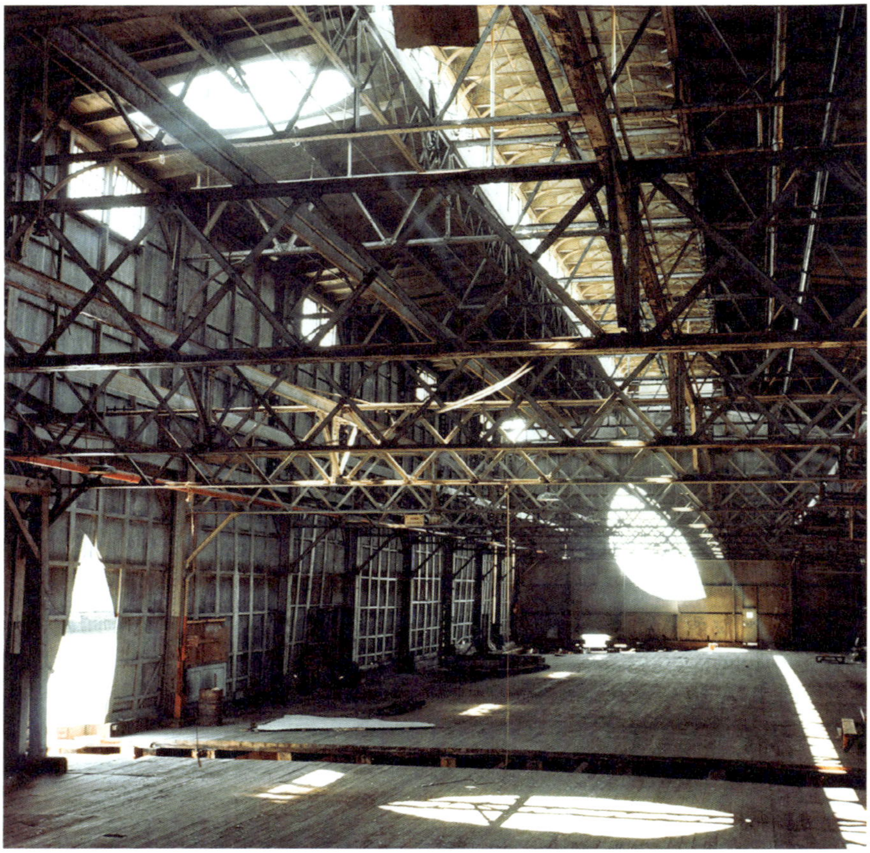

5. Gordon Matta-Clark, *Day's End*, 1975. © 2018 Estate of Gordon Matta-Clark / Artists Rights Society (ARS), New York. Photo courtesy The Estate of Gordon Matta-Clark and David Zwirner, New York / London / Hong Kong.

captured *Day's End* in their images. I was unaware of Matta-Clark's work; his cutouts blended into the area's general dereliction. Yet thirty years later, in 2002, a lecture by Thomas Crow on *Day's End* triggered the beginning of the research for this book.

At that time, I was a resident at the Getty Research Institute, where Crow was the director. Each year the Getty brings together a group of art historians, critics, and artists working on a given topic. That year's theme was biography and the role of the artist's life story in the creation and interpretation of works of art. I was just beginning my research on the East Village in the 1980s, in particular the art of David Wojnarowicz.

I had an autobiographical stake in this subject. In the late 1970s, I too was a denizen of the waterfront and a member of the queer subculture. In my late teens, I began to frequent the gay bars lining Christopher Street and leading down to the docks. I sketched and made paintings (fig. 6) based on the very same crumbling piers that inspired so much of Wojnarowicz's work.

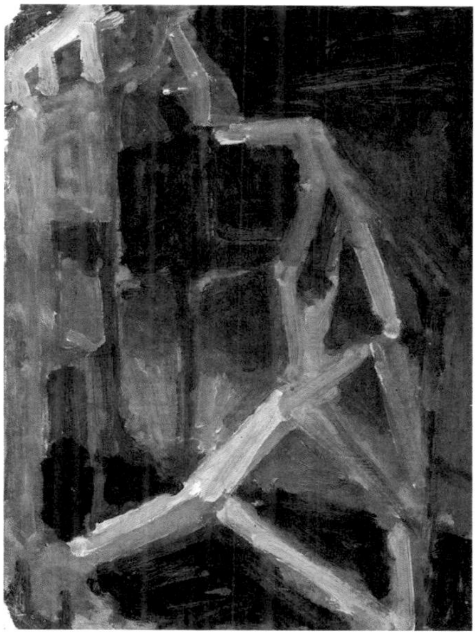

6. Jonathan Weinberg, *Pier*, 1978. Collection of the artist.

Crow began his lecture with Matta-Clark's 1975 *Day's End*, quoting at length Matta-Clark's tongue-in-cheek defense of his act of aesthetic vandalism against a city-owned site. Matta-Clark claimed that when he found the pier, it was already "a veritable muggers' play ground, both for people who go only to enjoy walking there and for a recently popularized sado-masochistic fringe." In Matta-Clark's view, the piers were "in a state of city-condoned anarchy": "In the midst of this state of affairs it would seem within the rights of an artist or any other person for that matter to enter such a premises with a desire to improve the property, to transform the structure in the midst of its ugly criminal state into a place of interest, fascination and value."[2]

Matta-Clark claimed that in the process of making *Day's End* he competed for the space with "the teeming s&m renaissance that cruises the abandoned waterfront." He had his "crew of henchmen boarding and barb-wiring up all the alternative entrances except for the front door in which I substituted my own lock and bolt."[3] Of course, it could be argued that Matta-Clark's seizure and "renovation" of city-owned property was far more criminal than the trespassing or lewd conduct of the gay men he sought to exclude from the site. Indeed, the police shut down Matta-Clark's project at its opening party, and there was talk that he would be arrested.

Crow's lecture raised several questions for me. How did *Day's End* relate to the queer subculture that Matta-Clark claimed he was saving the pier from? Was there any kind of equivalence between Matta-Clark's act of aesthetic vandalism and the sexually deviant behavior that was being temporarily locked out of the space? Was there an erotic component to Matta-Clark's acts of cutting that resonates with what he called an "s&m renaissance"? As I began researching Matta-Clark, I was surprised to find that these questions were barely broached. Writings on Matta-Clark tended to avoid questions of the erotics of his work, despite his fascination with voyeurism, as expressed in such projects as *Sauna View* and *Pier In/Out*, and the hypermasculine exhibitionism of his public acts of cutting and splitting.

Many of the photographs that document art made on the piers, such as Matta-Clark's own pictures of *Day's End*, show vast empty spaces. Similarly, the adjective "abandoned" is used again and again to describe these structures, and suggests emptiness—a place discarded, waiting to be rediscovered by the imaginative eye of an artist. Yet the more I learned about the piers, the more they seemed crowded with activity. If the piers were places for people to have sex and sunbathe, or for artists to create projects, they were also sanctuaries for the homeless. Matta-Clark's padlocking of Pier 52 as an act of rescue from the gays and the homeless was as much an act of hegemony as the police raid and shutdown of Matta-Clark's activities. In the end, Matta-Clark's padlocking was futile. The space was reclaimed by the gay cruisers and squatters. I like to think about *Day's End* as the backdrop for their clandestine activity.

Architecture

As I began researching the relationship between the art made on the waterfront in the 1970s and the gay subcultures of that time, I discovered a statement by George Segal that seemed relevant. Segal is not an artist one immediately thinks of in connection with Matta-Clark or with openly gay artists like Wojnarowicz. Yet one chilly night Segal found himself standing in aesthetic reverie amid the debris of a pier. He was brought there by a happening titled *Architecture* and created by Robert Whitman in 1972, three years before the unveiling of *Day's End*. Prompted by Whitman's happening, Segal made an inspired observation about art history in relation to contemporary art: "The experience of the early happening days was a physical one, where the observer had to walk through a space and have a set of responses, different responses including esthetic ones, depending on what he encounters. . . . I never made a happening but, accepting that premise of physical encounter, plus many other things having to do with plastic form in art, I still think there's a vast area for contemporary critics to examine connections between things that seem very diverse."[4] Central to this book is Segal's idea that connections can be made not only between artists such as Whitman and Wojnarowicz—artists kept separate in the history of art—but also between resistant subcultures typically seen as occupying different spaces and representing different identities.

The title of my book, *Pier Groups*, is derived from Arch Brown's 1979 gay porn movie, which is set on the waterfront and in which Matta-Clark's *Day's End* briefly and spectacularly appears. The pun of the title implies a relationship between Brown, the pornographer, and Matta-Clark, the site-specific artist, and also between the men Brown films who cruise for sex and the artists who made art in and *out of* the waterfront: all were *peers* on the piers. However, exploring the connections between these artists and subcultures neither equates their production nor—need I say it?—implies anything about their private sexual proclivities. The many artists discussed here, among them Vito Acconci, Gordon Matta-Clark, Arthur Tress, and David Wojnarowicz, had dissimilar backgrounds and ambitions. Yet they were all drawn to the piers as spaces of freedom seemingly outside social control. In their ruined state, the piers also served as metaphors for society at the end of the twentieth century.

In *Pier Groups*, some may see a leveling effect, a forged equivalence between the art of a pornographer like Brown and that of the site-specific artist Matta-Clark, or between the relatively unknown photographer Leonard Fink and the globally known Wojnarowicz. But to be among peers is not to be identical, as our jury system suggests. Indeed, the whole concept of a jury of peers in a democratic society is predicated on the idea that its members are diverse. It is precisely the multiplicity of the responses to the waterfront and the differences among the pier actors that fascinate me.

My own worries about this project have little to do with the way it might seem to equate very different kinds of art productions. Rather, my fear has been turning *Pier Groups* into yet another scholarly study of art in its so-called social context. I grapple with the problem that art history has rendered such works of art as Matta-Clark's *Day's End* or Wojnarowicz's *Arthur Rimbaud in New York* so familiar that they have lost their ability to astound. With each new study, these works become subsumed into coherent narratives about the past. Created to disrupt structures or to open new kinds of psychic spaces, this artwork has been used to reinforce the edifice of an increasingly standardized history of the art of the past fifty years. In juxtaposing the works of such varied artists in terms of quality, intentionality, and identity, my goal is to rescue the strangeness of the artistic production along the waterfront from the sanitizing and homogenizing effects of academic categorization and compartmentalization. Far from fixing its subjects in an all-knowing social context, the point of this book is to use a cacophony of images, reminiscences, and interpretations to defamiliarize and decenter the art of the waterfront. Like Matta-Clark, I want to cut into, or break out of, the narratives and theoretical constraints that have governed most approaches to the art of the period. If this study is brazenly promiscuous in its interconnections and relationships, it is not in the interest of a new commonality that is its own form of categorization. To quote Matta-Clark, I want to recover the piers as a site of "interest, fascination and value," and of risk and sexual adventure.

The visual materials and memoirs of those days are so compelling that initially I felt that all I needed to do was present them. In 2003, while still at the Getty, I wove together a chronological script of writings and images by the key participants, mixing the voices of artists, witnesses, and critics. I began with clips from Paul Strand and Charles Sheeler's 1921 *Manhatta*, which evokes the bustle and grandeur of the lower Manhattan docks at their commercial zenith; the inclusion of Brown's porn flick *Pier Groups* gave the flavor of the waterfront's ruin and abjection in the late 1970s. As an added twist, during a presentation of the material at the Getty's weekly seminar of works in progress, fellow scholars read the quotations aloud, giving the script's different characters different voices. At the end of my presentation, one horrified European art historian asked accusingly, "What would it be like in our seminar if everyone presented their sexual fantasies and obsessions?" I could not help replying, "A hell of a lot more interesting than it has been up until now!"

There have been many permutations between my 2003 hybrid lecture/performance and the book you have before you. I dropped the performers and fashioned more traditional lectures and fragments of essays out of my initial research. In 2012, with the assistance of the artist and curator Darren Jones, I had the opportunity to turn some of my research into an exhibition at the Leslie-Lohman Museum of Gay and Lesbian Art. And in 2016 I curated a show at the Hunter College Art Galleries that focused on Pier 34 in 1983–84, when it was briefly taken over by Wojnarowicz and his friends and used as makeshift studios and exhibition spaces. With these exhibitions and related texts, I realized that it is not enough just to point in wonderment to the piers and the art they inspired, expecting everyone to share in my awe and attraction. And yet, in conceptualizing my work in this book, the challenge was to devise a means of interpretation that would not bury my subject in abstract theory or sentimental nostalgia. I thus arrived at a hybrid: part journal, part scrapbook, part traditional art-historical narrative. I hope the shifting and mixing of modes will be truer to the strangeness and beauty of the piers than a more conventional history would be.

Wanting to Be There

I have often imagined meeting Vito Acconci in 1971 at the end of Pier 17 in the middle of the night. I have also wondered how *Day's End* might have looked on a summer's day in 1978, the specific sounds and smells of the Hudson, the changes in the light as the afternoon progressed, the characters sharing the space with me. The longing to have been there to experience works of art that no longer exist merges with the desire to walk along the waterfront, but not just as a young man in the 1970s. I want to walk along the piers when the port was on the verge of becoming the most active in the world, in 1916, and again in the 1950s, when the decay was beginning. All through this time, and even before, the waterfront was a site where men could pick up men. Indeed, I wrote in my first book, *Speaking for Vice: Homosexuality in the Art of Charles Demuth, Marsden Hartley, and the First American Avant-Garde*, about how gay artists like Demuth, Hartley, and Paul Cadmus, and poets like Hart Crane, were obsessed with representing sailors as objects of desire, and how men cruising the docks is a theme that runs through American culture from the nineteenth century on.

Given the importance of the New York waterfront as a theme in American art and literature, I was surprised by the relative paucity of visual and factual evidence about the pier structures when they were first constructed and throughout their varied history. When I began this project, I thought there would be equally enormous archives of pictures and architectural plans to study. But it has been surprisingly difficult to find such documentation. Take Pier 46 at the foot of Perry and West Streets, built by the city in 1929 and leased by the Savannah Line. In 1980, Pier 46 was probably the most popular of the so-called sex piers that bordered Greenwich Village. Pier 46 had none of the splendor of the Chelsea piers, beginning just above 14th Street, which were designed by Warren and Wetmore for the prestigious Cunard Line, yet it still was an impressive building. A picture in the New York City Municipal Archives documenting the brick façade when it was new shows that Pier 46 looked a lot like several other contemporary pier terminals built by the city—for example, Pier 34 at Canal Street and Pier 96 at 56th Street. They all share a slightly higher central entrance façade, with two lower wings, suggestive of a triumphal arch or gateway. Yet I have not been able to find the name of either the architect or the engineer who built Pier 46, or the original plans for its structure. Perhaps a more diligent and patient scholar with better bureaucratic connections could find such information, but the difficulty of the hunt suggests that such buildings, for all their functional importance, were not considered of aesthetic value. It was only in the late 1980s, after Pier 46 and many of its brethren were demolished, that people began to realize that these structures had considerable charm and, perhaps, architectural merit.

The Pier Project

From the outset, the great inspiration for this project has been Walter Benjamin's monumental *Arcades Project*, an unfinished literary work that focuses on Paris's covered passageways, which connect shops in ambitious iron and glass structures that look ahead to the modern shopping mall. Built at the beginning of the nineteenth century, at the dawn of modernity, they were the perfect site for Charles Baudelaire's flâneur, the artist who spends his time strolling through the city experiencing the crowd. By the 1920s, however, when Benjamin began his research, many of the remaining arcades had fallen into disrepair, and so the *Arcades Project* is obsessed with the relationship between the modern and the ruin. Benjamin describes his intentions: "Method of this project: literary montage. I needn't *say* anything. Merely show. I shall purloin no valuables, appropriate no ingenious formulations. But the rags, the refuse—these I will not inventory but allow, in the only way possible, to come into their own: by making use of them."[5]

Instead of Benjamin's arcades, my subject is the vast terminals that once serviced the ocean liners, ferries, and cargo ships of New York City. Their millions of passengers, sailors, and dockworkers passing to and fro are closely related to the arcades that so obsessed Benjamin. Benjamin described a "line of descent—arcades, winter gardens with their lordly palms, and railroads stations," finally "giving way to the hangar." We can locate the ship terminals between the railroad stations in Benjamin's genealogy of the arcades' descendants. Like Benjamin's arcades—"glass roofed, marble-paneled corridors extending through whole blocks of buildings . . . so that the arcade is a city, a world in miniature"—the piers were once an essential part of the fabric of urban life in New York. As Benjamin said of the arcades, "they were the hollow mold from which the image of 'modernity' was cast."

Like so many memoirs of the waterfront, Benjamin's reveries on the arcades are constantly overrun by a sense of their ultimate decay. Even as he evokes their splendor, he reminds us of their ruin. His descriptions of glass and iron merge with the later desultory uses of the spaces: "pimps are the iron bearings of this street, and its glass breakables are the whores."[6] Mirrored in the structures of the decaying arcades, Benjamin sees the structuring of society, or at least certain kinds of social and economic relations. In her *Queer Constellations: Subcultural Space in the Wake of the City*, Dianne Chisholm writes that, for Benjamin, "Paris presented a ready-made montage in whose architectural and archeological facades one could perceive the passage(s) of early industrialism and utopian socialism (arcades and *phalansteries*) in shattering juxtapositions with those of capitalist imperialism and failed communism (boulevards and barricades). . . . His disjointed notes . . . are calculated, at least covertly, to crystallize the contradictions of the era and to destroy the complacency with which future generations regard progress."[7] If these urban spaces allowed for certain kinds of freedom and new subcultural interactions, they also were sites of economic exploitation and desperation. The arcades are where capitalism and the commodity were most aggressively on display; and it is in their decay that their spell might be broken. All the objects that people longed to buy, but that in the end provided no real value, become dust-covered trinkets in the window displays of stores that people no longer frequented.

Unlike Benjamin's arcades, lined with stores where people passed hours window shopping and socializing, the shipping terminals from above the Battery to 14th Street were not meant for lingering; rather, they were built to facilitate the movement of people and things in and out of Manhattan. *Passage*, the French word for arcade, more aptly describes the porous nature of the pier buildings. They were the gateways where goods were handled, or literally *passed on* to the markets, among which were the department stores and shopping malls that were the descendants of Benjamin's arcades. To witness the waterfront's precipitous decline, ending in near abandonment in the 1970s, a mere twenty years after being the epicenter of the busiest port in the world, was to be given a premonition of what the end of modern commerce might look like. It was as if the entire logic of capitalism and the endless movement not only of things but of people coming in and out of the city might all be winding down. Of course, commerce didn't stop; it simply moved on to other, more efficient ports. But the fantasy of an apocalyptic stoppage, and

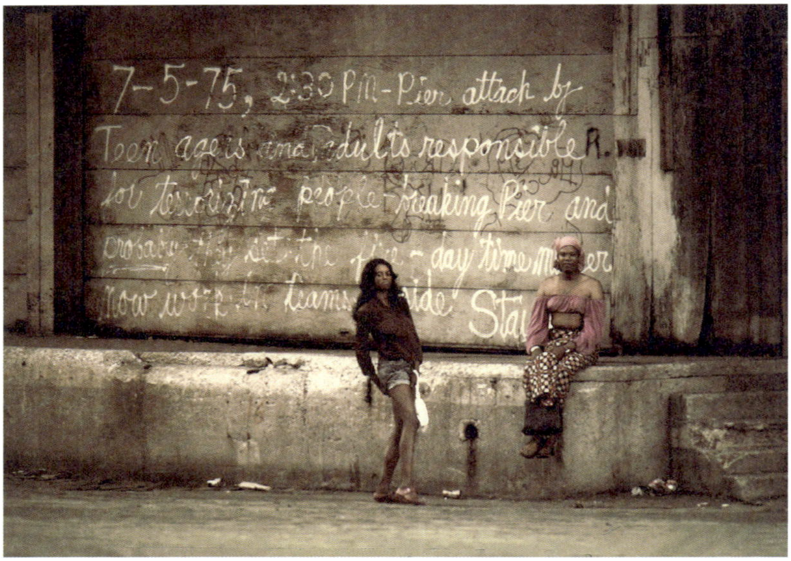

7. Shelley Seccombe, *Newspaper Wall, West Street*, 1975. © Shelley Seccombe.

an inkling of what that would mean for a whole way of being, hung over the waterfront's ruins. The city seemed to be unraveling at its edges.

As Chisholm reminds us, it was his description of Berlin, not Paris, that drew Benjamin closer to the experience of the piers and other queer sites in New York where clandestine sexuality and the city's ruins intermingled. Benjamin writes about his first attempt to approach a prostitute, an encounter that leads him to cross into impoverished and squalid areas of Berlin that had previously lain outside his upper-middle-class experience. "At the beginning . . . this was a crossing of frontiers not only social but topographic, in the sense that whole networks of streets were opened up under the auspices of prostitution. . . . In great cities, there are countless places where one stands on the edge of the void; and the whores in the doorways of tenement blocks and on the less sonorous asphalt of railway platforms are like the household goddesses of this cult of nothingness. So on these erring paths the stations became my special habitat, each with its outskirts like a city."[8] This passage reminds me of the transgender sex workers who frequented West Street at the foot of the piers. In Shelly Seccombe's 1975 photograph (fig. 7), two such figures, having taken up their posts in front of one of the entrances that connected Piers 46 and 48, offer their services to the passing traffic. Spray-painted on the wall behind them are words of warning about gangs of pickpockets. We have come to the part of the city where sex and danger mingle. The seduction of the sex worker brings men of all social classes—lawyers, pimps, truck drivers, sailors, and pickpockets—into the same space. The writer of the warning on the wall hoped to put on guard those who sought the pleasures of the pier, but of course the danger of this mix is part of the allure. Public sex on the waterfront not only violated codes of conduct; it cut across boundaries of class, race, and ethnicity. For queer writers like Samuel Delany, Guy Hocquenghem, and Wojnarowicz, among others, this was central to its revolutionary potential.

The ruins of churches and castles that fascinated the romantics took centuries to reach a suitably evocative state; industrial obsolescence driven by the need for ever greater profits and productivity transformed what had only recently seemed one of the most modern parts of the city into its most archaic. To wander among the pier ruins meant both to be aware of the past of a great maritime city and to sense an apocalyptic future. As Wojnarowicz put it, even our latest and greatest monuments "will all be picturesque ruins." And yet for almost all of the writers and visual artists who frequented the decayed spaces, the experience was not bleak. Disuse and collapse effectively opened up a part of the city to a range of uses and activities previously impossible. The waterfront, once a site of capitalist power, was at least for a brief time cracked open, overrun. Real estate that in the waterfront's heyday had costs millions of dollars to renovate and lease was appropriated by anyone who wanted to use it. And let us keep in mind that these structures were not in remote areas of the outer boroughs but were vast buildings within walking distance of the world's largest financial center.

Among the foundational texts of queer theory are Michel Foucault's writings on the way modern society constructs sexual identities. His observation, in the introduction to *The History of Sexuality*, that practices of censorship and confession intensify and heighten what they purport to repress is crucial to my discussion of Vito Acconci's work, and to the larger questions of desire and the body that are central to his art and to sex in America. Equally germane is Foucault's 1967 lecture "Of Other Spaces," which introduces the intriguing concept of "heterotopias," spaces that "suspect, neutralize, or invert the set of relations that they happen to designate, mirror, or reflect." Unlike utopias, which are fantasies of ideal spaces and relationships, heterotopias actually exist, but they have an in-between and indeterminate quality that makes them seem phantasmal. Cemeteries, brothels, prisons, and nursing homes are among the places Foucault offers as possible heterotopias. They exist amid our everyday spaces, but upon entering them we feel as if we have been transported outside the rules and categories of normal life. According to Foucault, gardens and movie theaters are also heterotopias, "capable of juxtaposing in a single real place several spaces, several sites that are in themselves incompatible." Where some heterotopias are relatively accessible, others require a kind of crossing over that involves risk or participation in some sort of ritual. For Foucault, ships are the ultimate heterotopias:

> If we think, after all, that the boat is a floating piece of space, a place without a place, that exists by itself, that is closed in on itself and at the same time is given over to the infinity of the sea and that, from port to port, from tack to tack, from brothel to brothel, it goes as far as the colonies in search of the most precious treasures they conceal in their gardens, you will understand why the boat has not only been for our civilization, from the sixteenth century until the present, the great instrument of economic development (I have not been speaking of that today), but has been simultaneously the greatest reserve of the imagination.[9]

Although Foucault makes no mention of them, the piers of lower Manhattan also fit his expansive criteria for heterotopias, on many levels. Neither land, nor water, nor boat, piers partake of qualities of all of these spaces. Piers are transitional, a means of getting from one place to another. Yet the gay men who came to the piers for sex and sunbathing, and the artists who found on the piers their subjects, or an arena for their performances, were not on their way to somewhere else. To use Foucault's terms, the piers along the New York waterfront "suspect, neutralize, or invert" the set of relations they were originally created to fulfill.

Did Foucault ever visit the piers when he was exploring the New York queer scene in the 1970s? I imagine him wandering the waterfront and cruising the trucks. I also think about the passage that concludes his famous essay "What Is an Author," in which he imagines a culture "where discourse would circulate without any need for an author. Discourses, whatever their status, form, or value, and regardless of our manner of handling them, would unfold in a pervasive anonymity."[10] This fantasy of a kind of promiscuous communication was, I believe, inflected by his experience of the anonymous sex that characterized the life of the piers at that time, but also of the gay sexual underground of San Francisco that Foucault knew well.

As early as 1972, Foucault's colleague Guy Hocquenghem made explicit the connection between the radicalism of the sexual practices of a newly visible queer subculture and a radically new understanding of human relationships and meanings:

> Possibly, when the anus recovers its desiring function and the plugging in of organs takes place subject to no rule or law, the group can then take its pleasure in an immediate relation where the sacrosanct difference between public and private, between the individual and the social, will be out of place. We can find traces of this state of primary sexual communism in some of the institutions of the homosexual ghetto, despite all the repressions and guilty reconstructions which these undergo: in Turkish baths, for example, where homosexual desires are plugged in anonymously, in spite of ever-present fears that the police may be present.[11]

To cite Foucault and Hocquenghem here is not to offer their ideas as master keys to unlocking the activities of the various pier groups. Instead, I hope to suggest a link between what was happening on the piers and the queer theory that was produced at the time. I employ the work of these writers to elucidate the visual material, and also to give their writings crucial context. As queer theory matures, we need to remember that it is not a transhistorical methodology; it is as much a construction as are the phenomena it describes and interprets. In other words, queer theory is very much a product of specific subcultural experiences of the gay underworld of the 1970s and '80s, in which anonymous sexual encounters were celebrated for their antibourgeois and antihegemonic potential.

Above all, I do not want to reduce the extraordinary variety of experiences and sensations of pier culture to a set of theories—or vice versa. But even as I insist that what happened at the piers was too extraordinary to be explained by theoretical constructs, I worry that my project will be overtaken by a sentimental nostalgia. A recurring theme in many memoirs of the period is that of the 1970s as a lost paradise (or hell) of sexual experimentation. Missing in some of these accounts is the cruelty and superficiality of much of the gay cruising scene, and how it put so much emphasis on looks and youth. In these stories, the HIV/AIDS epidemic that so devastated the gay subculture that flourished on the piers becomes a fall from grace. Sometimes likening the 1970s to a nonstop party that had to come to an end, memoirists unwittingly mimic a homophobic concept of HIV/AIDS as punishment for new forms of sexual expression and new ways of living. I have no patience for any version of history that sees a disease as some sort of retribution, divine or otherwise. And I want to emphasize that the period I am looking at in this book runs from the 1970s, before HIV/AIDS was even known, much less an epidemic, to the early 1980s, when the first cases of AIDS in the United States were just beginning to be diagnosed. Yet it is impossible to think of the gay past without looking at the devastation of the disease, if for no other reason than that so many of the key figures in this book died of it, whether image makers like Leonard Fink, Peter Hujar, Tava, and David Wojnarowicz, or writers like Foucault and Hocquenghem. Still, we must always remember that the ruins of the piers and so much of what went on there, sexual and otherwise, occurred before the plague of HIV/AIDS.

There is an equal danger of romanticizing the piers as a space of sexual liberation and the forging of new queer communities. We must never forget that the horrendous state of the docks was the result of economic disaster and the near bankruptcy of the city. The dilapidated waterfront was an apt metaphor for the loss of so many industrial jobs and the suffering that economic displacement wrought on so many lives.

As a ruin, the waterfront, particularly at night, was considered an unsafe place for women to venture, and so when we think about it as a site of liberation and experimentation, we must keep in mind that it served this purpose mostly for men. The photographs of Shelley Seccombe and the female artists of the Pier 34 group are notable exceptions. But Seccombe confided in me that she usually brought her husband along when she ventured inside the pier buildings. I learned of another exception when in the last stages of writing this book. In 1983, Morgan Gwenwald, whose S/M images appeared in *On Our Backs* magazine and in the anthology *Coming to Power: Writings and Graphics on Lesbian S/M*, took some photographs of the building on Pier 46. The most evocative of these pictures (fig. 8) shows her lover peering through a hole in the fence outside the ruined building. The photograph beautifully conveys the idea that even when they dressed in masculine attire—leather pants and jacket—women were not really welcome in the pier scene. When Gwenwald sent me this picture, she wrote: "miss those piers, they were not part of my life, and I did regret lesbians did not have such a space. They whispered dreams and adventures to you as you passed them, they held that special space in our imagination."[12] Gwenwald's comment suggests the exclusionary nature of the pier scene, but also how it exerted fascination and stimulated longing among people who never participated in it.

Of course, the danger of such longing is that it romanticizes the experience that was missed. While it is tempting to think of the waterfront as a laboratory for gay male sexual experimentation, the actual interactions that occurred

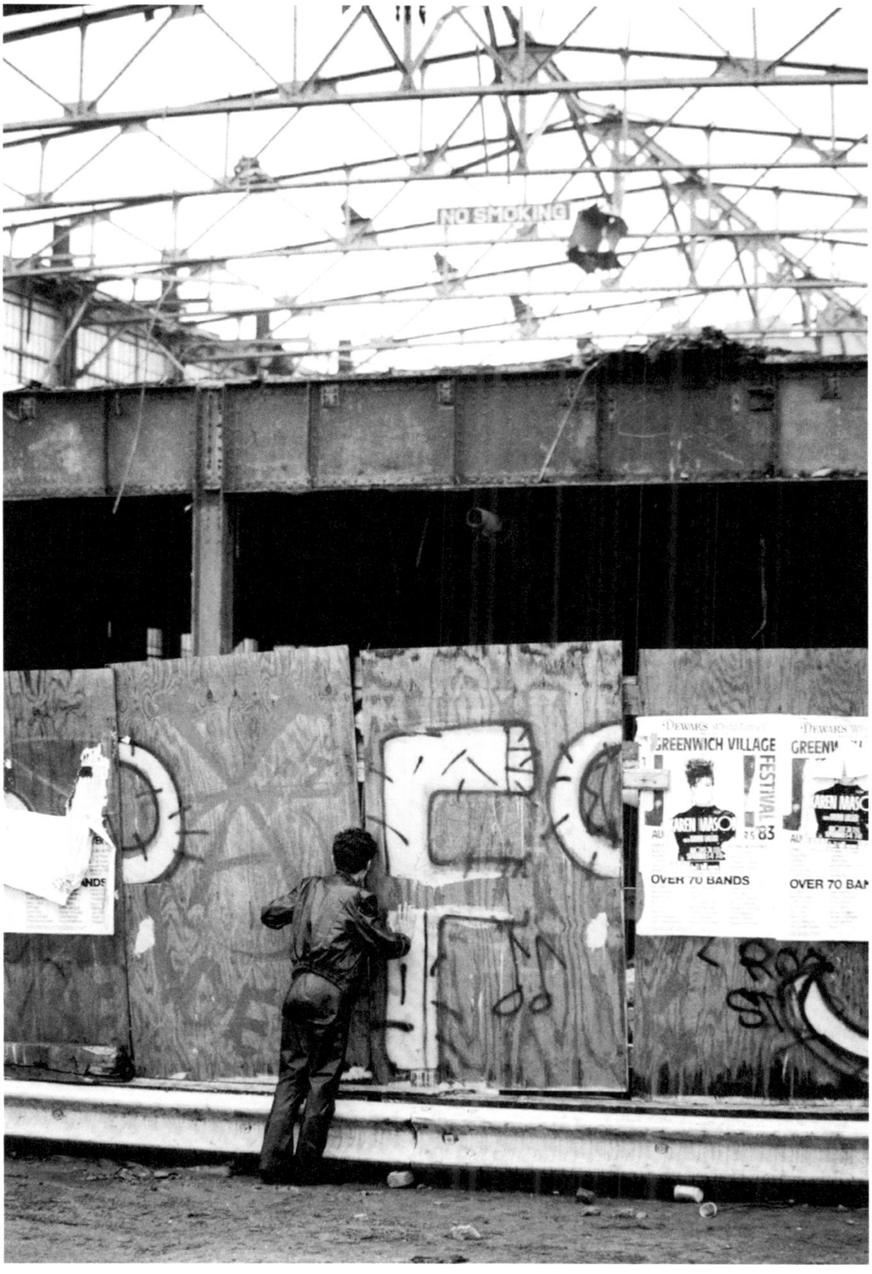

8. Morgan Gwenwald, *Untitled (Pier 46)*, 1983. © Morgan Gwenwald.

were often highly repetitive and circumscribed; participants did not suddenly shed all their social inhibitions and conventional behavior when they stepped onto the docks. Despite the exultant descriptions of orgies that are a staple of gay memoirs of the time, the trucks and the piers were not some utopian sexual community in which all gay men realized their ideal fantasies, or in which all were welcome to join. The hierarchy of youth and traditional notions of beauty that continues to determine sexual desirability on the internet or otherwise today was fully operable on the piers. Finding sexual partners along the waterfront was prone to be highly competitive and often frustrating, dangerous, and dispiriting. Writing and photographs, no matter how vivid, cannot convey the stench of excrement and garbage on a hot, humid July afternoon on the piers. The pier scene, ecstatic and liberating for some, for others was simply a scene of desperation. For me, it was both abject and exhilarating.

In their compelling book *If Memory Serves*, Christopher Castiglia and Christopher Reed confront the ambivalent ways in which we "unremember" the 1970s, under the influence of the trauma of HIV/AIDS and the various activist movements that arose to combat the epidemic and fight for the rights of LGBTQ people. Early in the book they quote at length two gay activists who had very different feelings about the sex with multiple partners that was so prevalent on the piers and the idea that such activity might be redemptive. The first and older of the two waxes wistful about what he claims is "the kind of intimacy you can experience in public sex spaces." His first experience of anonymous sex with a group of men evokes a reverie about what it might have been like in the period before the AIDS epidemic: "When someone stuck poppers under my nose for the first time . . . I felt like I was feeling what 'they' must have felt, our older (or dead) gay brothers (dare I use that term), some of whom were actually in the room, symbolizing the historical continuity that so often gets obscured by discourses of ageism. I felt like I had tapped into some eternal, carnal, homoerotic and brotherly stream of consciousness." In contrast, the second, younger man shows no interest in what he refers to as the "whore culture" of promiscuous sex that he implies is central to an older generation's notion about what it means to be gay. He declares that "it's time for gay men to stop thinking with their dicks . . . and start thinking about the future."

Wisely, Castiglia and Reed make no attempt to adjudicate the truth of these different accounts, but clearly their hearts are with the first memoir. Throughout the book they go on to embrace narratives of sexual liberation and of the radical nature of queer subcultures that "help us *in the present* to resist normativity (hetero- and homo-) and to enhance erotic and social imagination."[13] Likewise, I would argue that what happened along the waterfront in the 1970s and '80s is worth thinking about not because sexual encounters and cruising were necessarily more compelling or more real back then, but because they challenge us to reconceptualize sex and desire today and in the future.

We love to complain that the virtual world of the internet, computers, and cell phones has destroyed our humanity. Too many of our accounts of sex and romantic relationships today are built around a longing for a past when people supposedly had more authentic connections with one another. But in the 1970s, anonymous sex was often experienced and described as dehumanizing, in much the same way that cybersex is denounced now. My focus on the piers is not intended as a critique of the supposed alienation of the early twenty-first century; it is meant as a celebration of the possibility of creating moments of freedom and liberation in the most unlikely circumstances.

The seemingly anarchic and spontaneous nature of the experiences on the piers was a function of their impermanence: pier culture simply could not be sustained. But that is not to say that the piers cannot be models for new experiences and possibilities. And so what follows is a scrapbook or family album of the past, and also a possible blueprint for what to do with the future ruins and debris of our present.

Chapter 1

Initiations

It avails not, time nor place—distance avails not,
I am with you, you men and women of a generation, or ever so many generations hence,
Just as you feel when you look on the river and sky, so I felt . . .
—Walt Whitman, "Crossing Brooklyn Ferry"

In the introduction, I tried to convey my passion for the history of the New York City waterfront that runs along the southernmost section of the Hudson, what is sometimes known as the North River. I long not only to reconnect with my past, but to imagine what it would be like to wander along West Street and gaze out at the river at the beginning of the twentieth century, when New York City was becoming the busiest port in the world. This desire is tangled up with the hope that the pictures, descriptions, memories, and interpretations I present here will make the piers tangible to readers and viewers, as if they too could encounter a strange and wondrous place that has been at the edges of their consciousness all along. The hallucinatory pull of the waterfront is at the core of Whitman's ecstatic poem "Crossing Brooklyn Ferry" (1856), in which he imagines both past and future generations sharing his experience of the port and its "living crowd," even as he knows that his fellow passengers, who travel the same route every day, barely notice the dynamism of their surroundings. The poem is meant to change the way we see the harbor and our relationship to the modernity it represents; it forges a community across space and time ("others who look back on me because I look'd forward to them"), in much the same way that the ferry crosses the harbor, linking Manhattan with Brooklyn.

Whitman's call to awaken our senses to the waterfront and its cacophony of sensations, both frightening and exhilarating, was echoed more than a century later by a series of artists who created events that were fundamentally meant to change spectators, initiating them into a new community. AA Bronson, the Canadian-born artist and curator, remembers that during his first visit to New York City in 1973, his fellow artist Ray Johnson brought him to the waterfront in the middle of the night for a tour of its "artworks." The excitement of the journey was enhanced by a sense of danger: "We had to take a very particular route because he was very nervous about certain walks, and I remember, crossing 21st or 22nd, that he was quite scared. I could tell he was watching out who was in the doorways."

Once inside the pier building, Johnson led Bronson through a maze of rooms that differed enormously in size and function: "There were these smaller rooms in the front or maybe they were built for the offices that were built for the managers or something, little staircases and rabbit warrens and then all the walls had holes in them so you were always looking through layers and layers of walls." Just as Johnson's own collaged artworks distort and compress perspective, Johnson's tour of the piers telescoped and collapsed space: "It was a very sort of romantic environment and the moonlight would filter through the holes in the collapsing roofs and so on . . . very . . . very pretty. And we went up and down into the different levels of that particular pier. . . . There is an area where there was a platform that stuck out over the water that was not covered, it was open to the daylight and the guys would lie out in the sun in the early morning and have sex or just hang out and watch what was going on."

According to Bronson, the tour culminated at dawn in front of the enormous painted giants that the artist Tava (a.k.a. Gustav Von Will) had painted at the end of Pier 46, dramatically illuminated by the sunrise (fig. 9). These two-story-high nude men, both grabbing their erect penises, were so prominent that they could easily be seen from the New Jersey shore and from the Circle Line tourist boats that circled Manhattan. Indeed, in their day, they were far better known than Matta-Clark's *Day's End*. Yet very little has been written about these paintings or their creator, who died of AIDS in 1991. During his life, he certainly was no recluse, but for the most part he did not seem to be interested in forging a traditional art career. Rather than concentrate on paintings that could be hung in art galleries, he made site-specific

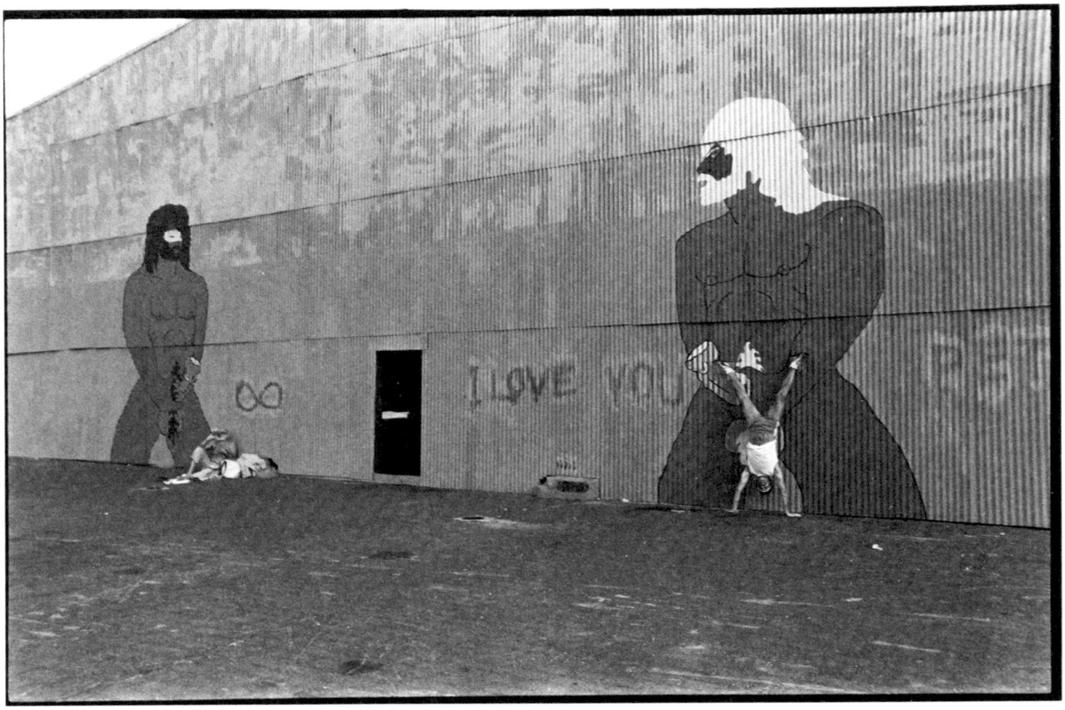

9. Leonard Fink, *Untitled (Tava Mural)*, 1979. Collection of the LGBT Community Center National History Archive.

murals that by their nature were temporary. For example, he depicted a fifth-century Greek orgy to decorate the Sleaze Ball dance, and the signature dolphin-riding nudes from his *Freedom or Death* series appeared on the decks of Pier 51 and in nightclubs like the Underground and the Flamingo. Tava is also remembered as an actor. In 1974, he played the hero of the X-rated film *Him*, which focuses on a young man erotically obsessed with Jesus Christ. This notorious film has completely disappeared, although film buffs, intrigued by its potentially sacrilegious content, continue to search for it and research its history.[1]

Frank Hallam took several photographs of Tava painting the figures of the Babylonian Gilgamesh and his beloved friend Enkidu on the end of Pier 46 (fig. 10). Hallam also documented how the murals were eventually covered with graffiti and bullet holes. In 1982, Tava painted a similar heroic male couple, the Athenian tyrannicides Harmodius and Aristogeiton, for *The Monument*

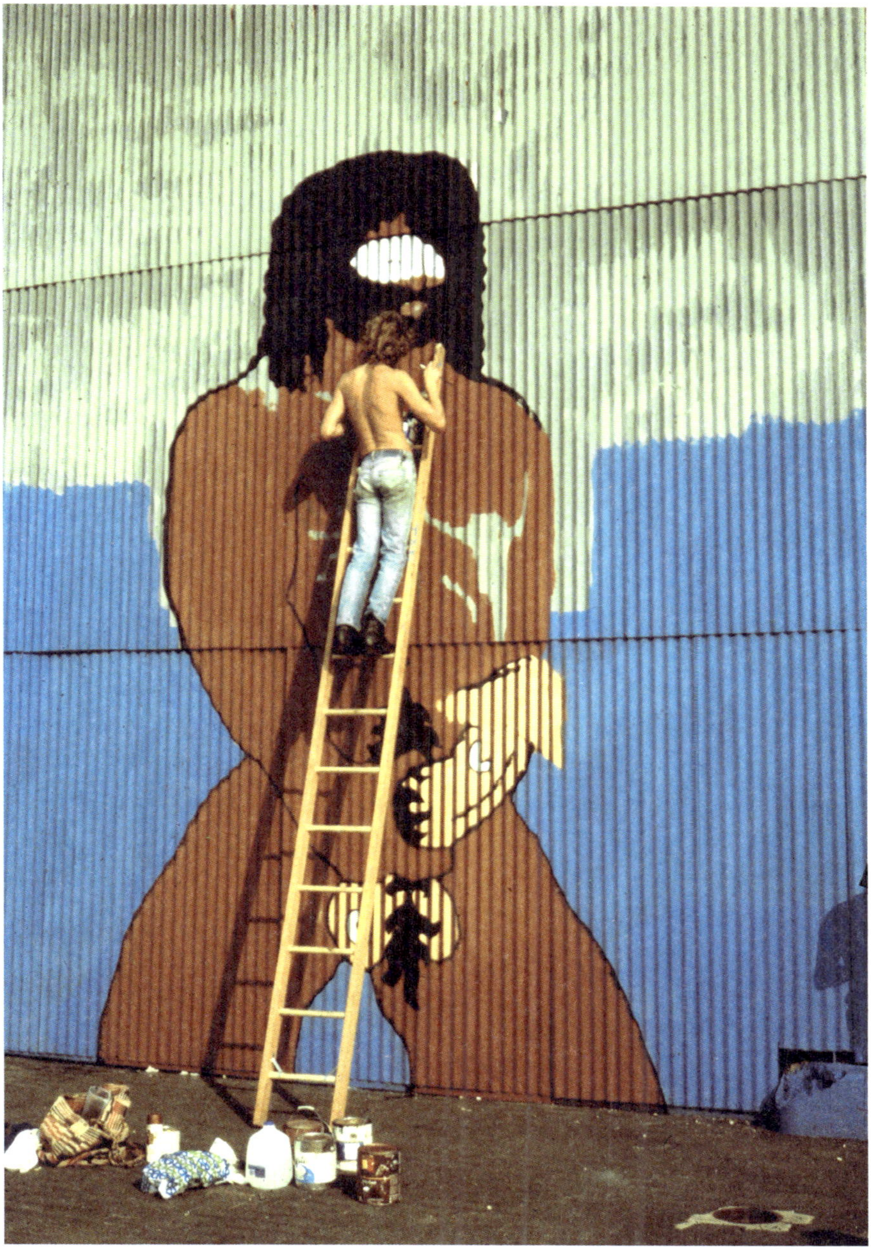

10. Frank Hallam, *Tava, Pier 46*, 1979. Private collection.

Redefined show in the Gowanus rail yards. Harmodius and Aristogeiton were lovers who fought for the cause of democracy against the Athenian system of tyrant rulers. For Tava, the couple symbolized freedom from the constraints of conformity and oppression. But they also embodied the idea that "the natural sexual order of things for men is to engage in sexual activities with other men to release energy and satisfy appetites and urges." While we cannot be sure of the content of *Him*, advertisements and reviews suggest that it depicted not only the potential erotic allure of Christ's body, which Tava's own nude figure evoked in the film, but Christ's homoerotic relationship to his disciples. With his mythological paintings, Tava was likewise making visual an argument popular with gay rights advocates going back to the homophile movement of the nineteenth century, namely, that same-sex relationships were sanctioned in ancient times and that homophobia and exclusive heterosexuality were, as Tava himself put it, "perverse."[2]

In essence, Tava created at the end of Pier 46 a monument to the homoerotic, which Ray Johnson wanted AA Bronson to see in the glorious light of the sunrise. But the details of Bronson's memory don't quite add up. Bronson could not have seen those particular Tava murals in 1973, because they were not painted until several years later. Bronson seems to have compressed what may have been a cumulative process of experiencing the waterfront over several visits and several years into one dramatic initiation story. As he put it, "it was so amazing, other than that everything muddles into a big jumble of public sex, I guess."[3]

In his memoir *The Motion of Light in Water*, the novelist Samuel Delany recounts a similar initiation into the public sex of the waterfront scene a full decade before Bronson's. Like Bronson, Delany was introduced to the area by an artist, the painter Simon Kestenbaum, but Kestenbaum didn't personally escort Delany to the area; rather, he told him to go there to check out the trucks parked near the piers for "instant sex."[4] The suggestion initially misfired, for when Delany arrived, he failed to see anything. The next day Kestenbaum chided him for being too shy: "you have to cross over and walk between them," he told him. Delany asked, "Isn't that kind of scary?" To which Kestenbaum replied, "You got it."

When Delany returned to the trucks, he made sure to "cross over." He discovered that every evening as many as 150 men were "slipping through and between and in and out of the trailers, some to watch, but most to participate in, numberless silent sexual acts, till morning began to wipe night from above the Hudson, to dim the stars, to blue the oily water."[5]

Delany returned several times to the waterfront, and for a time it became one of his favorite places to have sex. More than a convenient place for him to get off, the waterfront was profoundly transformative. The very title of his memoir, *The Motion of Light in Water*, evokes his experience of the river as if it encapsulated his entire career. In one particularly beautiful passage, Delany recalls having sex with a man just as the sun was beginning to rise over the Hudson: "I saw the black had taken a cobalt glaze. The water shook and shimmered with the cobalt reflection." The man, who he assumes is a truck driver, unzips Delany's fly and goes down on him. In the midst of sex, Delany is transfixed by the beauty of his surroundings: "Running across the stretch of dawn river just below us, two nets, one of shadow, one of light, on the wrinkling and raveling blue interlaced, interpenetrated, pulled endlessly one out of the other." Sex and the river merge into a single experience. "It seemed for a moment that both would become one, or would reveal themselves to be two aspects, differently lighted, of a complex singularity."[6]

Delany's description of the docks as a space of unfettered sexual pleasure and beauty, outside or beyond social control, is somewhat undermined by a police raid that occurred just as he was approaching the trucks. Surprisingly, what shocked him about the incident was not his near arrest but the enormous number of men fleeing the scene. The experience made Delany aware that homosexuality was not "a solitary perversion," as he had been taught growing up in the 1950s. The popularity of the sex scene at the docks, along with the "orgies" at the gay bathhouses that Delany was also beginning to frequent, "flew in the face of that whole fifties image": "what *this* experience said was that there was a population—not of individual homosexuals . . . not of hundreds, not of thousands, but rather of millions of gay men, and that history had, actively and already, created for us whole galleries of institutions, good and bad, to accommodate our sex."[7]

For Delany, Bronson, and so many other gay men, the lure of the waterfront lay in both the beauty of its ruins and the opportunities its derelict state afforded for same-sex encounters. Delany's phrase "you have to cross over" succinctly expresses the sensation that going to the piers at night was like entering a different world—a heterotopia, neither land nor water. The docks and waterfront structures marked the edges of Manhattan, yet for those who used them for sex or to create art, these spaces were *boundless*, their decayed and collapsing state inviting behaviors beyond the limits of public decorum and bourgeois morality. The celebration of anonymous public sex that is intrinsic to Delany's memoir and to so many other queer memories of the waterfront challenges the perception of public sex as pathological. To the contrary, these men embraced public sex as a rejection of the regulation of behavior by tradition and by various medical and legal institutions.

The December 1971 issue of *Gay*, one of the most widely read newspapers of the growing gay liberation movement, featured a passionate essay by the novelist Marco Vassi about the truck scene and its potential to transform society: "Something stronger than cocksucking was going on there. Important and entrenched taboos were being violated. Laws were being broken. The thing that society stridently abhors was being perpetrated, and the ensuing vibration was volatile. . . . There was as much real revolution taking place in that open crypt as in any other activity going on anywhere among the forces of life on this earth."[8] Writing two years later, the literary scholar and queer activist Charles Shively was even more emphatic: anonymous public sex between gay men was an act of revolution. According to Shively, the "indiscriminate promiscuity" of sex in the trucks and in other clandestine locations created a radical equality that heralded a possible socialism of sexuality. Shouldn't equality and freedom extend to our bodies and their physical relationships as well as to the economy? Shively's answer was that "we need to be *indiscriminate*": "No one should be denied love because they are old, ugly, fat, crippled, bruised, of the wrong race, color, creed, sex or country of national origin. We need to copulate with anyone who requests our company; set aside all the false contraptions of being hard to get, unavailable—that is, costly on the capitalist market. We need to leave behind the whole mentality of measurement; it is a massive tool of social control."[9]

Of course, in practice, anonymous sex was far from indiscriminate. Cruising the trucks or the piers was still competitive and was marked by some of the same biases against old and less traditionally attractive men that operated in gay bars and other settings. But Shively claimed that because such sex happened in the dark and was relatively quick, it was closer to his ideal of equality, where everyone is included and no one is found lacking. In this sense, his essay was as much a critique of gay men and their obsession with youth and the "blond, blue-eyed, Nordic" type as it was an attack on mainstream sexuality: "We are crippled by the pursuit of a false social ideal in sex—generally that of an Anglo-Saxon man. . . . Beauty needs to be appreciated in its multiplicity and many manifestations; it also needs to be freed from its market value, its power, its usefulness in getting what you want (a lover, money, love, attention, customers, etc.)."[10]

Although the lesbian poet Audre Lorde does not directly address male homosexuality in her groundbreaking essay "The Uses of the Erotic," she also offered a critique of the highly competitive, even capitalist, nature of sex as conceptualized in various gay male subcultures. Sex between men on the piers, in its very nature, might be transgressive of heteronormativity, but for Lorde, any form of sexual coupling that emphasized immediate sexual gratification was aligned with the pornographic, or what she insisted was "sensation without feeling."[11] Yet as influential as Lorde's writings were among radical lesbians, her emphasis on the erotic as a higher form of sustained connection was not universally embraced by all lesbians. Writing in the late 1970s and early '80s, Pat Califia, who co-founded the lesbian-feminist BDSM organization Samois, passionately advocated the transgressive power of public sex and the search "for an ever more forbidden orgasm."[12]

But there was no consensus about public sex among gay men either. For those who argued that same-sex desire was no different from heterosexuality, and that the legalization of homosexuality posed no threat to mainstream morality, the specter of men copulating with one another on the piers in broad daylight was an embarrassment. The assimilationist argument that gay men and women were essentially just like everyone else was at odds with the very public promiscuity that radicals felt was the vanguard of the sexual revolution. Yet even gay political leaders who had no moral or political qualms about such sex, such as Arthur Goodman, president of the Gay Activists' Alliance, wanted the trucks and the piers shut down for issues of safety. The men who cruised the waterfront at night and trespassed on the piers were vulnerable to arrest, easy prey for muggers and blackmailers, and at risk of falling through holes on the crumbling docks. Rich Wandel, the gay rights organizer, archivist, and photojournalist, was characteristically succinct: "if the condition of the building doesn't kill you, the local muggers will."[13] The menace of the piers is starkly conveyed in a photograph taken by Alvin Baltrop of police surrounding a naked body fished up from the river (fig. 58). It is unclear how the man was killed, but the image reminds us not only of the possibility of homophobic violence, but also of the docks' long history of organized crime, murder, and corruption.

Wandel's quip was quoted in a 1975 *Village Voice* exposé titled "Mayhem on the Gay Waterfront." The author was Arthur Bell, a founding member of the Gay Activists' Alliance and a writer of one of the first accounts of the 1969 Stonewall riots, but in writing for the *Village Voice*—the leading alternative newspaper in the United States in the 1970s, with a readership far beyond the so-called gay village—he was not addressing an exclusively gay audience. Bell began with a long description of an experience at the trucks very different from Delany's. His report centered on the sad story of Walter Kronwitt, a young man who worked by day in the hosiery department at Lord and Taylor department store. After work, Kronwitt made "a switch into a leather jacket, a transformation of character, and a night of cavorting at the gay bars on the waterfront." On 11 November 1973, Kronwitt's search for sex ended in an abandoned truck, where, "hit on the head with a heavy blunt instrument," he was robbed and left to die from his wounds.

Kronwitt's experience was not an isolated incident. With the advent of gay liberation, Bell reported, the fear of being arrested by the police had been replaced by "the boys with knives": "In the summer of 1973, the trucks were discovered by a group of hustlers passing themselves off as gay. They worked in pairs, mostly. One would proposition a gay man, feel him up, get him hot, pick his pocket, hand the stolen money or wallet to a nearby accomplice, and move on to another conquest."[14] According to Bell, the construction of a housing project directly across from the "truck action" shifted the sex scene to the building on Pier 48, which stood between Perry and West 11th Street. One of the oldest and grandest waterfront terminals below 14th Street, Pier 48 was built at the very beginning of the twentieth century. A double-spread illustration in the 11 May 1901 edition of *Harper's Weekly*, "Dock Improvement Along West Street," by E. J. Meeker, gives a sense of Pier 48's splendid youth as the epitome of a modern transportation hub. Its grand Italianate façade marks and celebrates the transition from water to land. Flags fly from the rooftops, and the streets are bustling with construction, delivery carts, and carriages. Meeker's picture symbolizes the vitality of the port, the quintessentially modern commercial city, and, most especially, the dawn of the new century itself. In contrast is an anonymous 1975 photograph of Pier 48, archived in the New York Public Library. Contemporary with Bell's article, the image is bereft of activity, and the Beaux-Arts façade, while still handsome, looks like the vestige of an era long past. For much of the twentieth century, Pier 48 had been leased by the Erie Railroad to service cargo that arrived and went out on ships; by the 1960s, the pier was outmoded and in decay. Essentially abandoned by the city, Pier 48 and its neighboring pier buildings had become erotic playgrounds for gay men. "Sex was, and is, available in all combinations," wrote Bell. "In twos, in fours, in clusters. Name the formula, name the mechanics. It's there. If the trucks were fantasy, the pier is nirvana."[15]

In a short essay in the gay magazine *Christopher Street*, Bell's contemporary, the novelist Andrew Holleran, wondered why gay men were drawn to such waterfront ruins for sex: "Why do gays love ruins? . . . Why is there that strange axis between the extremely aesthetic . . . and the extremely sleazy?"

A friend of Holleran's remarked that even if the waterfront was cleaned up, gay men would have to construct an artificial ruin on an island in "New York Harbor composed entirely of rotting piers, blocks of collapsed walls, and litter-strewn lots. Ruins become décor, nostalgia for the mud."[16] Holleran provided no real answers to his questions, instead emphasizing the general visual impact of the ruined piers. Whether seen as beautiful or filthy, it was their appearance as ruins that gave them their appeal as a locus of sex.

Strangely missing from Holleran's musings about public sex and dilapidated sites is the element of danger, the central focus of Bell's exposé. Bell understood that the piers were beautiful, and he described how at sunset the ruins were filled with pastel colors and "an aura of romance." But, he warned, "if you enter the place at night, you take your life in your hands": "You need the eyes of a cat to see a foot in front of you. There are holes in the floor that drop to the Hudson and stairs that lead to landings that lead nowhere. Accidents are frequent. A former hairdresser fell from a ramp and injured his kneecap. An out-of-work singer claims he was bitten by a rat. A publisher admits that while balling a guy in an upstairs room, he noticed that a couple of playful arsonists were setting small fires on the main floor."[17]

Bell's essay ends with a discussion of what to do about the muggings and other threats that waterfront sex posed to the welfare of the gay community. Should the police step in and arrest the gay men for their own good on the charge of trespassing? The men who participated in sex in the trucks and piers, Bell argued, were just as likely to be afraid of being "found out" as they were to be gay liberationists. Men victimized on the piers, therefore, rarely called the police or pressed charges, fearing both unsympathetic responses from authorities and exposure to public scrutiny, not only as gay but as promiscuous.

The dangers of the piers put leaders like Arthur Goodman in an uncomfortable position. Shutting down the waterfront sex scene would mean bringing police into the area—the very arm of government whose homophobia, brutality, and corruption had ignited the Stonewall riots. At the same time, as Bell reported, the police were powerless to prosecute criminals who preyed on gay men if their victims would not report them. But what if gay men acted to protect themselves? This was Jim Ryan's solution. Every few weeks in the mid-1970s, Ryan, a rehabilitation director by day, mimeographed thousands of copies of the *Warehouse Newsletter*, which reported the latest muggings and injuries sustained by gay men on the waterfront. Named after the Warehouse, a popular disco, and distributed in bars throughout the West Village, the newsletter was a curious mixture of news about events at the bars and diatribes about the danger of the piers and the foolishness of gay men who risked their lives there. For example, the weekend of 5–7 September 1975 issue featured this headline in all caps: "WAVE OF SERIOUS STICK-UPS WITH GUNS & KNIVES ERUPTS ON PIER 48 & 49. NITE TIME IS PRIME TIME FOR MUGGERS ON BOTH PIERS—WATCH OUT FOR YOUR BACK WHEN CRUISING 48–49. FIRE HAZARD CONTINUES ON ALL PIERS—YOUNG MAN KILLED BY TRAILER TRUCK THURS. EVE." Later in the issue, Ryan sarcastically suggested, "If getting ripped off, stabbed and held up a[t] gun point is a way of getting your rocks off that satisfies your desires, Pier 48 is just the place for you. . . . STAY OUT OF THE PIERS AT NIGHT—ALL OF THEM!!!!!!!!"[18]

Similar messages were spray-painted on the entrance gates and walls of the pier structures. Shelly Seccombe photographed one sign on the outside of Pier 48: "7-5-75, 2:30 PM—Pier attack by Teenagers and adults responsible for terrorizing people—breaking Pier and probably they set the fire—daytime muggers now working in teams. . . . Stay Out" (see fig. 7). The content and syntax of the message are so close to Ryan's that it was probably Ryan himself, or one of his friends, using the newsletter as a source, who spray-painted this warning.

In an interview with the weekly neighborhood newspaper *Our Town*, Ryan complained about gay men's apathy toward the dangers of the waterfront and proposed the creation of a patrol of volunteers or guards hired by the bars to prevent teenagers "invading the pier(s) to harass and intimidate & threaten people." He acknowledged the catch-22 that the situation posed for the police, "because no-one is supposed to be on the piers, at any time," but he rejected the idea that gay men's trespassing "gives these kids a license to harass anyone, on or off the piers." Despite Ryan's complaints about the apathy of gay men, *Our Town*'s reporter, John S. Turcott, saw in his warnings the signs of a nascent community and the possible bringing together of "a group of total strangers into a camaraderie that gives them the courage and strength to fight back against the muggers." Ryan himself noticed that people were becoming more likely to report to him crimes that were occurring on the piers.[19]

The pier buildings never became entirely safe at night, but with their growing popularity in the queer community came a certain safety in numbers. According to Frank Hallam, gay men did look out for one another even in the midst of cruising for sex. Hallam told me about an incident that occurred one summer afternoon when he was photographing on the roof of the terminal building on Pier 46 and felt threatened by a group of young men he thought were eyeing his camera. He was able to signal a man on a lower level who came to his rescue.[20] Just as Samuel Delany had suggested, the realization that homosexuals were not isolated, and that they had effectively made this area of the city their own, created a feeling of security and belonging, however illusory. And yet, paradoxically, it was the sense of danger and of crossing a line that was essential to the erotic thrill of the piers. Andrew Holleran's friend might joke about creating a simulated ruin for sex on an island off the coast of Manhattan, but to make public sex safe and legal would be to erase the excitement of breaking the rules. Arguably, homophobia and the prohibitions on homosexual acts heightened the erotic pull of the clandestine and the physically risky on queer desire.

Robert Whitman's *Architecture*

So far in this chapter I have focused primarily on erotic initiations and the sense of freedom mixed with danger that gay men felt when they discovered the sex life of the waterfront. What of the artists who were drawn to the waterfront not for sex but for its aesthetic and historical contexts? Many of these ostensibly "straight" artists consciously or unconsciously avoided the piers in the Greenwich Village area that were most frequented by gay men, preferring to create their performances and site-specific pieces further downtown, near the construction site of the World Trade Center. Nevertheless, they too saw in the area's neglect and ruin the opportunity to create new experiences not sanctioned by government or tradition.

On the frigid evening of 19 February 1972 at around 9:00 P.M., Robert Whitman initiated a small group of fellow artists into the nocturnal world of the piers with a "theater work" he titled *Architecture.* Not recorded on video or film, it is known primarily through an article published in the November 1972 issue of *Arts Magazine* (fig. 11). Simone Swan, who never actually witnessed the piece, introduced Segal's description of the performance. Although she showed up at the proper time and place, 9:00 P.M., at the corner of Chamber and West Streets, her feet became so cold that she decided to bow out after performing her role. Whitman himself recalled that he began the piece by telling his guests, who included the artists Jared Bark, Trisha Brown, Alan Kaprow, George Segal, Hisachika Takahashi, and David Tudor, that it was their choice whether to follow him into the pier structures. In contrast to what he called the "fascism" of many so-called audience participation happenings, in which spectators were coerced into particular actions, Whitman claimed that his "events" had "a kind of participation, but there is a great freedom." "There is always the freedom to go away. I told people who came, you can leave. It's really

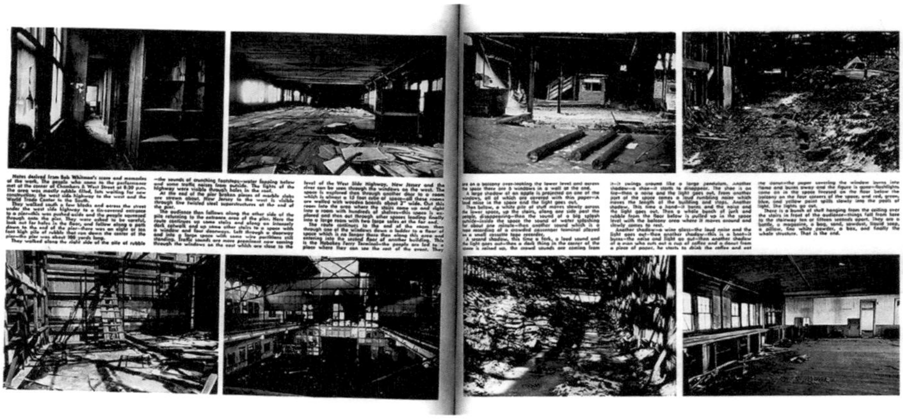

11. Robert Whitman, photographs of the interior of the Hoboken Ferry Terminal and surrounding pier buildings, as printed in George Segal, "On Whitman and Things," *Arts Magazine*, November 1972.

ferociously cold and the piece is this and this and this. You are free to depart."[21] Swan waited in Whitman's nearby loft to hear from her more intrepid friends what had occurred. Unfortunately, she later wrote in *Arts Magazine*, they were "too congealed to describe the event in any detail beyond it having been a 'fabulous, poetic adventure,' or 'groovy, a mind-blower.'" It was only later, over coffee at the Museum of Modern Art with the pop sculptor George Segal, that Swan got a sense of what Whitman's happening had been like. Segal described the evening so vividly that Swan asked him to record his memories on tape. In essence, this transcript, presumably much edited, accompanied by Whitman's own notes and a series of daytime photographs of the site, constitute the only public record we have of *Architecture*.

Surprisingly, the article in *Arts Magazine* privileges Segal's memory of the event over Whitman's own notes for the work. Described as being derived from the "score" of the work, as if it were a piece of music, Whitman's notes are nevertheless cast as a series of memories of what occurred, rather than as a score or script that could be repeated, and they are presented in a small font as a running commentary on the photographs of the event. Segal's description comes first and is printed in a bigger font, suggesting that the effect on the spectator, rather than the artist's conception, is the work's real content. Both Segal's account and Whitman's notes describe how the audience was warned about the potential risks involved in following the artist through the maze of rubble to the grand building that had once served as the Hoboken Ferry Terminal. In its heyday in the 1930s, the Hoboken Terminal had serviced thousands of commuters every day and transported goods and services back and forth between New York and New Jersey and other ports farther on. But now it was derelict. Segal remembers that "our guides, Bob and two young men, warned us not to step through these holes or we'd fall into the Hudson River directly underneath. It was extremely dark."[22]

The sequential photographs that accompanied the magazine article suggest the route by which Whitman led his friends through the collapsing building. But because they were taken in daylight, they cannot convey the sense of danger and disorientation that was an essential aspect of the nocturnal piece. Only Segal's words convey the feelings of unease and exhilaration of venturing into such dilapidated spaces in the dead of night: "You had to be careful not to step into danger. The space kept changing every few steps, you couldn't tell what the rubble was, what the building had been or any of its history; you were aware only of the quality of the space. Sometimes it was a narrow catwalk, other times a succession of shelves. The effect of nighttime and the ruin seemed to heighten the quality of the space divorced from whatever memory we have of its romantic ruinness." Eventually, Whitman led the group into the central waiting room of the old Hoboken Terminal building. "After more trudging through a succession of changing spaces we entered what appeared to be an amphitheater. It became obvious that this had been the waiting room of a ferry line. We stood on the second floor facing an enormous square opening, where a broad set of stairs led to a lower level. There was enough light from the sky, as the roof had mostly disintegrated. No railings kept you from falling off the ledge to the lower level, which was exhilarating; but you could see enough to stay clear. You could play at danger."

Segal's phrase "play at danger" links Whitman's happening to other site-specific works on the waterfront by Vito Acconci and Gordon Matta-Clark, and also to what gay men were experiencing in the "sex piers" a mile uptown. Unlike the workers who made a living on the piers—the stevedores whose labor put them in harm's way, or teamsters who ran afoul of organized crime—neither artists nor gay men had to be on the waterfront. They purposely sought the heightened sensation of putting their bodies, and the bodies of their initiates, at risk. In contrast to the repetitive daily task of loading and unloading boats, to say nothing of the dispiriting and dehumanizing process of looking and waiting for work, the artists and cruisers for sex went to the waterfront for pleasure and to disrupt routine. Labor on the waterfront was numbing, but after Whitman's happening, "everybody felt exhilarated and alive."[23]

At a key point in his performance, Whitman evoked the history of the site by playing a tape of bustling crowds that Segal thought might have been recorded in Grand Central Station. Whitman also introduced the sound of pulleys, suggesting the process by which longshoremen raised and lowered crates onto the ships. "It was not possible," Whitman remembered, "to go through these spaces without being aware of their former life. You are very aware of the ghosts."[24] But as the contemporary sounds of Grand Central attested, the bustle and congestion of the daily commute were not only in the past, even if most New Yorkers no longer commuted to work by ferry. In other words, Grand Central Station might easily face the same fate as the Hoboken Ferry Terminal building. Contemplating ruins is both nostalgic and predictive of the future. Only nine years before Whitman staged *Architecture*, the splendid Pennsylvania Station had been demolished, and officials were considering destroying Grand Central Station, or at least so altering it that much of its original design would be unrecognizable. In this context, Whitman's journey might inspire participants to think about what change might do to the rest of the city.

Whitman's tour of the piers culminated in the main waiting room of the Hoboken Ferry Terminal, an impressive space with vaulted ceilings and balconies reminiscent of a church or vast meeting hall (fig. 12). Whitman gathered his audience on one of the balconies, across from a series of windows covered with paper upon which, with candles and cut paper shapes, he projected a series of images, beginning with a large shadow of an apple: "A loud noise in the space and the light goes out. Then below, a white pile of stuff moves slowly across the lower space, up the stairs, along one side past the people, disappearing—then the sound of a big splash outside—inside the space the sound of water splashing for about one minute—then another sound which is a tape recording of a crowded passenger terminal played on a small cassette tape recorder."[25] For Segal, this series of images evoked "a slug, a prehistoric water monster," lumbering up the stairs. "It lurched, crept and scraped up the stairs onto a horizontal, disappeared and, of course, then we heard a splash, as it returned to the water." Whitman's own notes resist such metaphors. They describe a series of projections of oddly domestic objects and shadow-puppet-like gestures that appear briefly and then burn away as the cut shapes are set afire. The distinctly urban and public environment of the dilapidated terminal, once filled with a steady stream of laborers and office workers, becomes the backdrop for a series of images that suggest the home and private life: a fork, a shoe, a wine glass, a male figure drinking a cup of coffee with a donut, a magazine, a bar of soap. A few weeks later, as Segal tried to remember the happening, the experience was already becoming a jumble,

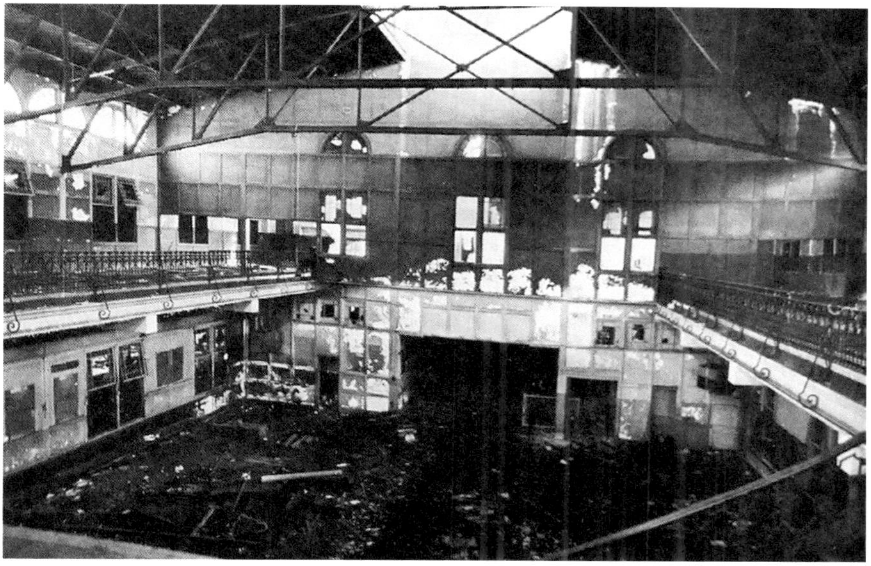

12. Robert Whitman, *Interior of the Hoboken Ferry Terminal*, as printed in George Segal, "On Whitman and Things," *Arts Magazine*, November 1972.

and the "sequences" became "all mixed up." For Segal, Whitman's work was not about "telling a coherent literary story," but more about "the plastic shape of the forms and the invisible rhythms connecting the images."

According to Segal, Whitman ended this peculiar performance with the declaration, "Well, that's it, folks. The piece is called 'Architecture.'" A title this broad defies the temptation to focus narrowly on the historical context of the space and its original contexts. The viewers' journey through the ruins of the terminal must have induced reveries about the past and questions about how such a grand place could have fallen into disrepair, but the odd series of projections at the end of the tour disrupted predictable narratives about the inevitable decline of fabricated things. Instead, the conclusion transformed the space into something new. To use a nautical metaphor suggested by the happening, the experience left Whitman's audience unmoored. Because the performance was not recorded, the transformation accelerates as it is remembered and recounted. Like Whitman's burning cut shapes, or the ruins of the piers themselves, the happening becomes mythologized by its verbal descriptions.

Another nautical metaphor comes to mind: drifting. Although Whitman led the participants through the pier, he did not control or contain their experience. Whitman's happening was profoundly disorienting, and the subsequent descriptions fail to fix the experience. Unmoored, drifting, disoriented—these are all states that relate to the situationists' concept of the *dérive*, which literally means *drifting*.

In 1955, Guy Debord advocated *dérive* as a fundamental situationist practice that involved "playful-constructive behavior and awareness of psychogeographical effects." The *dérive* involves a person, or a small group of persons, breaking out of their normal routines to explore new terrain with no set agenda or preconceptions. The goal is to "let themselves be drawn by the attractions of the terrain and the encounters they find there."

The piers would seem an ideal place for such creative drifting. In fact, Debord writes of the peculiar fascination of similar ruins and dark places: "slipping by night into houses undergoing demolition, hitchhiking nonstop and without destination through Paris during a transportation strike in the name of adding to the confusion, wandering in subterranean catacombs forbidden to the public, etc.—are expressions of a more general sensibility which is no different from that of the dérive."[26]

Whitman claims to have been unaware of the situationists, and although his happening relates to the concept of the *dérive*, I don't think he shared the situationists' goals of achieving a larger understanding of the urban environment's ecosystem or of unmasking the structure of capitalism itself. Interviewing Whitman almost four decades after the performance, I was struck by how reluctant he was to provide any kind of interpretation of the work that involved any sort of elaborate theoretical or political explanation. Inevitably, Segal's description, and even Whitman's own notes, turned the happening into a series of discrete acts. Yet Whitman insisted to me that the total experience should be read as producing a holistic image that was beyond linguistic interpretation. In this he was true to an interview he gave back in the 1960s: "I conceive of each piece as one image, and by the end of the piece the image is revealed through exposure of its different aspects. It is nonverbal theater, using a vocabulary of space, rhythm, scale, and formal plastic elements that communicate the image without words. The work of doing the piece is the work of revealing the image."[27] Just as AA Bronson's description of his pier initiation compressed many visits into one encounter, Whitman wanted the happening to cohere as a unified work that could not be taken apart or, in the end, adequately described. Radical disorientation, in which land and water, outside and inside, are confused, leads to a new form of sensory immersion that cannot easily be categorized or understood. But after the happening is over, the viewer feels changed. The emphasis becomes his or her experience of the event, rather than the artist's original intention. Unlike the situationist aesthetic, the goal doesn't seem to be a heightened understanding of the urban environment and the way it structures our lives. It is more akin to a Zen meditation, in which the categories of inside and outside, past and present, self and nonself, blur. In a sense, the situationist practice heightens the participants' critical faculties by disrupting routine, with the goal of creating a critique of modernity. Whitman's practice had no such ambitions; indeed, the breakdown of hierarchies and categories itself might undermine the viewer's ability to evaluate or interpret the experience. The goal of the happening was to be fully present, rather than to critique or interpret it (although, as Segal's account suggests, such interpretation is built into the process of remembering the piece). Rather than a stand-in for something else, the event is meant to *be*. For those who were lucky enough to witness it, the experience was potentially liberating. Whatever Robert Whitman's intentions, trespassing through a series of dark abandoned buildings and coming out alive must have been exhilarating, if slightly mad. Like the gay cruisers uptown, the artists who followed Whitman onto the piers risked life and limb in search of new sensations and the thrill of the forbidden and dangerous.

I began this chapter with Walt Whitman's famous poem about a ferry trip in New York, and I end it with Robert Whitman's poetic happening, set in the terminal of the Hudson Ferry Line. Although he denied having Walt Whitman in mind during the conception of *Architecture*, Robert Whitman told me that he believes his family is related to the poet, and that as a child he lived on a street named after Walt Whitman's mother, Louise van Velsor, and that it was within walking distance of her family cemetery. But if Robert Whitman is an heir of Walt Whitman, it is in the way that "Crossing Brooklyn Ferry" and *Architecture* strive to reconnect New Yorkers to their immediate environment of Manhattan—an island, as Robert Whitman noted, surrounded by water. In the work of the two Whitmans, and many of the other pier artists I will touch on in this book, the self becomes part of a larger dynamic experience that fuses the port's past, present, and future. The gay men who cruised for sex amid the mud and the ruins belong in that mix.

Just as you feel when you look on the river and sky, so I felt,
Just as any of you is one of a living crowd, I was one of a crowd,
Just as you are refresh'd by the gladness of the river and the bright flow, I was refresh'd.

Chapter 2

Material for Blackmail

If I tell you a secret, then I belong to you.

—Vito Acconci, *Untitled Project for Pier 17*, in *Diary of a Body, 1969–1973*

Sometime around midnight on 27 March 1971 in New York City, Vito Acconci stood before the dilapidated entrance of Pier 17, once used by ships delivering cargo to the New York Central Railroad (fig. 13). "I was afraid to go in," Acconci remembered, "and I thought, is it worth going in? Is it worth going in?"[1] Acconci found himself in this predicament because of a performance piece he had devised and set in motion by posting an announcement at the John Gibson Gallery: "From March 27 to April 24, 1971, 1 a.m. each night, I will be at Pier 17, an abandoned pier on West Street and Park Place, New York; I will be alone and wait at the far end of the pier for one hour. To anyone coming to meet me, I will attempt to reveal something I would normally keep concealed: censurable occurrences and habits, fears, jealousies—something that has not been exposed before and that would be disturbing for me to make public."[2] For Acconci, *performance* resonated less with traditional concepts of theater than with the idea of fulfilling a bargain, or *performing* the terms of a contract: "You say you are going to do something; now you are going to carry it through."[3] In this case, Acconci promised that whoever was brave enough to seek him out on the pier could make "any documentation he wishes, for any purpose; the

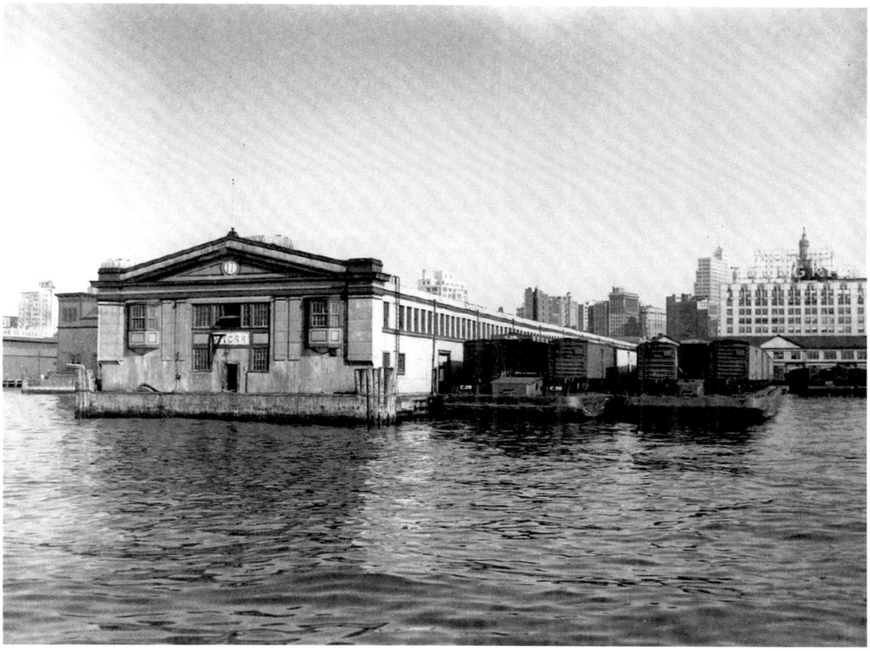

13. Unknown photographer, *Pier 17, North River*, 1951. Courtesy NYC Municipal Archives.

result should be that he bring home material whose revelation could work to my disadvantage—material for blackmail."[4]

Untitled Project for Pier 17 is frequently cited to demonstrate the eccentricity of Acconci's practice. For example, Michael Kimmelman, writing for the *New York Times*, bookends it between Acconci's *Conversions 1*, "in which he burned the hair off, and then pulled at his chest" to try and develop female breasts, and the "infamous" *Seedbed* of 1972, in which "he lay beneath a ramp installed in the Sonnabend Gallery in Manhattan and broadcast autoerotic monologues."[5] Rarely does *Pier 17* get a sustained discussion in its own right. The art historians and critics who have written about Acconci are remarkably incurious about what exactly happened on the twenty-nine consecutive nights that Acconci ventured out to the end of the pier to wait for visitors. Who went out to see him? What secrets were told? Did anyone make documentation suitable for blackmail? Reading through the Acconci literature, it is as if *Untitled Project for Pier 17* were a purely conceptual piece without a concrete presence or audience, and that its meaning had nothing to do with its setting or the various interactions it initiated.

Pier 18

In 2009, when I asked Acconci to describe what first drew him to Pier 17, he struggled to find an answer. Oddly, he did not mention the obvious impetus, namely, that Pier 17 was directly across from Pier 18, where only a month earlier he had participated in a project curated by the video artist and *Avalanche* magazine editor Willoughby Sharp. Sharp invited twenty-seven male artists to create works that would be photographed by the team of Harry Shunk and János Kender (a.k.a. Shunk-Kender). The pieces were executed in February and March of 1971. Shunk remembers that Acconci was "the most excited" of the artists about the project because he was in the process of creating his first performances.[6]

Sharp's intent in conceiving *Projects: Pier 18* was to inspire works of art whose scope and form could not be easily created in the studio or accommodated by the traditional museum or gallery. According to Sharp, most of the pieces were conceived in a matter of hours; "some were done in just a few minutes." Many took place on the uncovered section of the pier that jutted out into the Hudson River. Among the works that emphasized both the huge size of the dock and its limits are William Wegman's *Pier 18: Bill Wegman, Bowling*, in which the artist sent instructions from California for the dock to be used like a bowling alley, the ball eventually falling into the Hudson, and John Van Saun's *Freya Van Saun, 1965–1971*, in which white tape was laid down to mark the path of his child tricycling across the dock.

Sharp recalls that the project was done surreptitiously, without publicity or any kind of institutional support. He made no attempt to get official permission to use the pier, which is why no one outside the artists' immediate circles was invited to witness the events, and why it was necessary to document the proceedings with a camera. *Projects: Pier 18* was an attempt to disrupt conventional ideas of what constitutes an artwork, where it should be made, and how it should be viewed. Postindustrial sites like the pier, while larger, were not unlike the studios and galleries in which a new generation was making and displaying art. Sharp invoked Carl Andre's term "post-studio" to describe the entire Pier 18 project. But in many ways the artists' use of the once commercially bustling pier was one with the art world's colonization of the newly designated SoHo, the area south of Houston Street, where manufacturing lofts had been converted into studios and art galleries measured in the thousands of square feet. With Pier 18 and its various progenies, from Acconci's *Untitled Project for Pier 17*, to Gordon Matta-Clark's *Day's End*, to Mike Bidlo's and David Wojnarowicz's inviting their friends to turn Pier 34 into makeshift studios, artists were encroaching on the territory of commercial Manhattan. Industry and commerce gave way to forms of art that were impermanent and not for sale. But if the aesthetic gestures of Pier 18 and the various pier art that followed them were meant to undermine the profit-driven nature of the art market, the laying claim to such large expanses of space, even temporarily, was not free of ambition or the competitive spirit. Trading the square footage of an indoor studio for acres of waterfront could express seemingly unbounded freedom, but also, in many cases, unbridled ego.

Shunk-Kender

From the outset, the artists who participated in the Pier 18 experiment knew that the process would involve some sort of interaction with photography. Indeed, for all intents and purposes, the only means of access to the complete project is through the photographs of Shunk-Kender. The Shunk-Kender collaboration was responsible for documenting many of the most important conceptual and performance art pieces and exhibitions of the late 1950s, '60s, and '70s, including much of the work of the nouveaux réalistes, Harald Szeemann's 1969 exhibition *Live in Your Head: When Attitudes Become Form*, wrappings by Christo and Jeanne-Claude, and works by Yves Klein. Too often, photographs of conceptual works of art are thought of merely as documents, unmediated records of what occurred in the various performances. Yet in the case of the most famous image with which they are associated, Yves Klein's *Leap into the Void* (fig. 27), Shunk-Kender did not simply focus the lens and snap the picture. *Leap into the Void* is a composite picture that Shunk-Kender crafted in collaboration with Klein to create the effect that the artist had dived out the window and was caught midflight, perfectly serene, as if he were able to levitate. Likewise, Shunk-Kender's role in the Pier 18 projects went far beyond documentation, influencing the process of creation and, in the case of Jan Dibbets, Mario Merz, and Douglas Huebler, who were unable to come to the pier, actually carrying out the instructions of the artists themselves.

Of course, even if Shunk-Kender had just passively recorded the pieces they witnessed, their aesthetic decisions regarding selection, lighting, and cropping helped to package what we think of now as *Projects: Pier 18*. Perhaps John Baldessari was making this point when, in his contribution to the project, he used his hands to frame New York Harbor, in essence simulating the process of the camera composing a scene (fig. 14). Huebler was more emphatic in bringing the photographic team into the process. He asked Shunk-Kender to "establish the best 'aesthetic' shots of the pier and then mark the spots

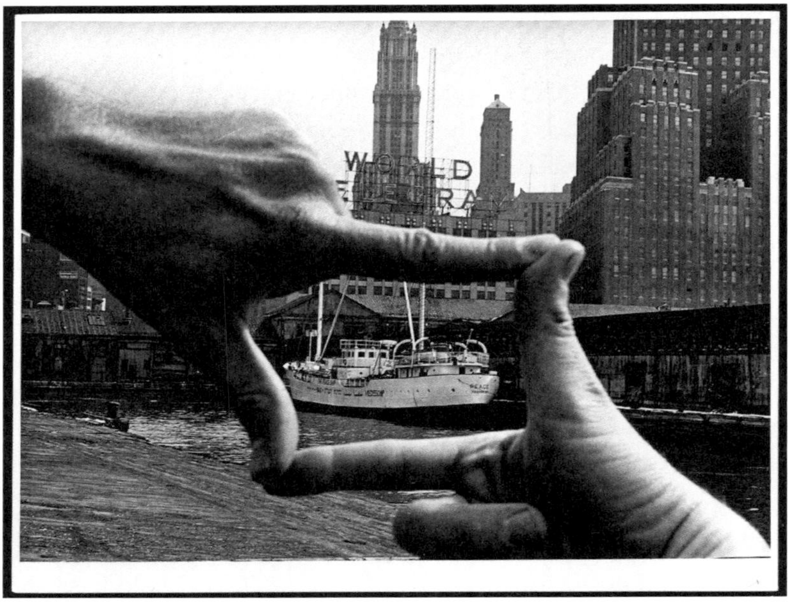

14. John Baldessari, *Pier 18: Hands Framing New York Harbor*, 1971. Courtesy of John Baldessari. Photo: Shunk-Kender © J. Paul Getty Trust. Getty Research Institute, Los Angeles (2014.R.20).

with an x." Ironically, the resulting photographs document the chalk marks, rather than the supposedly beautiful views. Richard Jarden's piece consisted of precise instructions about meticulously photographing the length of the pier, from the shed that fronts the street to the open docks that lead to the water. Dan Graham's contribution consisted of the artist's placing the camera at different locations on his body and taking pictures, almost, as Lynne Cooke suggests, as if he were a tripod. The resulting pictures of the sky, surrounding buildings, and pier seem uncomposed, the revolving camera creating a sense of disorientation and vertigo. In such a case, it is impossible to untangle the photographs from the performance.

In other examples, the photographers manipulated their images after taking the pictures, presumably in collaboration with the artists. Keith Sonnier's performance involved lining up groups of people, their backs to us, as if they had been rounded up by the authorities in some undefined authoritarian scenario. Shunk-Kender developed the pictures as both positive and negative images. The inversion of lights and darks, in the midst of the ruined pier, suggests the X-ray–like flash of an atomic explosion. The expressiveness of these images makes it clear that the camera did not just record events but aestheticized them and heightened their emotional impact.

Cooke argues that the photographs are so essential to *Projects: Pier 18* that Shunk and Kender are essentially collaborators with the artists. As she puts it, "a significant number of proposals required the making, as distinct from the taking, of photographs."[7] There is no question that Shunk-Kender's images shaped the reception of the Pier 18 projects. According to Shunk, it was a visit to their studio by Jennifer Licht and Kynaston McShine that led to the first public exhibition of *Projects: Pier 18* at the Museum of Modern Art in June 1971. Some two decades later, Shunk was again instrumental in resurrecting interest in Pier 18 when he helped supervise and catalogue an exhibition of the Pier 18 photographs for the Musée d'art moderne et d'art contemporain in Nice, France. Missing from the title page of the catalogue and its collection of essays by the curators and Shunk, however, was any mention of János Kender, Shunk's collaborator. Shunk's motivation for this erasure can only be guessed at, but the couple's bitter breakup in 1973, as both professional partners and lovers, might have had something to do with it. Shunk and Kender are no longer alive, and thus can neither explain their roles in conceptualism nor offer reasons for the abrupt end to their collaboration. To my mind, the violence of the erasure of Kender's name speaks of the way in which Shunk-Kender's role in the Pier 18 projects has been largely left unexplored. Given the context of this book's focus on the relationship between the art world and a newly visible queer subculture, it is intriguing that a same-sex couple was so actively involved in the first major art project along the piers. It raises the question: is there a queer subtext to Pier 18, or at least to the Shunk-Kender photographs?

Another characteristic of the Pier 18 project was the total exclusion of women creators, which puts the project firmly in the category that Eve Kosofsky Sedgwick termed "the homosocial." Looking through the pictures of *Projects: Pier 18*, and the way in which men worked closely together to create artworks, suggests a kind of intimacy typical of sports teams and other all-male institutions. Sedgwick's paradigm-changing analysis came in early feminist critique of the dynamics of male bonding, and the exclusion of women from the Pier 18 projects inspired an act of feminist protest in the form of Louise Lawler's 1972 *Birdcalls*, in which the artist warbled the names of several of the Pier 18 participants as she walked along the waterfront. As she described it to Douglas Crimp, *Birdcalls*

> originated in the early 1970s when my friend Martha Kite and I were helping some artists on one of the Hudson River pier projects. The

women involved were doing tons of work, but the work being shown was only by male artists. Walking home at night in New York, one way to feel safe is to pretend you're crazy or at least be really loud. Martha and I called ourselves the *dewey chantoosies*, and we'd sing off-key and make other noises. Willoughby Sharp was the impresario of this project, so we'd make a "Willoughby Willoughby" sound, trying to sound like birds. This developed into a series of bird calls based on artists' names.[8]

If Lawler is right that women contributed substantially to art on the piers, their exclusion from Shunk-Kender's photographs registers a form of decision-making that renders Pier 18 an all-male environment. But Shunk and Kender do more than capture the male bonding that was a pervasive aspect of the Pier 18 projects. I am struck by how often the photographs draw attention to the beauty of some of the artists, beyond what documenting the pieces might demand. For example, Dan Graham's pictures, which he described as a "spinoff" of his *Body Press* of 1970, fall into two groups (figs. 15–16). One set captures the handsome young artist from a distance, in a body-revealing A-shirt, as he positions a still camera on different parts of his body. In the other set are the images of the waterfront that Graham took as he pressed the camera against his feet, limbs, and torso. Despite Graham's notes, the results don't really seem like a spinoff of *Body Press* at all. In that work, a naked man and woman use a movie camera to film each other from different points of their naked bodies. The camera shakes and fragments their figures as if each were scanning the other's nakedness; the "handing off" of the camera from man to woman creates a sense of reciprocity that could be read as an allegory of heterosexual desire itself. Significantly, the film does not include a setup shot of the two in full figure from a distance, which would have helped normalize the proceedings. In contrast to *Body Press*, Shunk-Kender's documentation of how Graham's Pier 18 piece was made undoes the vertiginous effect of the pictures Graham took as he spun around. The emphasis shifts to the artist's lithe and bending figure in its totality and to the pressing of the phallic camera against his body, rather than the disorienting pictures his odd postures produced. Through the lens of Shunk-Kender's camera, the piece becomes all about Graham's body, rather than about empathetic sensations of our own body spinning in space.

The homoerotic becomes more overt in Shunk-Kender's documentation of Lee Jaffe's *Parallel Fears* (fig. 17). We witness Jaffe bound to a post on the water's edge. There is no sense of struggle on Jaffe's part, which makes the

15. Dan Graham, *Dan Graham—Pier 18* (from *Projects: Pier 18*), 1971. Reproduced courtesy of Dan Graham. Photo: Shunk-Kender © J. Paul Getty Trust. Getty Research Institute, Los Angeles (2014.R.20).

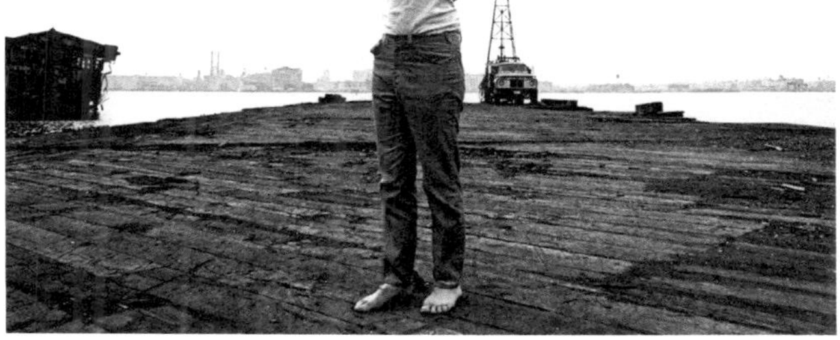

16. Shunk-Kender and Dan Graham, *Dan Graham—Pier 18* (from *Projects: Pier 18*), 1971. Reproduced courtesy of Dan Graham. Photo: Shunk-Kender © J. Paul Getty Trust. Getty Research Institute, Los Angeles (2014.R.20).

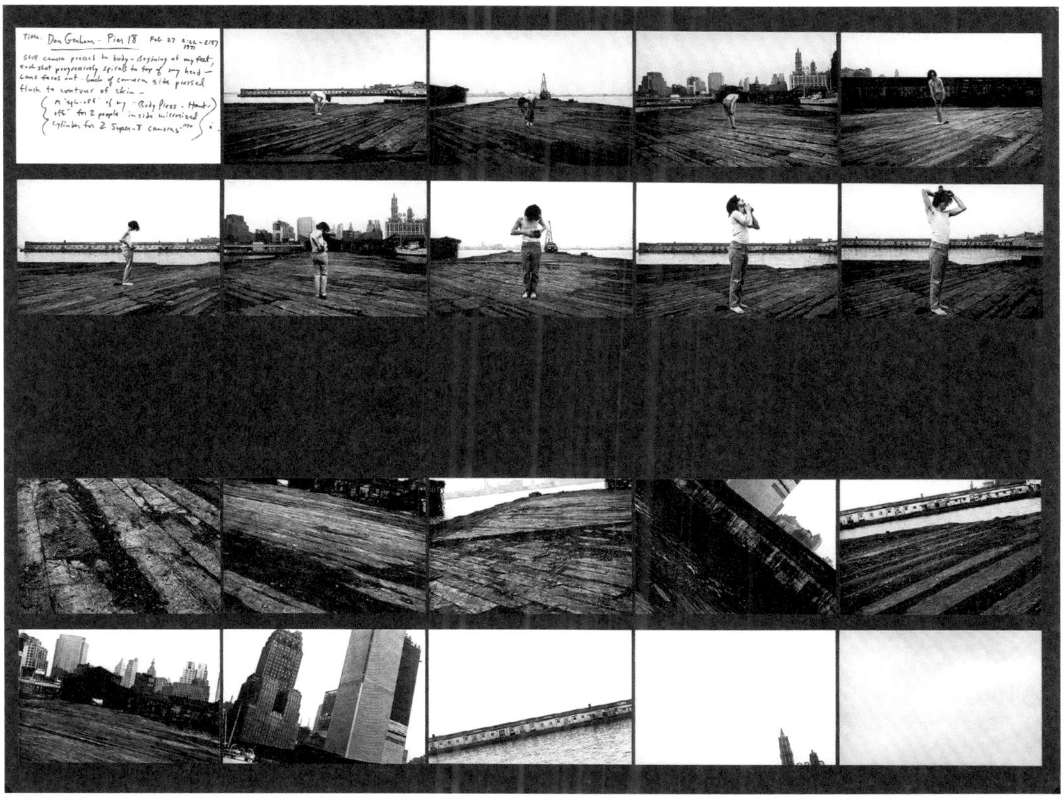

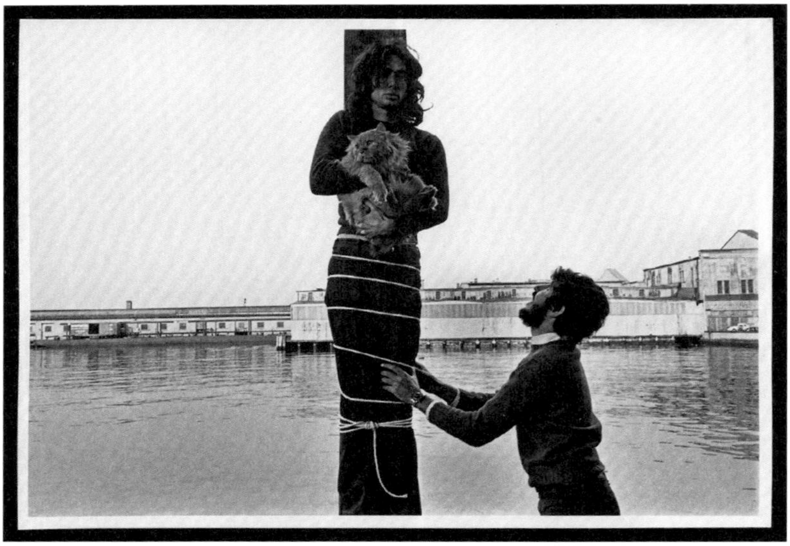

17. Lee Jaffe, *Parallel Fears* (from *Projects: Pier 18*), 1971. Reproduced courtesy of Lee Jaffe. Photo: Shunk-Kender © J. Paul Getty Trust. Getty Research Institute, Los Angeles (2014.R.20).

whole thing seem more akin to a sadomasochistic ritual rather than an act of anxiety-producing violence. Jaffe's long hair, his androgynous rock star features, and the cat that he clutches to his body add an element of gender ambiguity to the proceedings. Men with cats are often coded as gay, and the setup renders Jaffe passive and effectively *unmanned*. Despite the title, neither Jaffe nor his leonine cat seems particularly afraid. What exactly are the parallel fears the performance is supposed to reveal or express? Are they feelings of powerlessness and vulnerability, or does the bondage of such a willing and handsome victim suggest the anxiety of awakening illicit desires in the participants: Jaffe, the man tying him up, the photographer, and us, the viewers?

A similar potential for awakening homoerotic desires is built into *Security Zone* (fig. 18), Vito Acconci's contribution to *Projects: Pier 18*, which, interestingly, also involves Jaffe. According to Acconci's notes, the piece was used as an opportunity "to affect, improve, an everyday relationship," that is, his friendship with his fellow performance artist. Jaffe was to accompany Acconci to the end of the pier, blindfold him, and bind his hands behind his back. Earplugs were put into his ears. An avowed nonswimmer, Acconci asked Jaffe to make sure that he did not fall off the pier, even as he was escorted dangerously close to the edge. Adding to the anxiety of the performance were Acconci's "ambiguous feelings" about Jaffe; he claimed that he was not sure he trusted Jaffe: "I'm blindfolded, my hands are tied behind me, my ears are plugged: in my

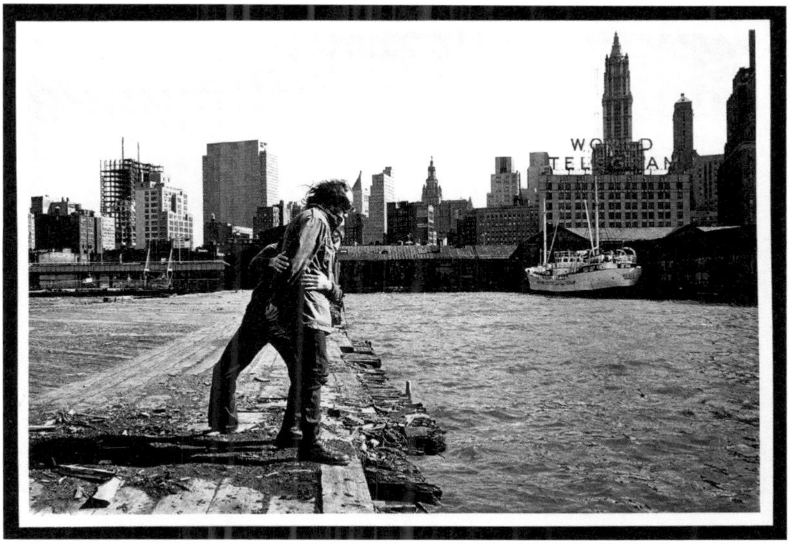

18. Vito Acconci (with Lee Jaffe), *Security Zone, Pier 18* (from *Projects: Pier 18*), 1971. © 2018 Vito Acconci / Artists Rights Society (ARS), New York. Photo: Shunk-Kender © J. Paul Getty Trust. Getty Research Institute, Los Angeles (2014.R.20).

deprived position, I'm forced to have trust—there's only one person here who can stop me from walking off into the water. The piece measures my trust; more than that, it builds up trust."[9] Theater students will recognize in Acconci's description a variation on a technique used in beginning improvisation classes to explore feelings of vulnerability and dependence and to build a sense of trust and collaboration. For example, a student is blindfolded and his partner leads him around campus, or the student is told to fall back limp into her partner's arms. Similar exercises are used in group therapy sessions to instill trust and break down inhibitions. But when we look at the photograph of the pier performance, it is hard to accept the dynamic between Acconci and Jaffe as some sort of therapeutic process of learning to trust a friend or stranger. Acconci may be tied up, but as he stumbles around the pier, testing its parameters, it seems to be Jaffe who is being led around by Acconci. Jaffe must exert enormous physical effort to keep Acconci from going over the edge. Several of Shunk-Kender's photographs are taken from a distance, so it is not even clear that Acconci is wearing a blindfold, or that his hands are tied. In these pictures, the two seemed locked in a peculiar dance. The "security zone" is not just the edge of the pier but the body itself, as Jaffe is forced to touch both his front and back midsection in order to save him. Rather than clear up the ambiguity of Acconci's relationship to his male friend, that relationship arguably becomes more fraught as the two artists become physically interlocked.

Acconci's photographic contribution to the Pier 18 projects once again calls into doubt the role of Shunk-Kender as blandly documenting the proceedings. Notes for the piece indicate that the "Pier 18 Show" was done "privately, without an audience," but of course Shunk and Kender were an audience. The presence of the photographers recording the scene profoundly changed the performance. They were there to witness whether Jaffe was adequately protecting Acconci; if the worst happened, they could help fish him out of the water. In this sense, the piece is not just about whether Acconci trusts Jaffe. Could he trust two gay men with his physical safety? Could he trust them with the integrity of the work of art itself and with his reputation as an artist? Acconci writes about extending the piece to include several meetings on the pier, which would become a place "in reserve for working our confidence, reliability." He is not describing his relationship to Jaffe as sexual or romantic, and yet this male relationship is instilled with enormous intensity. As Jaffe himself observed to me, all collaborations are erotic on some level.[10] At the same time, the piece expresses the difficulty of trust, given the anxiety and disapproval with which a homophobic society surrounds the idea of two men being physically and emotionally intimate.

Perhaps I am overreading the homoerotic tension of Acconci's *Security Zone*. If you had not read Acconci's notes about exploring a relationship and building trust between two friends, you might think the photos depict some sort of criminal activity, or perhaps a college fraternity's hazing ritual. Acconci's blindfolded and tied-up presence on the edge of an abandoned pier evokes associations of torture, kidnapping, even murder. In these scenarios, which I imagine through the mediation of film noir, the artist appears to be blindfolded not as a therapeutic or theatrical exercise but to maintain the security zone of the criminal's identity and the hideaway where he carries out his nefarious work. A month later, this clandestine quality, weighted with allusions to gangster films, spilled directly into Acconci's *Untitled Project for Pier 17*, in which the performance circulated around the idea of secrets exchanged in the middle of the night—and blackmail.

On the Waterfront

When I met Vito Acconci in his studio in 2009, I quickly discovered that we shared a passion for Hollywood movies. Warehouses and waterfront locations frequently provided the settings for gangster films, even before the heyday of film noir in the 1940s and '50s. For example, Josef von Sternberg's darkly expressionist film *The Docks of New York* dates from 1928. In my view, the movie that had the greatest influence on Acconci's Pier 18 and Pier 17 projects was Elia Kazan's *On the Waterfront* (1954). Although it was filmed mostly on the Hoboken side of the Hudson, it was based on a series of landmark articles written in 1948 by Malcolm Johnson in the *New York Sun* about racketeering in the longshoremen's union in New York City. Union leaders such as Joseph Ryan and his henchman John M. (Cockeye) Dunn effectively controlled most of the piers along the west side of Manhattan. They made millions of dollars forcing longshoremen to pay kickbacks in exchange for work. Challenges to this practice were met with violence and murder. *On the Waterfront* dramatizes the struggle to break the system of corruption and includes many scenes in which bosses punish workers who rebel against the system or report criminal activity to the FBI. Even more relevant to Acconci's Pier 17 performance and its themes of disclosure and blackmail is the film's emphasis on the idea of confession. One of the heroes of the film is Father Barry, a Catholic priest played by Karl Malden, who pressures Terry Malloy (Marlon Brando) to cooperate with the federal investigation of the piers. In his famous "sermon on the docks," Father Barry evokes Christ and his martyrdom to mourn the death of a longshoreman, killed for supposedly "snitching" to the police. For Brando's character, this speech crystallizes the moral imperative to betray his brother's trust by testifying about his own collusion in the waterfront corruption.[11]

I evoke *On the Waterfront* not to suggest that Acconci's pier projects were akin to mob movies but to highlight the ways in which his performances used the notorious past of the docks and their clandestine associations to amplify the themes of trust, confession, blackmail, and physical danger. Significantly, Acconci told me that the location was of no interest to him aesthetically. Unlike many of the artists and writers discussed in this book, Acconci did not go to the waterfront to explore the evocative beauty of its ruins. His emphasis was on vulnerability and physical terror, not the amazing view. After all, both of his pier pieces were built around the idea of limiting sight. In *Security Zone*, Acconci is literally blindfolded, while in the Pier 17 project, the blackness of the empty dock building endangers both the artist and the person courageous enough to meet him at one o'clock in the morning.

The Pier 17 Project

That first night of performing the Pier 17 project, Acconci claimed to have no idea whether anyone would actually show up. "I don't know if anyone is going to come anyway," he recalled thinking. "So the first night, I decided, I am going to stay outside and I am going to look around, and if I see someone coming, I am going to quickly go in." Asked to describe the dangers that he imagined would await him inside the abandoned building, Acconci responded, "I had gone in those piers in the daytime. I knew those piers had a nightlife. And I said, 'I don't know about this nightlife.' It's like the nice straight guy goes to prison. There were bars down the block called the Ramrod. . . . This was a particular time."[12]

Acconci's memory of fearing potential encounters with gay men in the darkness of the pier seems real enough, although his mention of the Ramrod is anachronistic; this famous waterfront leather bar actually opened a few years later. But his description of the era was accurate: in 1971, downtown New York along the waterfront "was a particular time" in which gay men were apt to display their sexual preferences with newfound aggressiveness. There were several gay bars along or near the river, including Choo Choo's Pier, Peter Rabbit, the Tool Box, and the Stud. If the names of these bars did not have the same in-your-face sexuality as the Ramrod, the fact that they were so easily identifiable and so well known to straight neighbors marked the new visibility of gay people and their institutions in New York City following the 1969 Stonewall riots. The Stonewall Inn, located at 51–53 Christopher Street, was not far from the piers and was the site of a murder at the epicenter of the scandals that inspired *On the Waterfront.* The riots began when the bar's patrons, many of them drag queens, stood up to government harassment and resisted the police raids that were part of homosexual nightlife at the time. Before Stonewall, gay bars tended to be highly discreet in their signage; after the riots, they became increasingly public, as gay men and women began to follow the call of the movement and "come out of the closet."

Even before Stonewall, the New York waterfront was known as a site for homosexual assignations. The 1968 film *The Detective*, starring Frank Sinatra, focuses on the brutal murder of a gay man and includes a key sequence in which the closeted killer cruises for sex amid the trucks parked along the piers. As Acconci suggested during our interview, the fear of being alone at night on the pier was wrapped up in the popular conception that it was a place where men had sex. And yet the pier Acconci chose for his performance was a mile south of the West Village piers and trucks popular with the type of gay men he imagined might accost him in the middle of the night. For all his anxiety during the run of the piece, Acconci says he never saw anyone at the pier other than members of his art-world audience and the occasional searchlights of boats patrolling the shore, his description of which evokes prison breaks or film noir police chases.

Though Acconci's Pier 17 project was far from the gay cruising scene in geographical terms, its theme of confession and blackmail trespassed into the psychic territory of the homosexual as conceptualized in a wide range of medical, legal, and literary discourses. Among blackmailable offenses in postwar America, homosexual acts would certainly rank high on the list. Acconci's emphasis on confession evokes, if not specifically homosexuality, all forms of deviant sexuality. I am not saying that Acconci's Pier 17 project is exclusively or even primarily about homosexuality, but rather that both its location and terms resonate and overlap with the contemporary gay subculture that was participating in similar nocturnal meetings. Acconci told me of a conversation he had with the artist and art critic John Perreault about glory holes, the openings drilled into the partitions between toilet stalls in men's rooms for peeping or fellatio. "At one point at this time," Acconci said, "John Perreault told me about gay bars and glory holes. And I thought I had to go to a gay bar and they can do whatever they want to me. And John Perreault said to me, 'You can't. You don't understand.'" According to Acconci, Perreault convinced him that the scenario he imagined would not be a performance—it would become too real, the implication being that Acconci would not be able to shrug off the effect of actually having gay sex. Or, as the visual culture historian Christopher Reed suggested to me, perhaps Perreault objected to turning the sexual practices of a gay subculture into art for an elite audience. Acconci's fascination with what gay men were doing in bathrooms and back rooms may have been due to a certain envy for the "authentic" marginality of such deviant behavior. Where Acconci and his avant-garde colleagues *performed* difference in opposition to the dominant culture, homosexuals literally embodied deviancy. Indeed, in his conversation with me, Acconci tended to exoticize the gay scene as if it were a foreign country: "I thought, 'I don't know this stuff.' I am like this little Catholic school kid, saying 'Let me traverse your world. Your world has rules. I am not part of this world.'" By evoking his childhood Catholic upbringing to explain his decision not to cross into the territory of gay sex, Acconci simultaneously touched on a link between the never-to-be glory-hole performance piece and Pier 17—namely, the Catholic confessional. The space of the confessional, two small compartments linked only by holes that preserve anonymity, is very much like the setup of peepshow booths, or toilet stalls linked by glory holes. Acconci's Pier 17 project converted the entire warehouse shed into a giant confessional, in which the viewer, or audience of one, listened to the whispers of the guilty artist.

What actually happened when Acconci met with his visitors out on the darkened pier? He claimed that he had not documented any of the meetings. But he had also said in his advertisement that "each visitor can make any documentation he wishes, for any purpose; the result should be that he bring home material whose revelation could work to my disadvantage—material for blackmail." So is there any such documentation? What did people do and say when they came to Pier 17? At my prompting, Acconci referred me to a mutual friend, the Fluxus artist Geoffrey Hendricks. As a gay man who had been married to a woman before coming out in the aftermath of Stonewall, Hendricks would have been particularly attuned to the idea of a secret that someone could use for blackmail. Here again, the Pier 17 project plays with the idea of shame, a concept that holds terrible power in the life of closeted homosexuals. In the end, though, Acconci's secret was not terribly embarrassing. According to Hendricks, "the secret that he shared with me was that he either wished Terry Fox was dead or that he had a fantasy that he was dead or was going to die." Fox was another performance artist of the era; he and Acconci were often spoken of in the same breath. Both had participated in Sharp's Pier 18 project, and both had been written about in *Avalanche* magazine. Clearly, Acconci was envious, or at least pretended to be envious, of Terry Fox's success. Of course, Hendricks himself was making performance art and was thus also a competitor of both Fox and Acconci.

Hendricks marked Acconci's confession by going back to his studio, where he made a work of art that plays with both words and images (fig. 19), combining in a collage an image of Giovanni Lanfranco's *Assumption of the Virgin*, a baroque fresco on the dome of Rome's Church of Sant'Andrea della Valle, and a photograph of Terry Fox, gazing open-mouthed upon Lanfranco's scene, which Hendricks inscribed with the title *Apotheosis of Terry Fox, for Vito*. A few days later, he went back to the pier and showed the collage to Acconci, who liked it so much that Hendricks reproduced it as a three-by-five-inch postcard and mailed copies to several friends. With this work, Hendricks magically transformed Acconci's envy and insecurity into an image of transcendence. In my conversation with Hendricks about the piece, and about the piers in general, I was struck by how he denied experiencing any fear of getting mugged or any psychic drama about shame or confession. Perhaps this had something to do with his familiarity, as a gay man, with the pier environment. If Hendricks's *Apotheosis* reflects the piers' role as sites for the transmission of creativity

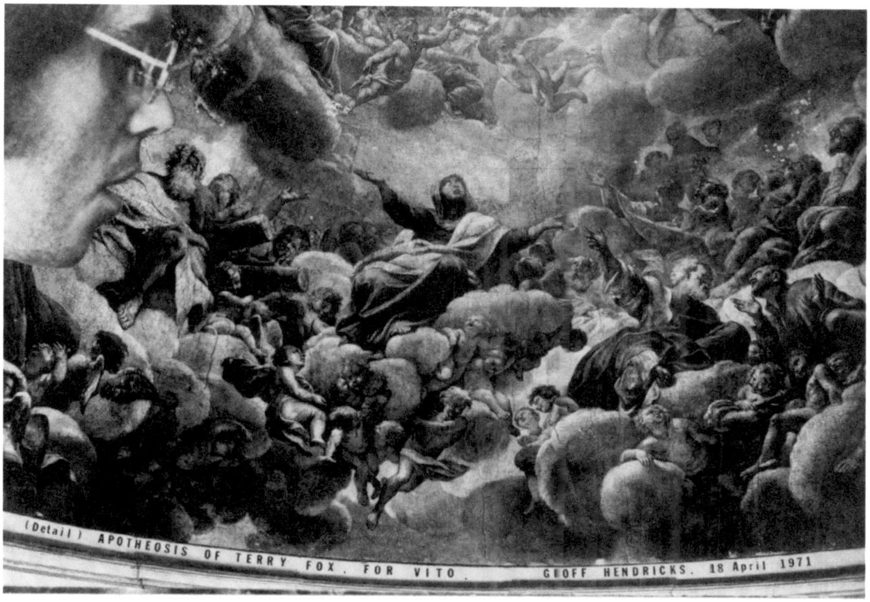

19. Geoffrey Hendricks, *Apotheosis of Terry Fox, for Vito*, 1971. Estate of the artist.

from artist to artist—in a bit of wordplay during our interview, he referred to his meeting with Acconci as an interaction between "peers on the pier"—as a postcard it also functioned as a token from a distant country, a place where Hendricks was a native and Acconci only a tourist.[13]

Acconci led me to another document that seemed to undermine his own notes on the Pier 17 project. He told me that someone named Larry Smith had complained about the project in the *Village Voice*. As part of a series inviting readers to respond to "subjects of artistic interest," Smith had written about his experience of attempting to visit Acconci on the pier after seeing Acconci's announcement at the John Gibson Gallery. Noting that anyone responding to Acconci's announcement would by definition belong to "a small part of an extremely specialized art public: that part of the Gibson Gallery–*Village Voice* audience who actually go to Lower Manhattan and walk down a long dangerous pier at 1:00 a.m. to participate in an art event," Smith offered a sophisticated critique of the constraints of Acconci's piece. "The artist and his milieu present a situation with an extremely low blackmailability coefficient," Smith wrote. "(What information would be so devastating? 'He's a junkie'? 'A pervert'? 'He cheats on his income tax'?) . . . What I am saying is that what at first appears to be a serious risk to the artist and a real decision for the participant is not much of either. The risk is symbolic and the decision is, on several levels, pre-determined." Despite being "scared," Smith went to the pier with a flashlight—"I was completely caught up in the work and clearly expecting a meaningful psychological ritual"—only to be disappointed:

> So what was there? Five guys—smoking, talking, laughing—one reading a piece of paper with a flashlight. They didn't seem to notice as I came up. Finally, I said to the one reading, "Are you Vito?" "Yeah," he said. He finished reading the paper and then slackly explained: "I usually like to talk to people individually, but on Friday and Saturday nights so many people show up that we usually have a party. . . . I've been talking to people during the week. . . . I try to tell them something revealing. . . . Sometimes I think it's not enough, but they seem satisfied . . . mostly . . . but now so many people show up . . . I really didn't intend to have a party."[14]

For Smith, the blackmailable offense was not a crime or perversion; it was that Acconci "lacked the nerve, the mental discipline, the understanding, or maybe just the endurance to complete his own work." Acconci had effectively betrayed Smith's trust, or what, on another occasion, he might have acknowledged were the "rules" of Acconci's world, turning what he had promised would be a thrilling and private clandestine encounter into a banal art-world gathering that the artist "slackly" acknowledged had left his potential partners at best "mostly" satisfied.

Needless to say, although Acconci himself told me about Smith's complaint, he saw things differently, and denied that he had said anything like what Smith alleged.[15] Yet even in the official notes for the project, Acconci mentioned running out of secrets to confide: "I don't have enough secrets; there are only a few things worth telling—the rest, it wouldn't bother me at all if they were revealed." Also, he noted that there was often a line to hear his confessions, especially on weekends.

One virtue of Smith's story, true or not, is that it raises the question of the differences and similarities between avant-garde transgressions and the kind of forbidden acts that can destroy a career or a family. As Smith suggests, the identity of avant-garde artists—their supposed proclivity for sex, drugs, and alcohol—shields them from being blackmailed for deviant behaviors. Even before Smith went to meet Acconci on the pier, he was primed for disappointment. The increasingly bizarre aspects of performances by Acconci that followed the pier pieces, and their testing of taboos (culminating in the public, or quasi-public, masturbation of *Seedbed*), might be understood in the context of Smith's disappointment and the increasing difficulty of shocking the audience for contemporary art. At what point do certain kinds of deviance become the norm within the art world and, I should add, its extensions into academia? How do these acts of deviance compare with the prosecutable forms of sexual activity and display associated with an increasingly visible gay culture? What does radical transgression actually look like?

In this context, Christopher Reed has suggested to me that Acconci's confession to Hendricks that he envied Terry Fox might be "a displacement for another kind of envy: an envy for what, in comparison to the scripted, increasingly institutionalized alienation of the avant-garde, seemed like the more radical alienation of Stonewall-era gay men imagined as the rightful denizens of the piers in the middle of the night."[16]

Whatever we think of Smith's and Hendricks's responses, they are not mere footnotes to Acconci's piece. As Smith insisted, the terms of *Untitled Project for Pier 17* depended on an interaction between the artist and his audience. As Acconci put it, the Pier 17 project was a performance in the way that we speak of performing a contract. It requires an exchange between two parties for its completion and evaluation. Scholars of Acconci's work need to pay more attention to the nature of such exchanges and the ways in which Acconci's audience interacted with his pieces. But whether Acconci failed to keep his end of the bargain is not as important as the idea that the Pier 17 project occurred in a particular place and time, and that its effects and meanings cannot be measured by merely consulting the artist's notes or analyzing his concept.

I have suggested that Acconci turned the dock warehouse of Pier 17 into a giant confessional, but the confessional in turn suggests the therapeutic couch. Increasingly, in the modern period, the psychiatrist has replaced the priest as the chief confessor. Like the priest, the psychiatrist hears, and must keep, all kinds of secrets. But whereas the priest gives dispensation for sins, the psychiatrist effects a cure. In both models, confession is redemptive. As Smith's story suggests, however, and as Acconci's notes attest, in the Pier 17 project, telling a secret does not redeem the artist or make him a better person. But it does have the potential to change the person who gives and the person who receives the secret. "This piece isn't about secrets," Acconci wrote. "It's about searching for secrets, making secrets, using secrets as an excuse—a device—for forming a relationship. If I promise to tell you a secret, then you and I can meet; if I tell you a secret, then I belong to you."[17]

Chapter 3

Degenerate Structure

Sure, it's still there. In fact, the other day I went back and there was this fantastic moment where a storm hit the west side, and the wind and rain poured in, a very visible column of air and water through the opening. And so its life goes on but it's a secret life.
—Gordon Matta-Clark, radio interview with Liza Béar

An oft-repeated story about Gordon Matta-Clark's work is that at the artist's untimely death from cancer at age thirty-five, "only one building intervention, *Office Baroque*, remained."[1] But as various photographs and even a porn film attest, *Day's End* was also still in existence (fig. 20). As it happened, the artist's death in 1978 came on the three-year anniversary of the "opening" of Matta-Clark's colossal work on the waterfront. What better way to pay homage to the memory of the artist who died so prematurely than to trace his footsteps to Pier 52, at the end of Gansevoort Street in the West Village? Like him, you would disregard any warnings about muggings posted on the façade of the building. Stepping over debris and winding your way through various barricades, cut fencing, and broken doorways, you would eventually find yourself in the presence of the remnants of *Day's End*, Matta-Clark's single largest architectural project. Unfortunately, by 1978, city officials had removed the barrier of wooden debris that originally slowed the viewer's progress and formed a bridge of sorts over the canal below, but Matta-Clark's signature cut at the west wall of the vast shed was still intact, as were the various openings in the

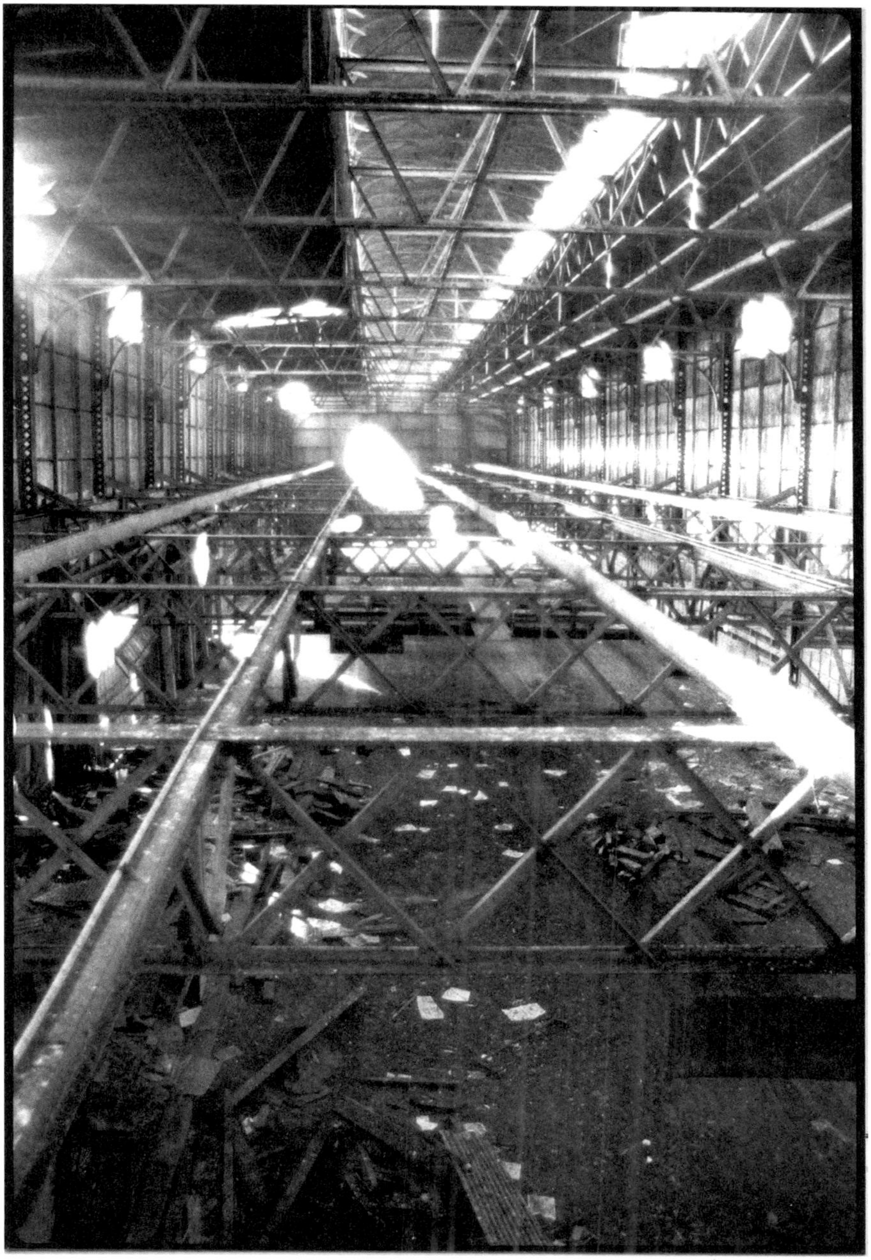

20. Leonard Fink, *Interior of Pier 52 (Matta-Clark's Day's End)*, 1977–78. Collection of the LGBT Community Center National History Archive.

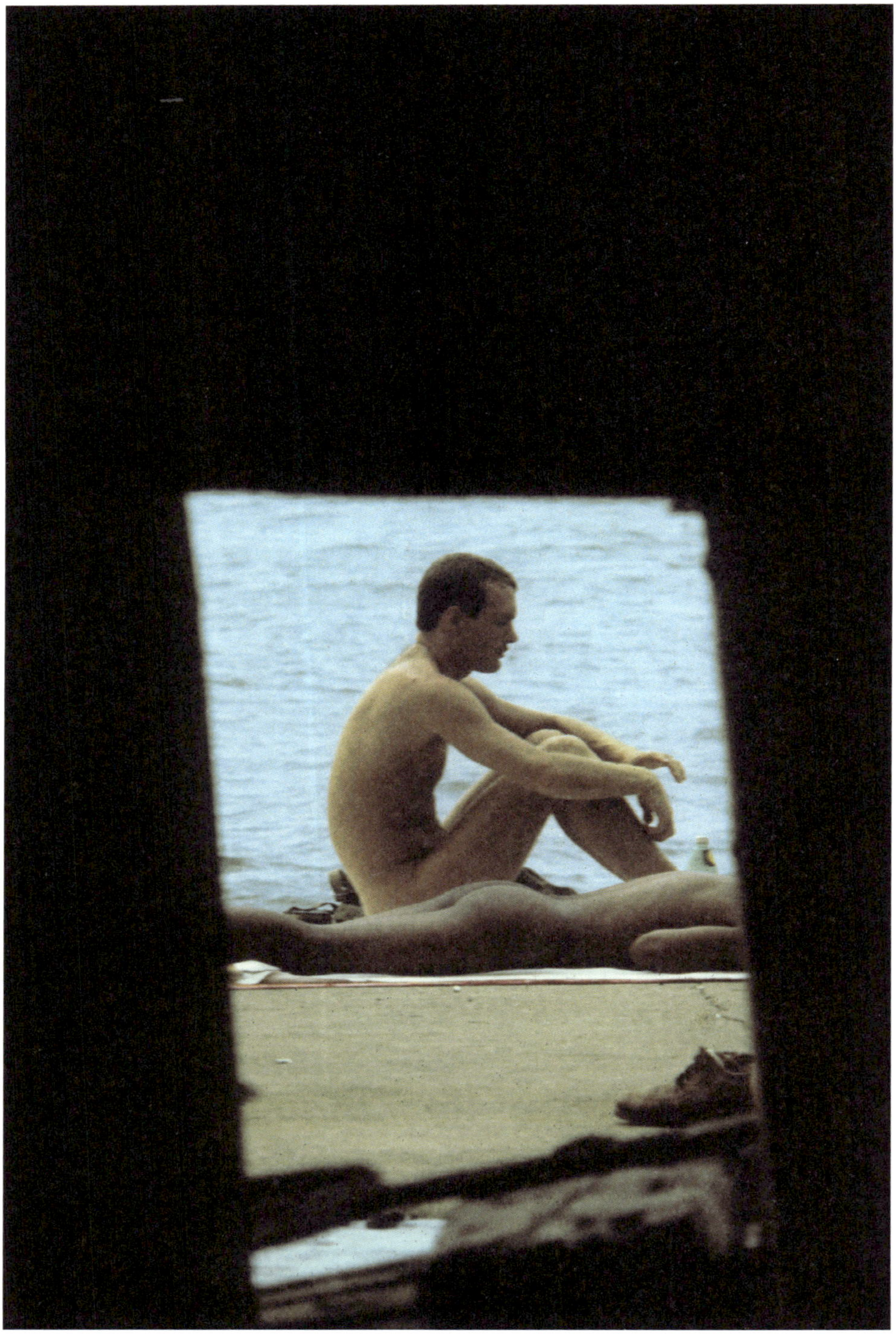

sides and ceiling. Chances are you would not be alone, although few of your fellow visitors would be mourners. Instead, they would be gay men cruising for sex, members of what Matta-Clark called the "sado-masochistic fringe," whom he and his collaborators locked out of Pier 52 when they started the project.[2]

Frank Hallam was at the piers on the day Matta-Clark died, 27 August 1978. It was a Sunday, so Hallam was free from work and able to pursue his hobby of photographing what the gay world called "the sex piers." Did he wander onto Pier 52? Hallam didn't remember, and unfortunately, he didn't take pictures of it that day, but he took several of neighboring Piers 49 and 51 (fig. 21). Given the scantily dressed people in his photographs, it must have been a hot summer afternoon in New York City. Hallam knew nothing about Matta-Clark, but his photograph of two naked men taken through a rectangular break in the wall has a Matta-Clarkian feel. Taken from inside the structure on Pier 51, this picture suggests one of Matta-Clark's signature cuts in the way it stages the idea of surreptitious viewing. Hallam's picture could be said to make literal the qualities of desire, exhibitionism, and voyeurism that are fundamental to Matta-Clark's practice of cutting or holing through but that have been downplayed or neglected in so much of the literature on his art.

21. Frank Hallam, *Biracial, Pier 51*, 1978. Private collection.

Hallam was not unique in his ignorance of Matta-Clark's work, even though he spent a good deal of time in and around Pier 52. The professional photographer Shelley Seccombe, who lived in Westbeth, the artists' housing project directly across from the piers, and who took some splendid pictures of Pier 52 from the outside, told me that she also knew nothing of *Day's End* (fig. 22) back then. In 1978, I too was ignorant of Matta-Clark, despite my newly minted bachelor's degree in art history and my frequent visits to the waterfront. I must have seen Matta-Clark's cuts in the exterior walls of Pier 52, but they didn't register as art. That all these frequenters of the piers, myself included, could have been unaware of the existence of *Day's End* seems particularly surprising given its prestige and notoriety today. Along with *Splitting*, which it followed almost immediately, *Day's End* now figures as the most significant work in Matta-Clark's extraordinary career. Its importance has much to do with its outlaw status; few artists in the history of the avant-garde have committed a criminal act on the scale of *Day's End*. Marcel Duchamp may have taken the role of an outlaw in his *Wanted: $2,000 Reward* poster, and Ed Ruscha may have fantasized about setting the Los Angeles County Museum of Art on fire, but in cutting enormous holes into the walls and floors of the city-owned Pier 52, Matta-Clark risked actual criminal charges that, if pursued, would have landed him in jail for years. Even to visit the site to look at *Day's*

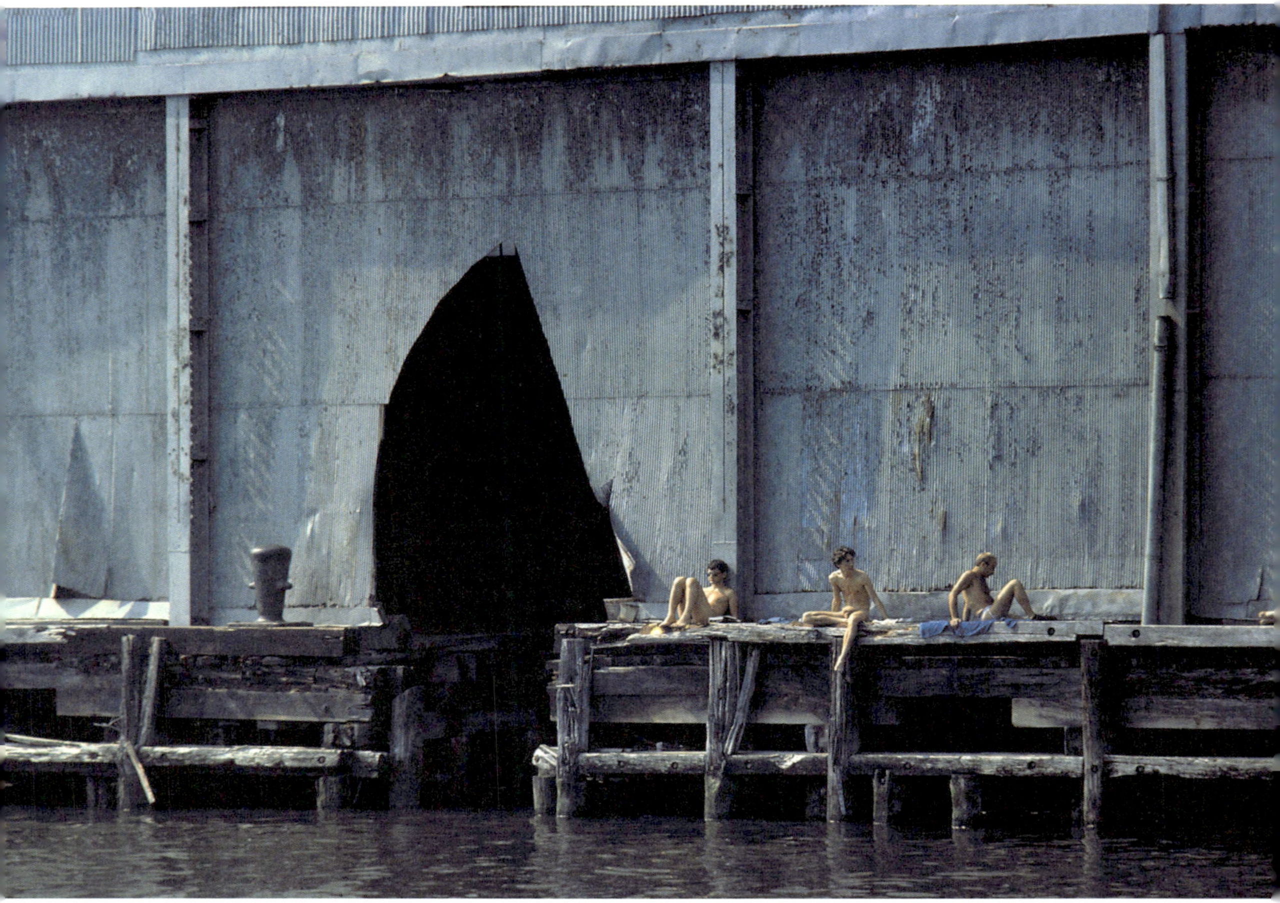

22. Shelley Seccombe, *Sunbathing on the Edge, Pier 52 (Matta-Clark's Day's End)*, ca. 1977.
© Shelly Seccombe.

End was to risk being mugged or arrested for trespassing. And then there were those like the sculptor Joel Shapiro and his young daughter, who felt "put upon" by the sexual exhibitionism characteristic of the pier's gay cruising: "this crazy naked guy was masturbating in a corner," Shapiro recalled.[3]

Whether members of the art world stopped making the pilgrimage to *Day's End* because they thought the city had shut it down or because it was deemed too dangerous, Matta-Clark's masterpiece increasingly became a thing of the past. In March 1976, less than a year after the completion of *Day's End*, Matta-Clark's interviewer, Liza Béar, was surprised to learn that it was still accessible and that the artist himself had ventured back to see what had become of his work. Turning his own crime of destroying city-owned property on its head, Matta-Clark complained that the "authorities"—that is, the agents of the Department of Ports and Terminals—had "vandalized it [laughter]."

> They put railings up and they put a very neat little bridge across the place that I cut in half—I cut the pier in half at the midway point. And then they sealed off all the surface entrances—anything that could allow approach from the outside.
>
> They can't stop the sun coming in through the sickle shape in the back though. . . . No, the basic nature of the space is there except that the pigeons have taken it over again. Or whatever kind of debris floats in or blows in has just filled it up. Where once it was clear that there were a certain number of well-intended interventions, now that intervention has now become little mediated by . . .
>
> Bureaucracy. Well, by bureaucracy but also by droppings—pigeon crap.

Obviously, official attempts to cordon off the building or "confiscate it," as Matta-Clark put it in the same interview, did not keep him or others from entering the site. As he confided to Béar, "Sure, it's still there. In fact, the other day I went back and there was this fantastic moment where a storm hit the west side, and the wind and rain poured in, a very visible column of air and water through the opening. And so its life goes on but it's a secret life. . . . The fact that it's transitory is another contradiction between it and architecture, or it and a lot of other more formally established work."[4]

Strangely enough, what it might be like to risk such a visit to Pier 52 and get a sense of its "secret life" is best conveyed not by the artist's own documentation or some art text but by a pornographic film. Arch Brown's *Pier Groups*, filmed in the months following Matta-Clark's death, contains brief but spectacular footage of *Day's End* and its environs. It tells the story of two handsome men, one gay and one presumably straight, who live in the same walk-up apartment in Greenwich Village. One goes to the waterfront to cruise for sex; the other, partnered to a woman, is sent there by his construction company to survey Pier 52 and come up with a bid for its demolition. As the hypermasculine construction worker carefully inspects the dock, getting down on his knees and even on his stomach to measure various elements of the structure, he repeatedly encounters gay men cruising or in the midst of sex. These men are drawn to his manly physique and intrigued by his suggestive poses. At the same time, the construction worker's attention to his work often seems to falter, and he voyeuristically watches the men copulating.

Of course, *Pier Groups* is not a documentary about Pier 52; many of the film's sex scenes were not even shot on the waterfront. And, like Hallam and Seccombe, Brown himself told me that he had never heard of Matta-Clark or guessed that he was in the presence of a monumental artwork when he filmed *Pier Groups*.[5] Nevertheless, the brief appearance of *Day's End* in Brown's film strikes me as more evocative of the lived experience of the work than Matta-Clark's own film, which captures the actual cutting, or the extensive video footage made by Jack Kruger under Matta-Clark's direction before and during the opening. Matta-Clark's film is most effective in the way it conveys the physical effort that went into the cutting. The artist and his assistants, wielding an oxyacetylene torch and a chainsaw, literally become the type of construction worker the brawny star portrays in Brown's *Pier Groups*. The blatant eroticism of Brown's movie reminds us how Matta-Clark's adoption of the tools of a hypermasculine laborer was itself an erotic performance during the years when the construction worker was considered an ideal of desirability both within and outside the gay community.

But Brown's film does more than help us appreciate how Matta-Clark performed, however unconsciously, a fantasy of machismo; *Pier Groups* effectively extends the history of *Day's End* beyond the actual process of its making and the few days in 1975 when Matta-Clark invited friends to witness the piece. However brief its appearance, we see *Day's End* existing over time, and in a context entirely outside what is usually considered the art world. Brown's film is particularly apt at evoking the inside/outside dynamic of pier spaces; framed by doorways and windows, sky and water are always in movement. Figures stand against wooden beams, silhouetted by the dazzling light of the skyline and the reflections that bounce off the river. We also hear snatches of river sounds and the traffic outside on West Street (or at least simulations of such sounds). As with Hallam's photograph of two naked men sunbathing, scenes of men having sex are spied through windows or cracks in the wall. Such cropping of bodies both piques our interest and frustrates our viewing. We feel protected by our clandestine position in the shadows: we can see, but the objects we long for cannot see us. Or can they? Several times, the gaze of the supposedly straight construction worker is returned by a man engaged in sex. In the logic of the film's camera angles, the voyeur's gaze is returned, as if to say, "I know you are watching me, but I don't mind. It might even turn me on." Brown enacts a series of such encounters, taking us through dark, confined spaces and passageways, until in one brief moment the camera pans back and we watch men cruising in the vast space of the interior shed, illuminated from behind by Matta-Clark's enormous cut, filled with the light of the setting sun. It is by far the largest hole in a film in which holes are everywhere—holes in the wall, ceiling, and floor, and also in the bodies exposed and pleasured in sex. Filling the screen for a few dazzling seconds, Matta-Clark's cut functions in the film like an emblem of voyeuristic desire—like a giant eye, or a keyhole in the sky.

Pier Groups reminds us that *Day's End* changed not only in relation to the position of the sun but also in terms of who interacted with the space. In so much of the official documentation of *Day's End*, Pier 52 is depicted either as empty or as inhabited only by the artist and his friends. In Brown's film, by contrast, and in photographs by Baltrop, Fink, and Seccombe, Matta-Clark's cuts are in constant interaction with the local gay subculture. For example, in a wonderful picture by Baltrop, we see two men cruising the central space of Pier 52, with the sunlight pouring through the large cut (fig. 23). The jacket and boots of the bearded figure suggest that the picture was taken in the late fall or early spring. It must have been quite chilly, yet the pier is so suffused with light from the various openings in the walls and ceilings that it seems warm. Even more inviting is Seccombe's picture of several naked men sunbathing next to Matta-Clark's sail-shaped cut, taken from outside at the height of the summer (see fig. 22). As Matta-Clark himself said, after the building was shut down, "a lot of people took it on themselves to break in and so keep the work in some kind of public domain."[6] How ironic to evoke this concept of antiprivatization when it was Matta-Clark and his cohorts who for several months seized or "squatted in" what was after all a publicly owned structure, keeping out anyone else who wanted to use it. And what are the implications for the concept of audience and site specificity when the public of "public domain" changes from

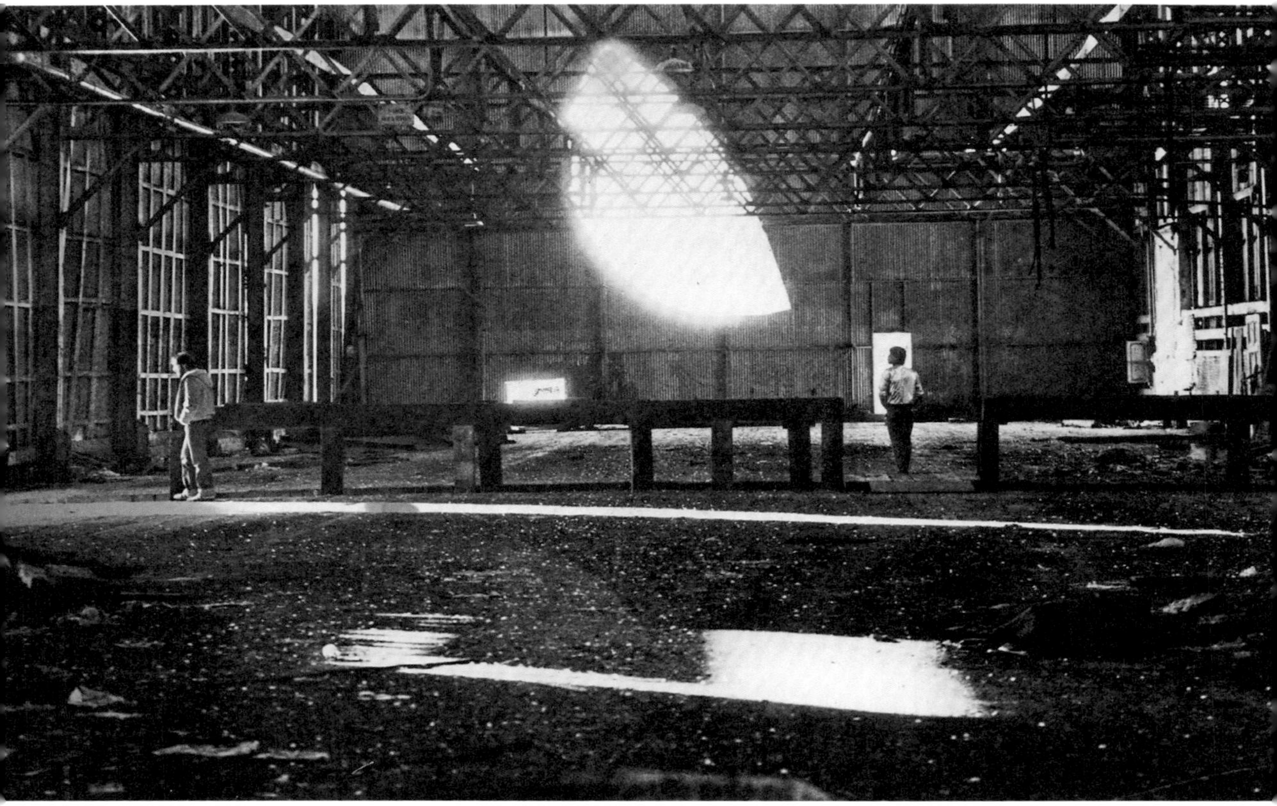

23. Alvin Baltrop, *The Piers*, n.d. (1975–86). Photograph used courtesy of The Alvin Baltrop Trust, © 2010, The Alvin Baltrop Trust and Galerie Buchholz. All rights reserved.

art-world insiders to gay men sunbathing and cruising for sex? Consideration of the ways in which Pier 52 was used in the years after its completion by those who knew nothing about Matta-Clark, let alone the history and theory of the avant-garde, allows us to take seriously the artist's own claims of site specificity, albeit in ways that he himself may never have imagined.

Site Specificity

Since the controversy around the removal of Richard Serra's *Tilted Arc* from Manhattan's Federal Plaza in 1989, the popular conception of site specificity has been dominated by the idea of a work of art so completely designed for a particular space that to move it, or drastically change its environment, is effectively to destroy it. As Thomas Crow suggests, however, this concept of the sanctity of the original location and context invests the site-specific sculpture with the very quality of modernist autonomy that the ideal of sculpture embedded in the world was supposed to challenge or resist. Matta-Clark had a far more social and profoundly antimodernist concept of site specificity. Seeking to engage the peculiar contexts and histories of a place by creating "deep metamorphic incisions into space/place," he insisted, "I do not want to create a totally new supportive field of vision, of cognition. I want to reuse the old one, the existing framework of thought and sight." Such a transformation would not be the final work of art; rather, it would become "a special stage in perpetual metamorphosis, a model for people's constant action on space as much as in the space that surrounds them."[7] Crow posits that this "strong" conception of site specificity was augmented by the limited duration of most of Matta-Clark's architectural cuttings and performances: "his sculpture tended to leave so minimal an imprint on the world that it precluded fixation on formal particulars by the simple measure of barring most of its interested audiences from ever seeing it. . . . The actual duration of the strong work is limited because its presence is in terminal contradiction to the nature of the space it occupies. Contradiction is the source of its articulateness, so brief duration is a condition of meaning and is presupposed in its founding stipulations."[8] Crow's analysis fits well with Matta-Clark's critique of the egotism and commercialism of so much modern sculpture and architecture. Matta-Clark's stated goal was to create "non-monuments" and "anarchitecture."

But while Crow's argument that Matta-Clark's work's site specificity requires the work's almost immediate destruction makes sense for some of Matta-Clark's pieces (such as *Splitting*, where the artist knew the building he was working on was scheduled for demolition), it does not apply to *Day's End*'s open-ended span of existence. Nor does limited duration account for the powerful aesthetic pleasure *Day's End* elicited in its viewers, an effect of the piece's sublime scale and the way it used the changing light of the sun. These effects did not depend on the work's imminent destruction. At the same time, Matta-Clark's own utopian aspirations for his work contradict Crow's emphasis on negation. Matta-Clark insisted that he was interested in augmenting or revealing aspects of the original historical and social context of the structure. He even fantasized to Donald Wall about working on some future project that "would no longer be concerned with just personal or metaphoric treatment of the site, but finally responsive to the express will of its occupants."[9] In Crow's emphasis on the role of opposition and negation in Matta-Clark's practice, the buildings the artist acts on are surrogates for a repressive society. Indeed, many of Matta-Clark's pronouncements encourage Crow's emphasis on negation. When Matta-Clark declares in a typewritten statement, "much of my life energies are simply about being denied," he shifts the focus away from the analytic to a matter of frustrated desire: "There's so much in our society that purposely intends denial: deny entry, deny passage, deny participation, etc. We would still be living in towers and castles, if we hadn't broken down some of the social and economic barriers, inhibitions, and restraints."[10] In these final lines, Matta-Clark evokes the idea of the artist as a rebel who, by breaking taboos and conventions, points the way to a freer and fairer society.

Realizing that such an antiauthoritarian bent and quest for personal liberation would not be Matta-Clark's best defense against the charge of vandalism of city-owned property, his lawyer convinced the artist to draft a statement in which he cast himself as the enemy of the waterfront's seemingly "city-condoned anarchy," in which muggers victimized pedestrians and "a recently popularized sado-masochistic fringe."[11] In this statement, Matta-Clark claimed that his goal was not to undermine the integrity of a government-owned building but to "improve the property" by letting in more light, thereby making it safer for the public. In another statement, Matta-Clark made analogies between Pier 52 and a Christian basilica, referring to the enormous cut at the west end as a rose window.[12] Whether this account of his motive was sincere, it is hard to see how cutting out sections of the floor improved the building's safety. Following Matta-Clark's lead in emphasizing the positive aspects of his peculiar renovations, friends, colleagues, and critics repeated the rhetoric of his religious trope, his evocation of light casting out darkness, as one of the central themes of *Day's End*. Jane Crawford, the artist's widow, set the tone: "the alchemist has transformed the dark and derelict behemoth into an indoor park that shimmered with light reflecting from the water inside and out, lit by half-moon and full-moon shapes at the western end and bisected by a cut through the width of the pier ending in a sail shape. . . . Light from the sun setting in the west would pour in through Gordon's cut as if through the rose window of a cathedral, animating the interior with light."[13] *Day's End* collaborator G. H. Hovagimyan is every bit as ecstatic in describing the way the "circular removal revealed the sky and at the edge of the 'interior canal' a jaunty cut-out seemed to mimic the outline of an unfurled sail. Light, air, sky and water. Everything was alive with motion and light."[14]

Among the accolades of the friends and admirers who witnessed *Day's End*, the reminiscences of sculptor Joel Shapiro strike a somewhat sour note. His remarks stand out for their ambivalence and their focus on the work's paradoxes and problems. Shapiro insists that although it "was probably the most successful of the pieces" he had seen by Matta-Clark, *Day's End* was nonetheless "frightening":

> Gordon's pieces were dramatic—subtracting chunks and big parts of buildings. I recall thinking, whose building is this? It is dangerous. I did feel put upon when I went into the pier with my daughter, and this crazy naked guy was masturbating in a corner. Where was Gordon? . . .
>
> To go into an abandoned place and chop it up—I don't know what I thought about that. The destructive aspect, I mean. Who owned the building? What was it being used for? Was it really abandoned? The willful aspect, I don't know. The piece was dangerous to the viewer. Why did he do it? It was spectacular. It was large; it had scale. He was creating some kind of edge—flirting with some sort of abyss. It wasn't like the earthworks of the same time. It was urban, it was in an existing, degenerate structure. There was a city sense. I sensed rage and anger, but never really talked to him about it.[15]

Shapiro calls the building a "degenerate structure," but it is not entirely clear whether he is referring to its condition before or after Matta-Clark was through with it. I assume that by degeneracy he is referring to the way the building was used for gay cruising, but in the context of the larger statement and his worries about the project, some of this degeneracy rubs off on Matta-Clark as well. Like the men who use the piers for sex in the middle of the night, when they could easily plunge to their death or fall victim to muggers, Matta-Clark is flirting with the edge, risking the abyss.

Despite the fame of *Day's End*, it seems to me that many of Shapiro's basic questions about the piece have not been adequately answered. Above all, whose building was it? Had it really been abandoned? Shapiro talks of feeling "put upon," as if Matta-Clark himself was responsible for the degenerate behavior he and his young daughter encountered at the pier. Surely it is unfair to blame Matta-Clark for the acts of sexual exhibitionists. And yet, as Shapiro implies, the totality of *Day's End* as a work of art resided not just in the cuts but in the "degenerate structure" that contained them, and for which it was, in some sense, the ideal setting.

Pier 18

What was it that drew Matta-Clark to Pier 52 and the waterfront in the first place? According to the radio interview he gave with Liza Béar in March 1976, the artist and a small group of friends had been searching the city for an abandoned building much larger than the suburban house he famously cut in half in New Jersey and titled *Splitting*. The Beaux-Arts façades originally drew him to the piers: "Driving down the pier along that empty highway in front, the façades are an incredible, animated grouping of different eras and different personalities. . . . And I wanted to deal with one of the earlier ones . . . a turn-of-the-century façade."[16] Oddly, he makes no mention of two earlier waterfront pieces—his untitled performance on Pier 18, and one of his earliest cuttings, *Pier In/Out* of 1973. Neither of these efforts manifested the scale or ambition of what he accomplished on Pier 52, yet both were closely related to it in theme and aesthetic. In this context, *Day's End* seems far more deliberate than Matta-Clark himself let on. It was the culmination of several years of experimentation, rather than a work devised on the spot in response to a fortunate set of circumstances. To put it another way, Matta-Clark recognized the potential of Pier 52 in part because of his experiences working on these two earlier projects.

As with Vito Acconci, it was Willoughby Sharp's invitation to join his Pier 18 project that first drew Matta-Clark to the waterfront. In response to Sharp's call for works of art that broke through the confines of the art gallery and museum, Matta-Clark originally envisioned creating small ecosystems of trees and other plantings on barges and parking them along Pier 18. This concept of a movable park was probably inspired by Robert Smithson's 1970 scheme, "Floating Island to Travel Around Manhattan Island." Matta-Clark's drawing *Parked Island Barges on the Hudson*, with its bushy trees and arched bridges, is so reminiscent of Smithson's precedent that it could be thought of as an homage to Smithson, who had only recently died and whose work was so important to Matta-Clark. Whether because of the anxiety of influence or the expense and difficulty of obtaining suitable barges, Matta-Clark abandoned his Edenic dream of a flotilla of floating gardens. Instead, he created a onetime performance (fig. 24) inside the pier shed that was recorded by the photographic team of Harry Shunk and János Kender. On top of a pile of dirt and debris, he planted an evergreen. He then climbed a ladder to the structure's ceiling beams and proceeded to hang from one leg, upside down, over the tree. In putting his body at risk in this way, Matta-Clark may have been in conversation with his close friend Lee Jaffe's Pier 18 contribution, *Parallel*

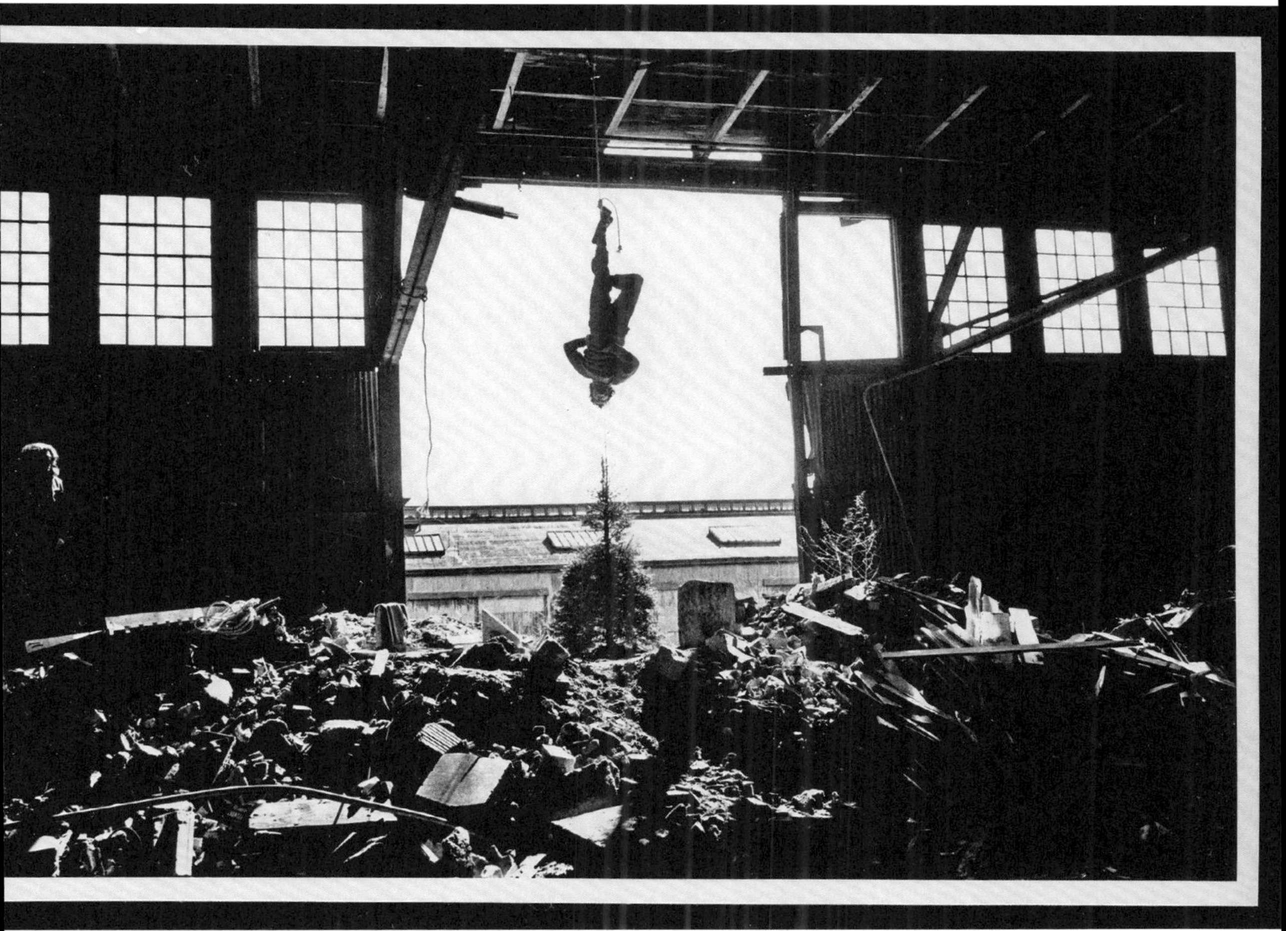

24. Shunk-Kender and Gordon Matta-Clark, *Project for Pier 18*, 1971. © 2018 Estate of Gordon Matta-Clark / Artists Rights Society (ARS), New York. Photo: Shunk-Kender © J. Paul Getty Trust. Getty Research Institute, Los Angeles (2014.R.20).

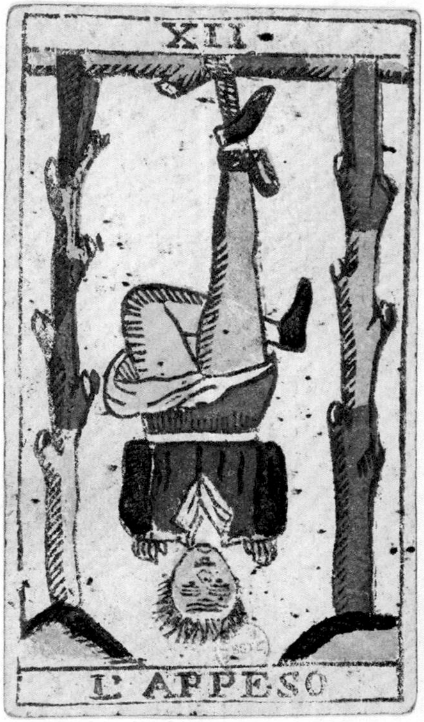

25. F. F. Solesio, *The Hanged Man, Piedmontese Tarot Deck*, 1865. Photo: Wikimedia Commons.

Fears, which also involves a man suspended over the water. While the tree element remained, like a remnant of the original barge scheme derivative of Smithson's project, Matta-Clark shifted the focus of his version of an earthwork to his own physical labor and his seeming ability to defy gravity. In *Project for Pier 18*, at the very inception of his career, the artist was already manipulating earth, air, light, and water in feats of physical endurance and danger that, if they didn't directly involve cuts to a building, were about revealing aspects of its structure and the latent potential in its decay and imaginative reconstruction.

Matta-Clark's act of suspending himself upside down from one leg was meant to evoke the Hanged Man (fig. 25), the hero of the twelfth card of the Tarot, or so Tina Kukielski reports in her essay in the catalogue for Matta-Clark's 2007 retrospective at the Whitney Museum of American Art. Although she mentions that the Hanged Man card is often associated with "life in suspension," Kukielski has little to say about its highly charged history and contested symbolism, nor does she remark on the significance of Matta-Clark's foray into the Tarot.[17] I share her reticence about going too far into the strange world of Tarot interpretation, particularly when we know very little about Matta-Clark's investment (or lack thereof) in its systems and beliefs. Nevertheless, certain basic themes surrounding the Hanged Man card are not in dispute, and they are relevant to Matta-Clark's practice and, perhaps even more, to his mystique. Above all, whether villain or hero, the Hanged Man is a risk taker. The card is also known as the Traitor because during the Renaissance rebels were hung upside down after being executed as a form of humiliation. The Hanged Man is also said to evoke Odin, the chief Norse god, who dangled upside down for nine days as a means of obtaining ultimate wisdom. It is also associated with Saint

Peter, martyred upside down on a cross in an inversion of Christ's crucifixion. I wonder whether Matta-Clark had Caravaggio's spectacular painting of Saint Peter's death in mind as he assembled the elements of his own simulated martyrdom. Caravaggio conceives of Peter's crucifixion as if it were happening not in a large outside space but in a tightly contained, dimly lit area; the taut rope that flips Saint Peter upside down and the emphasis on the structural element of the enormous beams of the crucifix come together to make a theatrical image of a body in tension that might have appealed to Matta-Clark.

God, saint, outlaw—these are the foundational figures upon which the cult of the romantic artist is based. Whether Matta-Clark sought to summon these attributes to himself or to make fun of them, they seem important in understanding the later trajectory of his art. But as with Matta-Clark's interest in alchemy, a fascination with the Tarot and its association with 1960s hippie mysticism may not fit well with various attempts to claim Matta-Clark for the cause of poststructural critical theory and/or architectural deconstruction. Certainly, any interest Matta-Clark might have had in the Tarot is at one with his exploration of alchemy "as an answer to his acute personal and artistic dilemmas through a theatrical simulation of its arcane physical procedures," as Crow aptly puts it.[18] In discussing Matta-Clark's intense exploration of the history and methods of alchemy, Crow documents the artist's exploration of the writings of Carl Jung, who believed that the imagery of alchemy and the Tarot offered a particularly vivid way to explore the symbolic process of what he called archetypes of transformation. Although Jung himself did not write an extended analysis of the Tarot, interpreters of the Tarot frequently offer Jungian explanations for the meaning of the individual cards. It has been noted that Jung's famous description of the search for self in *The Archetypes and the Collective Unconscious* is suggestive of the Hanged Man's state of suspension:

> The meeting with oneself is, at first, the meeting with one's own shadow. The shadow is a tight passage, a narrow door, whose painful constriction no one is spared who goes down to the deep well. But one must learn to know oneself in order to know who one is. For what comes after the door is, surprisingly enough, a boundless expanse full of unprecedented uncertainty, with apparently no inside and no outside, no above and no below, no here and no there, no mine and no thine, no good and no bad. It is the world of water, where all life floats in suspension; where the realm of sympathetic system, the soul of everything living, begins; where I am indivisibly this and that;

where I experience the other in myself and the other-than-myself experiences me.[19]

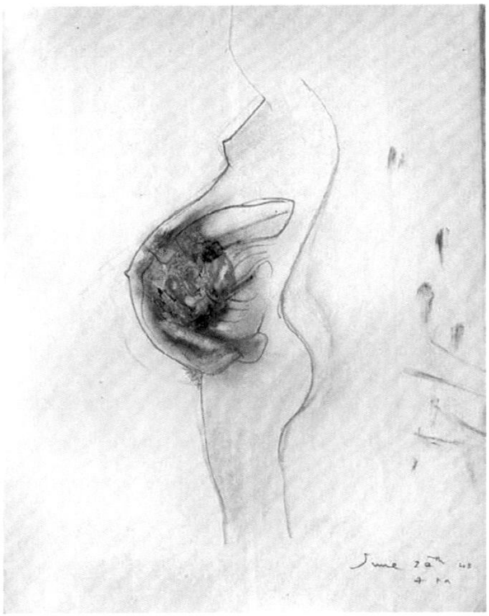

26. Roberto Matta, *Study for the Hanged Man*, 1942. Photo courtesy of Ramuntcho Matta.

It is remarkable how this passage reads like a description of Matta-Clark's artistic process, in which architectural spaces are cut or dug into, or the artist's body is suspended in air in a high-wire act. Matta-Clark's work frequently involves a sort of passage that leads to a "boundless expanse . . . of uncertainty," where sky and water are framed in such a way as to leave "no inside and no outside, no above and no below." For all of Matta-Clark's later attempts to engage the political and economic contexts of the sites that he manipulated, his work always seems animated by a Jungian quest, some bodily struggle with archetypal elements of air, earth, fire, and water, in which, as Matta-Clark put it, "the microcosmic self is related to the whole."[20]

Whatever we may think of Jung's writings, they had an enormous influence on the history of modern art, beginning with the generation of Matta-Clark's father, Roberto Matta. In fact, if we want to look for possible origins of the Hanged Man motif in Matta-Clark's work, we need look no further than his father's own painting *The Hanged Man* of 1942 and its related drawings (fig. 26). Matta was fascinated with the Tarot and kabbalah. According to William Rubin, "free association" with the Hanged Man card "induced in Matta's mind an image of the fetus 'hanging' in the abdomen of his pregnant wife."[21] In 1942, the year of Matta-Clark's conception, his father was fantasizing about the birth of a son who would take up the god/outlaw role of the Tarot card. Some three decades later, dangling from a rope on a rotting pier, Matta-Clark accepted that mantle.[22]

Perhaps no two men could have been more primed to witness Matta-Clark's daring act on Pier 18 than Harry Shunk and János Kender, who had collaborated in 1960 on Yves Klein's famous *Leap into the Void* (fig. 27). Is there another image that so aptly encapsulates the ideal of the avant-garde artist who risks life itself to explore new experiences and possibilities? Of course, *Leap*

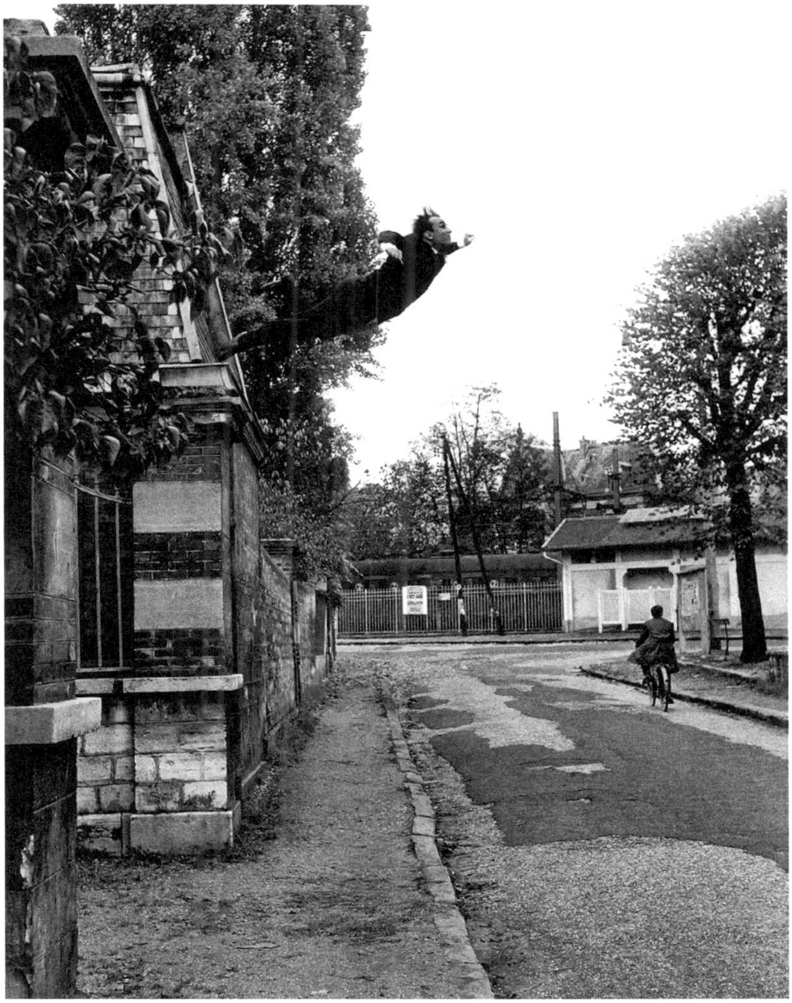

27. Yves Klein, *Saut dans le Vide (Leap into the Void)*, 1960. Artistic action by Yves Klein © The Estate of Yves Klein c/o ADAGP, Paris 2018. Collaboration Harry Shunk and János Kender © J. Paul Getty Trust. Getty Research Institute, Los Angeles (2014.R.20).

into the Void is a fake—a montage of negatives that makes it look as if Klein is magically suspended in the air without a safety net to catch his falling body. By contrast, Shunk-Kender's photographs of Matta-Clark document the awkward and tricky process by which Matta-Clark had to slip the rope around his body and then somersault around to dangle precariously from the rafters. In a project that both emulates and critiques Klein, Matta-Clark reveals the string that suspends him over the void.[23] True to the origins of the Hanged Man motif in the humiliation of traitors, Matta-Clark's performance must have looked by turns ridiculous, as when his legs were splayed like a wishbone; frightening, as

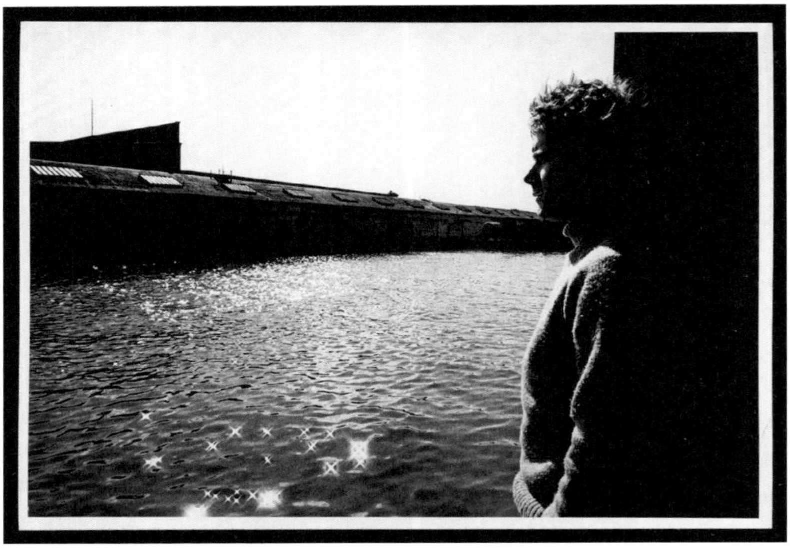

28. Shunk-Kender and Gordon Matta-Clark, *Project for Pier 18*, 1971. © 2018 Estate of Gordon Matta-Clark / Artists Rights Society (ARS), New York. Photo: Shunk-Kender © J. Paul Getty Trust. Getty Research Institute, Los Angeles (2014.R.20).

when he first climbed the ladder and confronted the rope as if it were a noose; and, finally, positively exhilarating, as when he centered himself in the pier's window, perfectly suspended above the crown of the tree. How many artists could perform this level of gymnastics? Could Yves Klein actually have done this? These questions lead to another. As gay men, were Shunk and Kender particularly open to the kind of exhibitionism displayed by Matta-Clark, and Klein before him? Their series of photographs does seem to play up the eroticism of Matta-Clark's performance. One striking image shows Matta-Clark in profile (fig. 28), accentuating his almost classical nose and forehead. Sunlight falls across his curly locks and makes starlike reflections on the glistening water. In his lumpy sweater, he shares the glamour of such contemporaries as the football player Joe Namath and the rebel movie star Peter Fonda of *Easy Rider*.

For me, the most amazing thing about Shunk-Kender's photographs of Matta-Clark's earliest pier piece is their premonition of the monumental cuts in *Day's End*. In one striking picture of Matta-Clark hanging from the rafters (fig. 29), the contrast between foreground and background is so stark that the image almost reverses itself. The black shape of Matta-Clark's body looks like an empty black silhouette that has been cut out of the flat white sky. Klein's physical leap into the void has become the void of Matta-Clark's own body. Matta-Clark will make cuts, but he himself is already a kind a cut, a jagged hole the viewer is invited to fill in.

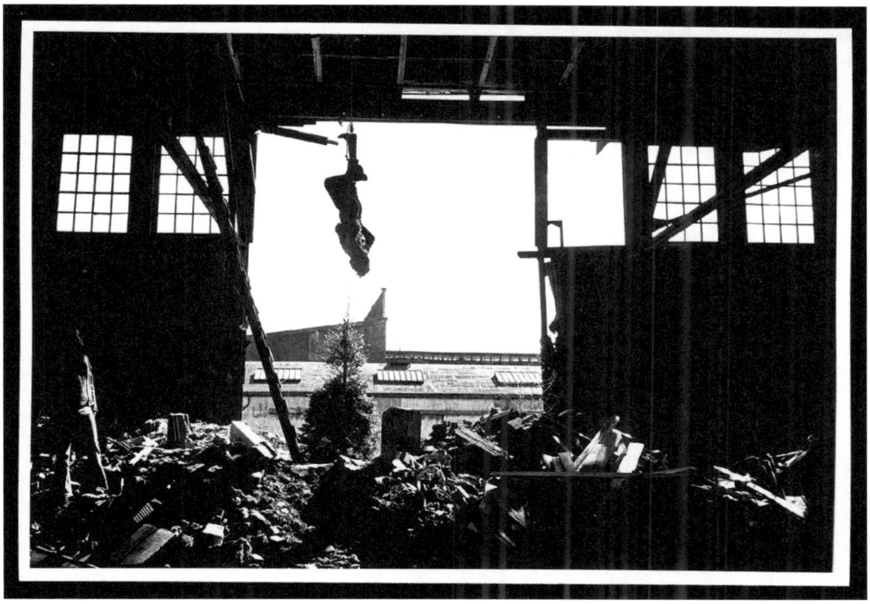

29. Shunk-Kender and Gordon Matta-Clark, *Project for Pier 18*, 1971. © 2018 Estate of Gordon Matta-Clark / Artists Rights Society (ARS), New York. Photo: Shunk-Kender © J. Paul Getty Trust. Getty Research Institute, Los Angeles (2014.R.20).

Pier In/Out

There is another kind of void that Matta-Clark's Pier 18 performance and so much of his later work risks, which is not about the great unknown or the chasm above which he dangles, or even the blank spaces created by his cuts. This void is the one left by the fact that so much of his art no longer exists. There is a disconnect between the grand scale of Matta-Clark's great effort to bore through buildings and the relative smallness of the documentation that these efforts left behind: the photographs, sketches, and crude videos and films. Of course, Matta-Clark's willingness to spend so much energy on such impermanent works of art was part of his radicalism. By leaving so little to exhibit and sell, he undermined the commodity nature of the monument and the masterpiece in the art world. And yet, like many other performance and conceptual artists of his generation, he was reluctant to abandon the art object completely. Even if he found walls in themselves far more interesting than the pictures made to hang on them, he created elaborate photographic collages drawn from images of *Day's End* that were meant to be displayed in

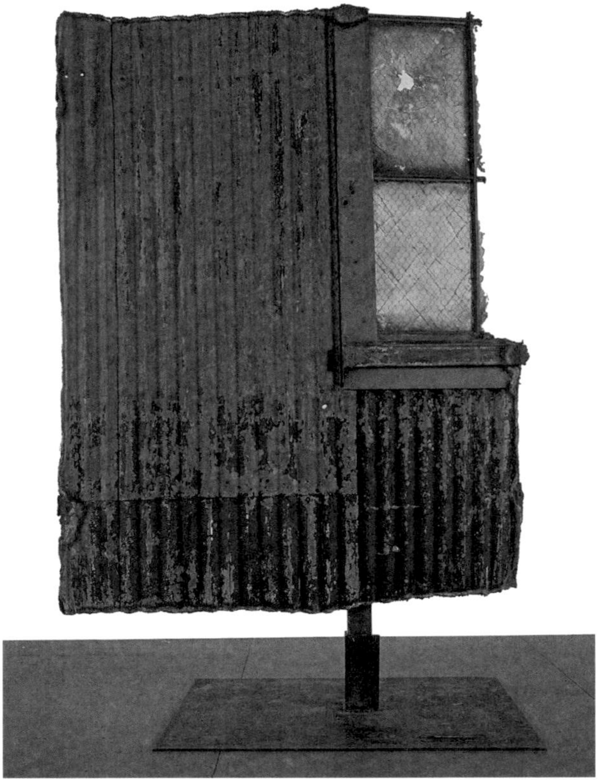

30. Gordon Matta-Clark, *Pier In/Out*, 1973. Collection of John and Thomas Solomon. Photo courtesy The Estate of Gordon Matta-Clark and David Zwirner, New York / London / Hong Kong.

galleries and museums. Matta-Clark also saved and exhibited a few building fragments left over from his cuttings, most notably corner pieces from the Englewood, New Jersey, house of *Splitting*. *Pier In/Out* (fig. 30) is one of the earliest of these remnants. It was cut from the façade of Pier 14, which stood at the end of Fulton Street, four blocks south of Pier 18, where Matta-Clark had created his first pier performance. In its heyday, Pier 14 served the Fall River Line steamboats that traveled to and from Boston and other New England ports. Although various other shipping lines used the pier into the 1960s, it never regained the importance of its days as the gateway to what Roger McAdam calls "the floating palaces" of the Fall River Line steamboats, with their elegant parlors, dining rooms, and sleeping cabins.[24] By the time Matta-Clark made his cuts, the pier was slated to be buried by landfill for the massive Battery Park City project, which would also cover Pier 17 and Pier 18.

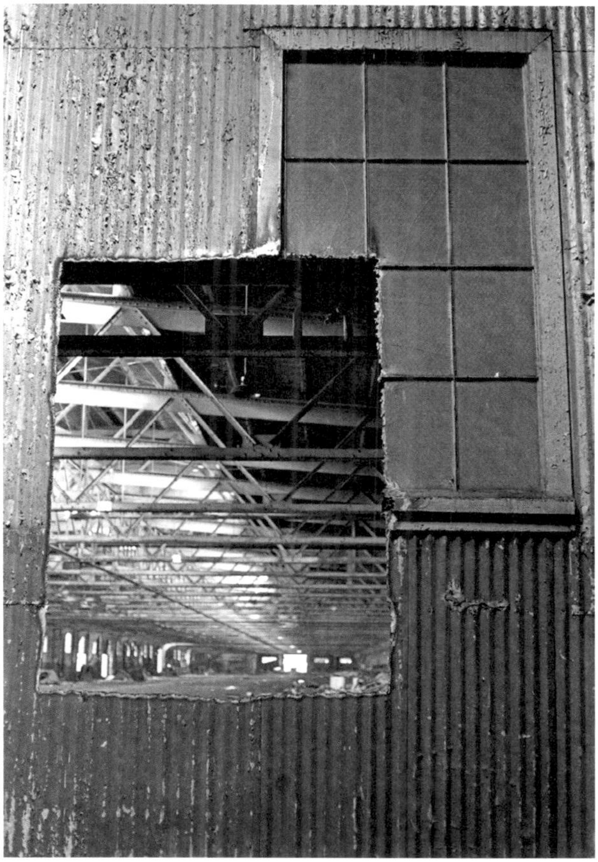

31. Gordon Matta-Clark, *Pier In/Out*, 1973. © 2018 Estate of Gordon Matta-Clark / Artists Rights Society (ARS), New York. Photo courtesy The Estate of Gordon Matta-Clark and David Zwirner, New York / London / Hong Kong.

I have described *Pier In/Out* as a remnant or fragment because it appears to be taken from a larger piece. Unlike the corner chunks of the Englewood house, which represent only a part of the work of *Splitting*, however, *Pier In/Out* represents the entirety of Matta-Clark's architectural cutting. Also unlike other building fragments that Matta-Clark exhibited, *Pier In/Out* reads as a work of art in its own right. Its pedestal, no matter how awkward, gives it a quality of autonomy—it is literally freestanding. Of course, it is meant to be considered in the context of the documentation of its creation: a photograph that shows the space left behind by Matta-Clark's audacious cut in Pier 14 (fig. 31). Like so much of Matta-Clark's documentation, the photograph shifts attention from the object to the history of its making, or in this case specifically to the space it left behind. Comparing the photograph with the object makes us wonder what constitutes the work of art. Is it the section that Matta-Clark cut out of the façade, or the opening in the façade itself? The void created by cutting out a section of the façade of the warehouse turns into the void, or melancholy lack, that viewers experience because we were not present to witness the work's coming into being, a drama that is intrinsic to its meaning.

Given that actual sculptural objects are rare in Matta-Clark's career, I am surprised that so little has been written about *Pier In/Out*. The piece gets trotted out in Matta-Clark exhibits, if for no other reason than to give the audience something three-dimensional to look at, but relatively little has been said about it. My guess is that what makes it useful to curators—its materiality—makes it something of an embarrassment for those who see Matta-Clark's project as a dismantling of the autonomous art object. Ignored is how well this work speaks to so many of the themes and paradoxes of the artist's practice. Its awkwardness is eloquent. The pier's history of decline adheres to the forlorn quality of Matta-Clark's fragment; he has not transcended it by making over an industrial ruin into a handsome piece of sculpture. He did not create out of rusty steel or splintered wood a heroic work of abstraction in the manner of a Mark di Suvero or Richard Serra. Nor is the work a critical comment on the pretenses of monumental industrial sculpture alone; *Pier In/Out* relates to modernist painting as well. As if in reply to the quip that sculpture is what you bump into when you back up to see a painting, sometimes attributed to Barnett Newman, Matta-Clark created a sculpture that reads like an abstract painting (albeit more like a Diebenkorn than a Newman). In response to the idea beloved by certain minimalist artists that the wall is more interesting than the pictures hanging on it, Matta-Clark literally gives us a piece of wall.

In its apparent reference to painting, *Pier In/Out* refuses the Greenbergian command that the artist be true to the specificity of his medium. It can even be read as a witty reply to Clement Greenberg's famous essay "Modernist Painting," which by 1973 had become required reading for anyone claiming knowledge of contemporary art. Central to Greenberg's thesis was the claim that modernist painting, in its flatness, resisted the tendency of the Old Masters to treat their pictures as if they were windows into real spaces. *Pier In/Out* breaks Greenberg's rule about medium specificity by being a sculpture that is flat, like a painting, while mocking his idea about the Old Masters by literally inserting a window into its structure. Matta-Clark's entire practice goes beyond figuratively cutting through the picture plane to literally make holes through the wall, and the ceiling and the floor, so that the very concept of medium—along with the boundary between art and life—becomes blurred.

To focus on *Pier In/Out's* critique of formalism, however, is to miss one of the work's major themes, which is the relationship of desire to the visual. Significantly, the title's pun equates Matta-Clark's criminal act of cutting a hole with the act of voyeurism. The physical pier is converted into an act of peering, and, as in so many later Matta-Clark pieces, a site becomes all about sight. But what exactly did Matta-Clark see, or hope to see, when the chunk of wall was removed? Not much. Given the waterfront's notoriety as a site of violence, corruption, drug use, and sex, the photograph is a disappointment. Shot from below and at an angle, it reveals little more than a cavernous space and the truss work of the ceiling of a largely empty bulkhead warehouse. The crime *Pier In/Out* allows us to see is not an act of bribery or murder but the work of art itself. A trophy of an illegal act, it reminds us that if we had been there to watch Matta-Clark make this cut, we would have witnessed a felony. If the making of *Pier In/Out* was a crime, how much more so was *Day's End*?

Pier In/Out succinctly raises another neglected aspect of Matta-Clark's practice, namely, his obsession with voyeurism. One of his earliest videos, *Chinatown Voyeur* of 1971, focuses on what you can learn about the private lives of New Yorkers if you train a close-up lens on their windows at night. That this video lineage includes movies like Alfred Hitchcock's *Rear Window* (1954), Michael Powell's *Peeping Tom* (1960), and Brian De Palma's *Hi, Mom!* (1970) does not change the fact that what Matta-Clark was doing was illegal. Watching *Chinatown Voyeur*, we become complicit in Matta-Clark's act of peeping. The suspense in viewing the footage resides in the hope that someone will do something worth watching. That nothing much occurs doesn't mean that the filmmaker isn't playing with our desires—turning his voyeurism into our voyeurism.

Matta-Clark's *Sauna View* continues in the same vein, but it is both funnier and more obviously titillating. The artist cut a hole in the side of the sauna through which he videotaped his naked friends as they came and went. The low viewpoint positions the viewer as a child peeping through a keyhole at its parents. Unlike a traditional movie, in which the characters would be cropped in such a way as to avoid showing us their private parts, the waist-level viewpoint of Matta-Clark's video frequently reveals breasts and genitals; rarely do we see an entire body, nor are we able to reliably connect specific body parts to the people who are talking. The quality of infantile voyeurism and the nervous giggling of the participants might lull us into thinking that *Sauna View* was just a silly one-off, but this video occasioned Matta-Clark's first architectural cut. That his practice of cutting holes in buildings had its origin in voyeurism should come as no surprise to those who have read the artist's interviews. Around the time he was working on *Day's End*, he wrote that his interest in abandoned structures started "small almost to the point of peering through key holes for a better eavesdrop view."[25] In an interview with Donald Wall, Matta-Clark confided that from a young age he "wanted to be a voyeur." He claimed that when he was four, his parents gave him a dollhouse, implying that all his work was related to his childhood activity of playing with and making toy houses. Prodded to consider whether there is "anything sexual about this," Matta-Clark replied, "Yeah. The thing that is most sexual about voyeurism is the thing that is most sexual about sex, to some degree; (there) is as much anticipation as there is gratification."[26] *Sauna View* perfectly expresses this feeling. As we watch, we wonder whether the naked figures in the sauna will "get it on," and if they do, will we be able to see from our obstructed viewpoint? The video both elicits and frustrates our desires. Viewership in *Sauna View* is as much about blindness as it is about sight, just as *Pier In/Out* is about what we can and cannot see.

Matta-Clark's obsession with voyeurism might not seem immediately relevant to *Day's End*, even though the site itself was implicated in the kind of sexual activity that is usually the focus of surreptitious viewing. After all, the scale of the holes in Pier 52 has the effect of bringing light into a darkened space, presumably discouraging any form of clandestine activity. But the videotaped documentation of the project, filmed from a small boat on the Hudson River, which Matta-Clark directed, heightens the sense of voyeurism. Jack Kruger shot the actual video, while Matta-Clark steered the boat and barked directions. At one point, he warns Kruger not to get too close to Pier 51, where gay men are sunbathing, referring to it as "ass-crack beach." Weirdly, he masked the camera lens in such a way that the resulting footage appears to be shot through a semiround portal. The effect is that we view the great outside cut of *Day's End* through another cut.

This process of cropping or framing the viewpoint in the documentation of *Day's End* is reminiscent of two of the Pier 18 projects. Richard Serra cut a trapezoid shape out of cardboard and then had Shunk-Kender photograph the surrounding pier and river through the opening. The "trick" of Serra's project is that Shunk-Kender positioned the camera at such an angle that the resulting picture appears almost perfectly square. John Baldessari's crop was simpler: he merely used his thumbs and his fingers to frame a view of a boat in the harbor, in much the same way that a movie director might convey a shot to a cameraman (fig. 14). These gestures make us hyperaware that taking a picture with a camera is a matter of cropping the scene—creating a fragment of the world—and that the camera itself is a machine with a viewfinder that we look through. When we use a camera, we are in essence looking inside, or through it, to look out. In this respect, Matta-Clark's "porthole" effect eloquently conveys the sense of being both inside and outside, almost as if we were somehow contained within the camera. The circular shape makes us think about the relationship between seeing and our actual eyes. We get the sensation that our body, like the boat and the camera, is a shell or container out of which we look. I would argue that whereas both Baldessari and Serra, in collaboration with Shunk-Kender, used the frame to think about the aesthetics of picture taking, space, and illusion, Matta-Clark is interested in the physicality of vision and above all in the compulsion to look. As Kruger holds the camera, Matta-Clark repeatedly tells him not to move it around and to keep the focus static, as he maneuvers the boat closer and closer to the pier. At one point, they regret that they cannot change the lens. Kruger becomes annoyed because the wide-angle lens makes it seem as if they are farther from the pier than they want to be. The camera brings them in only so far. Like the crop, it enables and constrains vision.

What is it that compels us to look? The most dramatic element on both the outside and the inside of Pier 52 is the great cut on the western façade (fig. 32). Its enormous size can only be appreciated from the vantage point of the water. Surely we are meant to marvel at the abstract beauty of its form, but that pleasure cannot be separated from the outrageous act of its creation. As with *Pier In/Out*, we marvel at the audacity of Matta-Clark's crime. The video makes us feel as if we are discovering it, or spying on it, or perhaps voyeuristically complicit in its criminality. The pleasures and meanings of Matta-Clark's piece are hard to fathom. The iconic shape at the center of the west wall, in particular, defies description. The art historian Pamela M. Lee calls the cut "almond-shaped" and, more eloquently, a "gargantuan, misplaced oculus."[27] Others compare it to a cathedral rose window, a cat's-eye, and a solar eclipse. Matta-Clark equated the cut with a sickle, and thus by implication with the act of cutting itself, with additional associations of communism; more mundanely, he related the process of cutting to removing wedges of pie.[28] Yet none of these forms quite does justice to the intriguing nature of the shape created by the overlapping of two circles, or a circle and arc of different radii; interestingly, the precise technical term for such a shape is a lens.[29] Given that our best access to the now destroyed piece is through photographs, "lens" is a

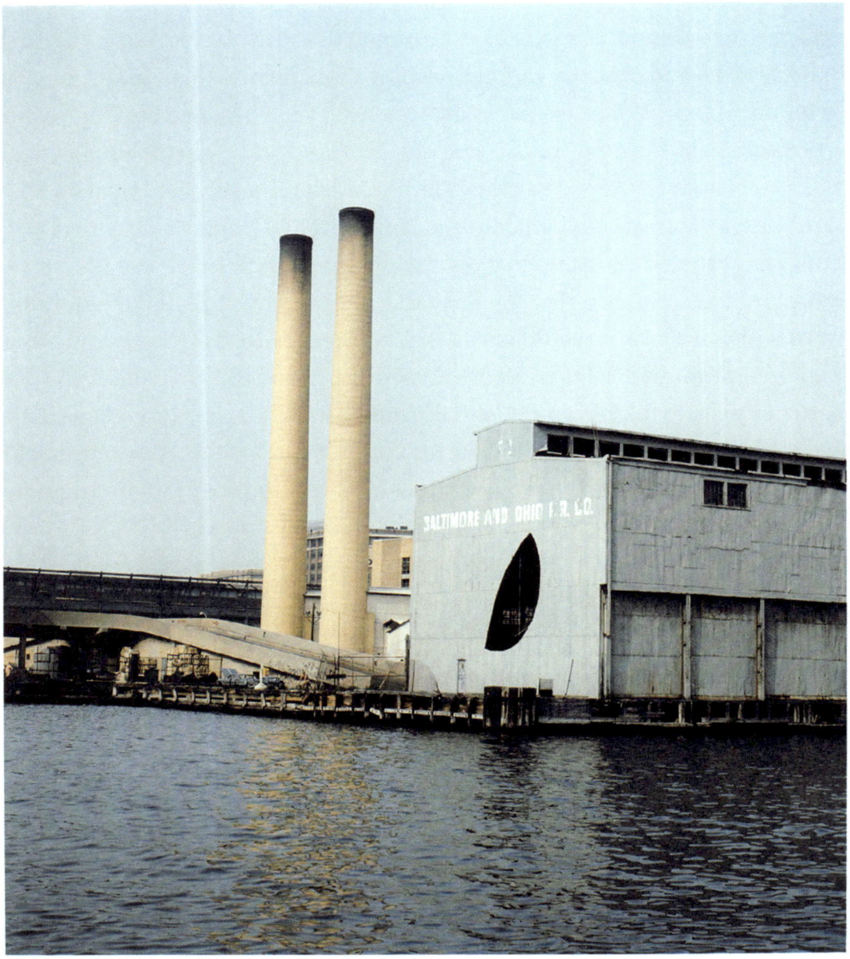

32. Gordon Matta-Clark, *Day's End*, 1975. © 2018 Estate of Gordon Matta-Clark / Artists Rights Society (ARS), New York. Photo courtesy The Estate of Gordon Matta-Clark and David Zwirner, New York / London / Hong Kong.

particularly apt description and metaphor in the way it makes us think of the entire project as an enormous camera or eyeball into which the viewer walks.

According to the artist, the geometry of the piece had a complex genealogy. Matta-Clark told Liza Béar that he was originally thinking of cutting out "wedges" of the "empirical New York waterfront." He was aware that the piers in the Meatpacking District were "overrun by the gays," and of their earlier history of "ex-stevedore violence and things like that." But more important was that "since the 19th century robber baron American railroad pier was cutting up American business and American holdings throughout the country, it would be appropriate to take a pie-like slice out of it." The original idea was for the shape to be more evocative of a sickle, thus infusing the piece with an anticapitalist message.

As Matta-Clark interacted with the space, however, his conception shifted away from past uses of the building to the axis of the earth itself, and the process of the sun making its way across the horizon: he began to see "associations and references to the sun and earth surface relationship." The large cuts on the west and south walls and on the floor of the pier came after he had made an initial cut in the ceiling. He then spent time watching how the sunlight penetrated the space throughout the day and thinking about how the angle of sun would change over the course of a year. Béar asked Matta-Clark if he was influenced by the way Mayan monuments acted like solar calendars. Indeed, from the outside, the shape is reminiscent of a partial eclipse of the sun. Matta Clark did not reject the association, but his poetic observation that the piece was "in pursuit of the sun's setting" makes it sound less like an enormous solar calendar, which charts the predictability of the seasons, than a melancholic reverie on the way time swallows everything, including the sun.

Crucial to Matta-Clark's intention for the piece was that it be experienced "in a peaceful enclosure, totally enclosed in an un-menacing kind of way. That when they went in there, they wouldn't feel like every squeak or every shadow was a potential danger. . . . I wanted it to be more of a joyous situation." And yet even during the opening, when there were many people around, Holly Solomon reported feeling uneasy about being led across a break in the pier.[30] A few weeks later, when Joel Shapiro visited the site, he and his daughter felt vulnerable. Such reports of unease evoke not only the literal danger to the body presented by the pier and its cuts, but also the embodied nature of Matta-Clark's work. The intense physicality of the cuttings gets lost when we look at them in photographs or on screens. If we think only about geometry or the effects of light as dictated by the course of the sun, we forget how violent the act of making the cuts was in the first place. The entire piece was founded on the illicit acts of trespassing and squatting, that is, moving one's body into a space illegally and then holding it. Matta-Clark himself described the act in the most bodily terms: "squat, yeah, kind of deep-squat, deep-knee squat."[31] There is also an erotic aspect to Matta-Clark's practice of "holing through." One of the virtues of thinking about *Day's End* in the context of Brown's porn film

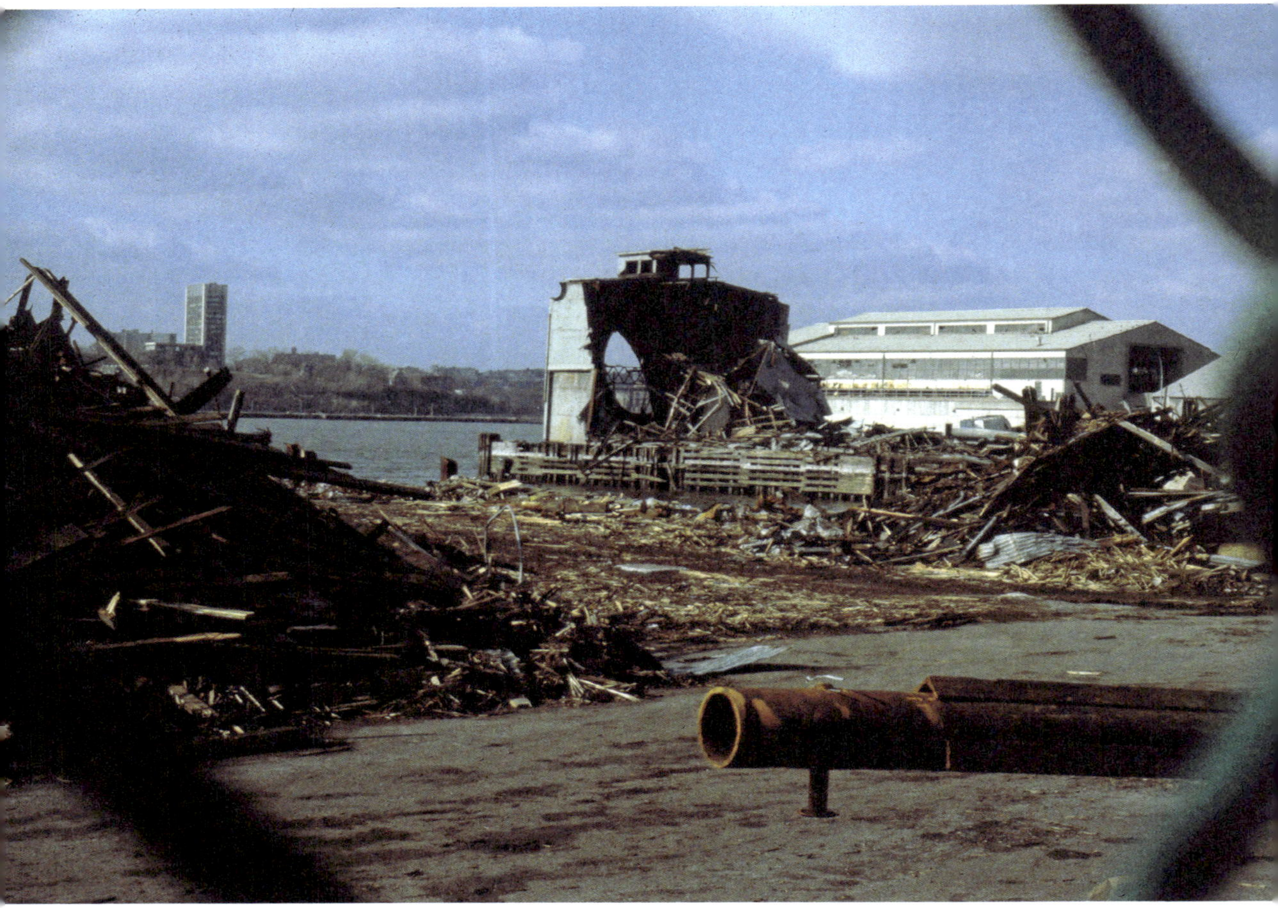

33. Frank Hallam, *Pier 52 Coming Down*, 1979. Private collection.

about sex on the piers is the reminder that Matta-Clark's cuttings are potent metaphors for penetration and voyeurism.

Reinserting the physical and the bodily into *Day's End* does not negate its potential joy and transcendence: the abjection of the site heightens the sublimity. I do not share Matta-Clark's worry that the potential "paranoia of being in a space where you didn't know who was there" would detract from the power of the piece. As Brown's porn movie suggests, in that brief moment when the camera pulls back and the shining splendor of *Day's End* illuminates the gay cruisers, the very dereliction of Pier 52 only intensified the ecstatic beauty of Matta-Clark's art.

I began this chapter by evoking a late-summer fantasy pilgrimage to Pier 52 upon hearing the news of the artist's death. But to be true to Matta-Clark's memory and to the full experience of the trajectory of *Day's End*, you would have had to return to Pier 52 at least once more, in January 1979, to witness the demolition that was only predicted by Brown's film. Fortunately, Frank Hallam was on hand to make the pilgrimage for us. In a picture taken from behind a fence (fig. 33), Hallam shows a moment in which most of the shed of Pier 52 has come down, leaving standing only the west wall, with Matta-Clark's great cut framing the sky. No longer a window that illuminates a dark space, the shape defined by the radii of two different arcs, with its remnant of a pediment and gable above, evokes a gateway, or triumphal arch, the perfect memorial for the fallen artist/hero. Not even the photographer realized that he was witnessing the death of a great work of art, so completely had *Day's End* become one with the piers and their melancholy fate. But isn't this what Matta-Clark wanted all along in his concept of the "non-monumental"—a work of art that, at its most monumental, would appear to be no monument at all?

Chapter 4

David Wojnarowicz in New York

If those floorboards could talk, if those streets could talk, if the whole huge path this body has traveled—roads, motel rooms, hillsides, cliffs, subways, rivers, planes, tracks—if any of them could speak, what would they remember most about me? What motions would they unravel within their words, or would they turn away faceless like the turn of this whole river and waterfront street, all of its people, its wanderers, its silences beneath the wheels of traffic and industry and sleep, would it turn away speechless like faces in dreams, in warehouses, pale wordless faces containing whole histories and geographies and adventures?
—David Wojnarowicz, *In the Shadow of the American Dream*

One of my earliest experiences doing archival research for this book was visiting what were then the very cramped quarters of the Lesbian, Gay, Bisexual and Transgender Community Center National History Archive sometime in 2002–3 on West Thirteenth Street in New York City. Among its treasures is the estate of the photographer and lawyer Leonard Fink, who died of AIDS in 1993. Fink's great subject was the way the Stonewall riots had made gay life visible in New York. Fink used his camera to document gay bars, the annual Pride marches, and his favorite location, the sex piers at the end of Christopher Street. Browsing through the various boxes that contain hundreds of pictures of the waterfront, many of which feature Fink and his friends acting out sexual fantasies in various stages of undress, I came across one particular pier photograph that gave me pause. Among all of Fink's outrageous images of naked men fucking, and evocative pictures of waterfront piers collapsing into the Hudson River, this one stood out for me for its innocuous quality. The photograph shows a lone young man walking down the street toward the underpass of the West Side Highway, just in front of Pier 46. Tall and quite thin, he is dressed in a leather jacket and has his hands in his pockets, as if he felt a slight chill. As he moves down the street, he turns his head toward the viewer, perhaps sensing that he is being observed (fig. 34).

So many of the men Fink photographed remain unidentified, their names and biographies lost with Fink's untimely death. But here among the photographs of anonymous men was someone who looked familiar to me. Was he someone I used to see at the bars along Christopher Street, or did I cruise him on one of my many sketching trips to the waterfront? Although in the picture he doesn't look traditionally handsome—his face is unusually gaunt, almost skeletal—there is something sexy about his gait and his gawky adolescent look. Suddenly I realized that this young man was the artist David Wojnarowicz.

Did Fink know Wojnarowicz? The picture was probably taken in the late 1970s or early '80s, before Wojnarowicz had become famous; if Fink recognized him, it was not because he was a celebrity but because they had spent so much time at the piers. Had they talked, or even had sex? Perhaps Fink was aware that Wojnarowicz was also making art on and about the piers. Or perhaps Fink simply recognized him as a familiar presence—like a neighbor, someone you nod to but don't necessarily know by name. According to his own journals, Wojnarowicz wandered the waterfront so frequently in those years that he must have become part of the general landscape. At times he all but lived on the piers, which remained a central motif and metaphor in his writings and visual production long after his favorite waterfront haunts were destroyed in the mid-1980s. Given Fink's similar obsession with the piers, it stands to reason that the two men would have seen each other constantly, even if they never spoke.

Fink's photograph of Wojnarowicz may seem unremarkable, but for me it eloquently reiterates a theme of this book, namely, the ways in which visual and aesthetic productions on and about the piers overlapped and coincided without their makers necessarily being aware of one another. And yet for all the pleasure I take in knowing that two of my favorite pier artists encountered each other, at least for the moment it took to take the photograph, it is not this aspect that I find most compelling. Drawing me to the photograph again and again is the sensation it gives of the double take of recognition: that I too

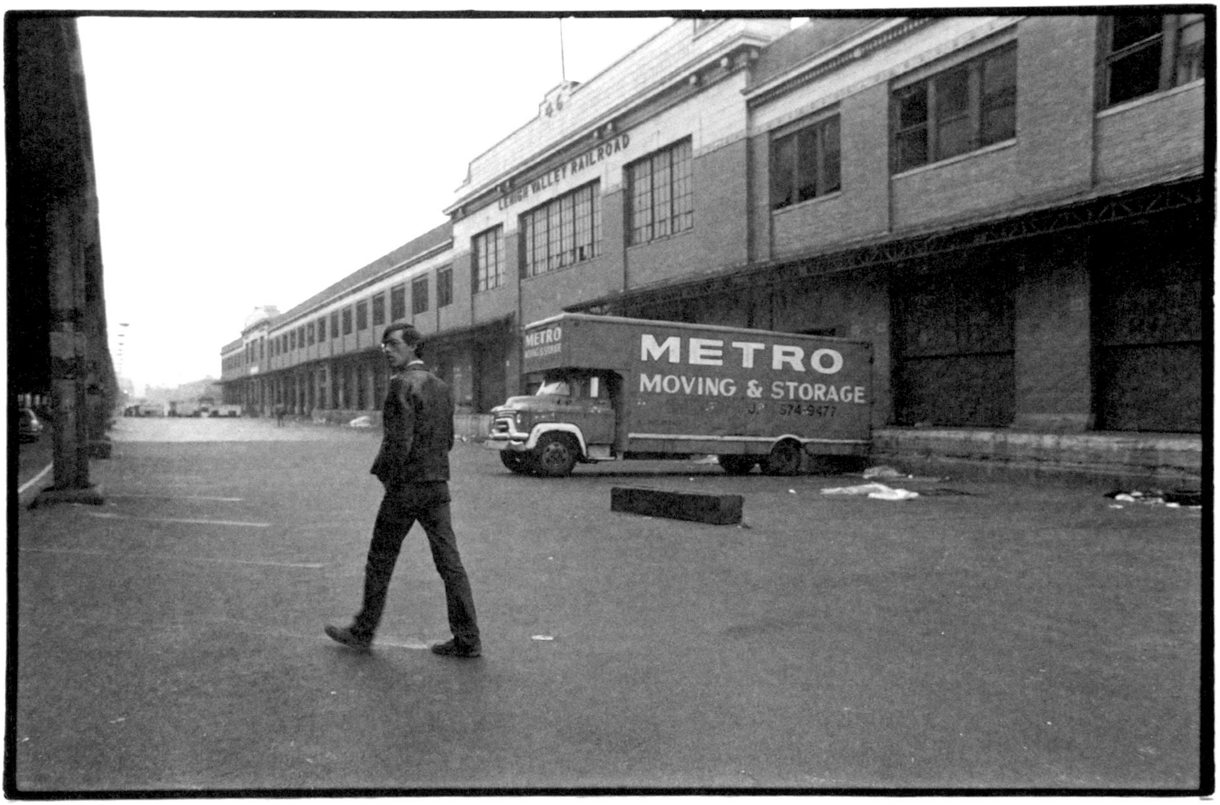

34. Leonard Fink, *David Wojnarowicz*, ca. 1980. Collection of the LGBT Community Center National History Archive.

might have walked down that street and had that same momentary encounter with Wojnarowicz . . . and then walked on.

I wonder what Wojnarowicz was up to when Fink captured his likeness. Perhaps it was that very day in 1980 that inspired this entry in Wojnarowicz's journal: "Afternoon brings me down to the river, a lazy afternoon with the highway traffic rushing along past me, bringing with it all concerns of the working world, schedules blown away in that traffic, in the breeze from the river as I pass beneath the West Side Highway in between slow-moving columns of cars."[1] In a previous entry he described long walks downtown: "Restless walks filled with coasting images of sight and sound, cars buckling or bucking over cobblestones down quiet side streets, trucks waiting at corners with swarthy drivers leaning back in cool shadowy seats and windows of buildings opening and closing, figures passing within the rooms, faraway sounds of voices and cries and horns that roll up and funnel in like some secret earphone connecting me to the creakings of the city."

During such rambles along the streets of the waterfront, Wojnarowicz sometimes followed men into the pier interiors:

> Stooping beneath the half-raised doorway (loading doors) I saw him walk further into the darkness and then turn suddenly and squat down, motioning me towards him with a single wave of his large hands. Rubbing my palms around the base of his neck over and over, feeling the bristle of his shaved skull against the sensitive undersides of my wrists, movements like birds in a stationary flexing of wings, my hands riding his forehead, smoothing along his jacket, over his hard shoulders and muscles. . . . His face buried itself beneath my shirt and rose upwards like an enormous fisted hand, tongue easing out between slightly parted lips so I could feel the coolness of a breeze follow his motions. I freed the buckle on my belt and then the button of my overalls, and he followed up with a series of movements of his hands, sliding the zipper down and his face leaning first back and then forward into my belly. I wrapped my hands around his body, my arms pressing against his sides, the wind moving closer and the lights of turning cars spreading beneath the slight cracks in the wall where it joined the concrete floor.[2]

In these journal entries, the experience of the city streets merges with encounters on the crumbling piers, turning inside and outside into one vast, continuous interior space. Almost any man peering through a window, or standing on a corner, or sitting behind the wheel of a parked truck, is a potential sexual partner. Sometimes the ramble is meditative; Wojnarowicz contemplates his life and feelings as he walks. Sometimes it is restless, as he scans his surroundings, searching for sex with strangers.

Tony Kushner attributes the inversion of public and private in Wojnarowicz's writing, its descriptions of streets and the piers seeming like an extension of his home, to an adolescence spent on the streets escaping from his dysfunctional parents, especially his violent father.[3] But arguably Wojnarowicz's attachment to the waterfront was a kind of return to family, a connection to his father's profession as a merchant seaman. One of Wojnarowicz's few happy memories as a child was going down to the docks to watch his father's ship, the colossal transatlantic cruise ship the SS *United States*, set out to sea.[4] This must have been in the early 1960s, when transatlantic ocean liners still lined the Manhattan waterfront. Wojnarowicz incorporated images of cruise ships in several works of art, most explicitly in the painting *Dad's Boat*. This eight-foot-square picture provides the backdrop to the *Burning Child* installation of 1984, in which a map-covered youth in flames runs across an apocalyptic landscape, as if trying to escape the oncoming ship. In the *Sex Series* of 1988–89, a cruise ship is juxtaposed with porthole-like circular images of fellatio, making us privy to the erotic lives of some of the crewmen or passengers who are traveling the sea.

In this context, it is tempting to see Wojnarowicz's propensity for cruising mostly older and hypermasculine men along the waterfront as a search for a father figure. Even the use of the word "cruising" to denote men seeking sex relates to his father's maritime job. Yet to read Wojnarowicz's art about the waterfront and queer sex as compensation for his father's cruelty and absence is limiting and ultimately normalizing. Wojnarowicz, like so many queer writers before him, was inspired by the sexual energy and surprising moments of intimacy that he found with strangers during his sexual adventures on the piers. Giving too much interpretative weight to Wojnarowicz's unhappy childhood and search for parental love also ignores the social and political dimensions of his interest in the waterfront as a reflection on the larger transformations occurring in New York City during the devastating recession and hyperinflation of the late 1970s. Wojnarowicz's firsthand childhood experience of the commercial waterfront when it was a vibrant port made him hyperaware of the collapse of the piers as symptomatic of the disappearance of entire industries and professions in the process we now call globalization. In a 1989 interview, Wojnarowicz interpreted references to his father's career as way to confront enormous technological changes and the anxieties they produce in us. Describing his recently completed picture *My Father Was a Sailor, My Father Was the Century*, Wojnarowicz said, "it's about him as a sailor, but it's also about transportation, about moving out where a century ago most people wouldn't know what was beyond the bend in the road outside their door. Now you turn on the TV and you're in China, you're a thousand feet below the ocean looking up at things that exist there, or whatever. The painting touched on that idea of collapsed distances, but also, more personally, it touched on the psychosis and danger of the world—like my father's psychosis—a world bent on death and destruction."[5] If Wojnarowicz saw the abandoned piers as a site for aesthetic reverie, a sexual playground, or a huge artist's studio, he was also alert to their decay as a symbol of the psychic disjunctions wrought by the dislocations and inequalities of late capitalism. The piers are one of the key spaces in Wojnarowicz's art that give form to an overall sense of "disintegration," and of what it was like to feel oppressed under "the shadow of the American dream." The piers double in Wojnarowicz's art as a place of liberation, outside the hegemony of what he called "the one-tribe nation," and as a warning of impending disaster. They prophesy an apocalyptic future in which the ostentatious signs of American wealth, the skyscrapers, the highways, the suburban sprawl, would all be laid low. "Soon all this will be picturesque ruins," the subtitle of one of his most influential essays predicts.

In 1982, not long after Fink and Wojnarowicz had their photographic encounter, Michel Foucault sat down to talk with Jack O'Higgins about homosexuality in words that, for the philosopher, were unusually personal and improvisational. Did Foucault ever wander the piers? Given his documented interest in the leather scene of Paris and San Francisco, I would like to think that he must have ventured to the Manhattan waterfront. Certainly, he was speaking from personal experience when he mused that the most erotic aspect of anonymous or casual gay sex was not the act itself but the memory of it as you were leaving the scene: "it is when the act is over and the boy is gone that one begins to dream about the warmth of his body, the quality of his smile, the tone of his voice." "This is why the great homosexual writers of our culture (Cocteau, Genet, Burroughs) can write so elegantly about the sexual act itself," he claimed, "because the homosexual imagination is for the most part concerned with reminiscing about the act rather than anticipating it."[6] Although such a sweeping generalization risks limiting and stereotyping the many varieties of sexual desire and identity, Foucault's words speak to an aspect of Wojnarowicz's memoirs, which, after all, were profoundly influenced by at least two of the writers Foucault cites, William Burroughs and Jean Genet. Wojnarowicz sought out a friendship with Burroughs, and he was so obsessed with Genet that he pursued a man on the waterfront simply because he resembled the French author. He associated the waterfront deeply with these two authors, comparing the interlocking rooms and passageways of the pier sheds, and the anonymous sex that went on there, to "live films of Genet and Burroughs," unwinding in a "stationary kind of silence."[7]

In Wojnarowicz's journals, as in Genet's novels, the briefest sexual encounters are described in such explicit detail that they seem jotted down on the spot, though given the circumstances, they must have been recorded hours or even days after the fact. The significance of a blow job or of merely brushing against a stranger's body is amplified by memory. As in Samuel Delany's memoir, *The Motion of Light in Water*, images of the surrounding Hudson merge with the experience of touching bodies: "This desire, so small a thing, becomes a river tracing the drift of your bare arms, dark mouth, and memories of strangers." In Wojnarowicz's stream of consciousness, the real river just outside the window becomes the liquid of ejaculation: "Something silent and recalled, the sense of age in a familiar place, the emptied heart and light of the eyes, the white bones of streetlamps and autos, the press of memory turning over and over and I'm coming."[8] Studying Wojnarowicz's waterfront stroll in Fink's photograph, I wonder if he was in reverie about a recent sexual encounter. As he looks back down the street, is he cruising for sex, hunting for yet another adventure with a stranger to provide the material for more memories and more writing?

I realize that in spending so much time unpacking this seemingly bland photograph, I am beginning to fixate on Wojnarowicz less as an artist and more as someone I might have known. I cannot escape the sensation that not only have we met before but we share some kind of deep connection.[9] I find myself having to resist calling him simply David, a liberty I would never take with Vito Acconci or Gordon Matta-Clark. Of course, it is not just Fink's photograph that creates this sensation of familiarity but the nature of the art and personae that Wojnarowicz forged in his brief career. To engage fully with his work is to feel as if nothing is withheld of the artist's feelings and life experiences. *X-Rays from Hell*, another of his memorable titles, encapsulates his project of exposing the injustice of the American system, but it also signals his broader attempt to convey what it feels like to strip off the skin of appearances. If Wojnarowicz often positioned himself as a deeply alienated figure driven by anger, his sense of alienation is countered by the way his art is about connections to strangers—not just the men he has sex with on the waterfront but the strangers who make up the audience for his vividly autobiographical art. But in fact Wojnarowicz's journals leave out all kinds of crucial information about his life and art. Cynthia Carr, in her wonderful biography, notes that Wojnarowicz rarely mentions Tom Rauffenbart, his longtime companion, in his journals, nor does he write much about the making of art itself. Nevertheless, the effect of his writings, in their stream-of-consciousness style, is to make the reader feel that he is telling all. I am well aware that any autobiographical enterprise contains elements of fiction—that it is a construction designed to make us love and admire its author—still, the best of the genre, and I count Wojnarowicz's journals among the best, makes us feel as if we are the author's confidant.

Arthur Rimbaud in New York

As it turns out, the fantasy I indulge in while contemplating Fink's photograph—that I might meet face to face a dead hero/artist amid my own day-to-day experience—is central to one of David Wojnarowicz's most compelling works, *Arthur Rimbaud in New York*, a series of photographs of some of Wojnarowicz's most intimate friends wearing a cardboard mask of Arthur Rimbaud (fig. 35). The effect of the mask, made from a photocopy of an 1871 portrait photograph by Étienne Carjat (fig. 36), is to resurrect the French poet on this side of the Atlantic and make it seem that he is following or leading Wojnarowicz in his treks through New York City, from Coney Island to Times Square, on the subway, in front of porn theaters, and repeatedly to the piers.

If, by the artist's own calculations, *Arthur Rimbaud in New York* is his earliest mature work of art, then arguably it can be considered one of his last as well.[10] Although Wojnarowicz took the photographs that compose the series in 1979, he made public fewer than twenty of the pictures over the following year.[11] Four photographs were printed in the centerfold of the *SoHo News Weekly* to preview the publication of a sixteen-image portfolio in Dennis Cooper's journal *Little Caesar*. The project was then largely abandoned, and many of the negatives remained unprinted until 1990, when Wojnarowicz rediscovered them and made an edition of twenty-five prints, which were exhibited at the P.P.O.W. gallery in New York in November. Seven months later, Wojnarowicz succumbed to HIV/AIDS. In 2004, under the supervision of the Wojnarowicz estate, several more images were printed from the original negatives and included in the series. In this way, *Arthur Rimbaud in New York*, from its

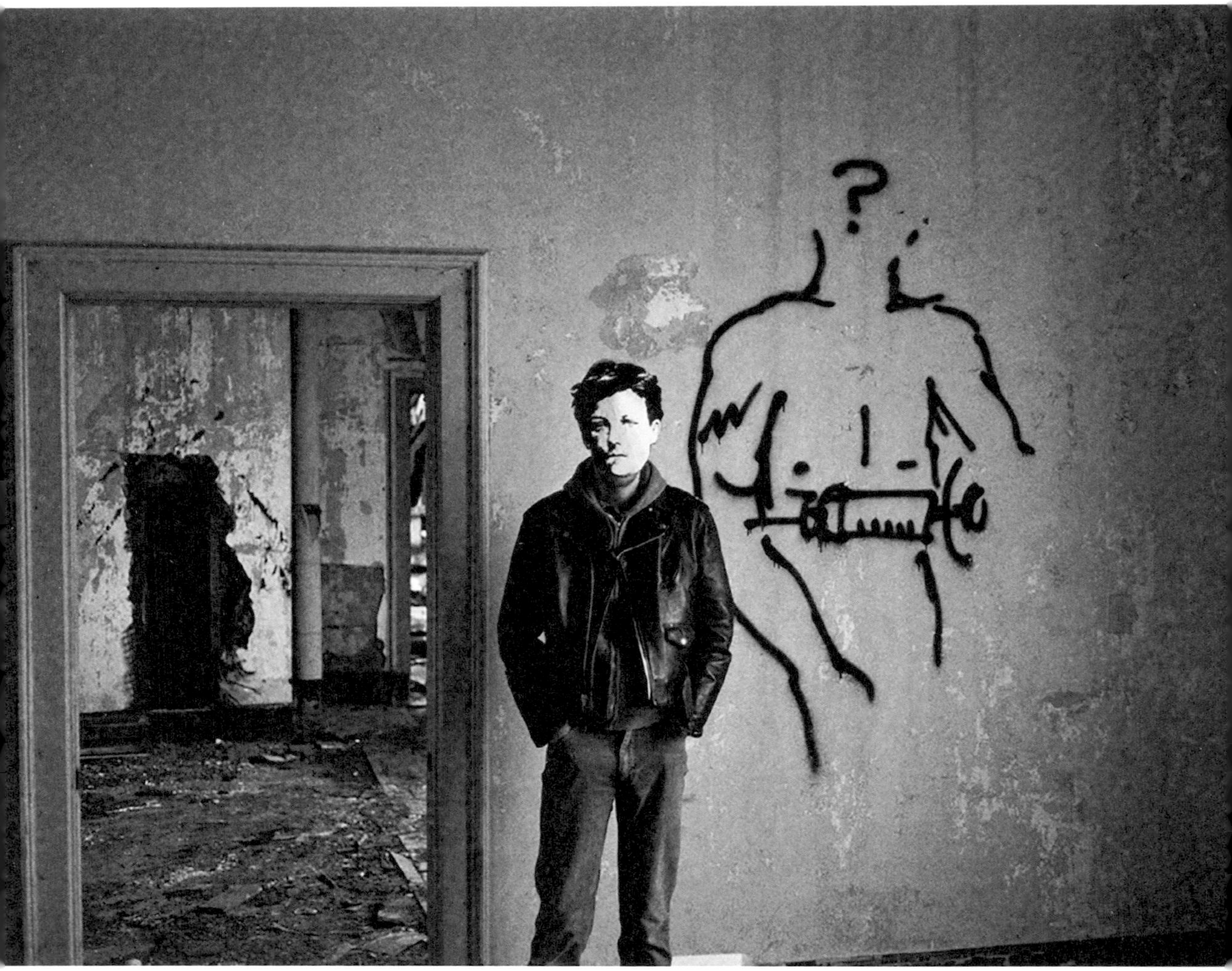

35. David Wojnarowicz, *Arthur Rimbaud in New York*, 1979–80. Photo courtesy of the Estate of David Wojnarowicz and P.P.O.W. Gallery, New York.

gestation to its most recent form, spans Wojnarowicz's career as an artist and continues even after his death. Its theme of the resurrection of a dead artist resonates with his estate's decision to imagine what further images Wojnarowicz might have chosen to print had he lived. Yet, in focusing on the expanded series of prints created at the end of Wojnarowicz's life or after, little attention has been paid to the form and context of the series when it was first made and shown to the world in 1979–80, or to Wojnarowicz's intentions when he was taking these photographs, several of which were never published by Wojnarowicz or his estate.[12]

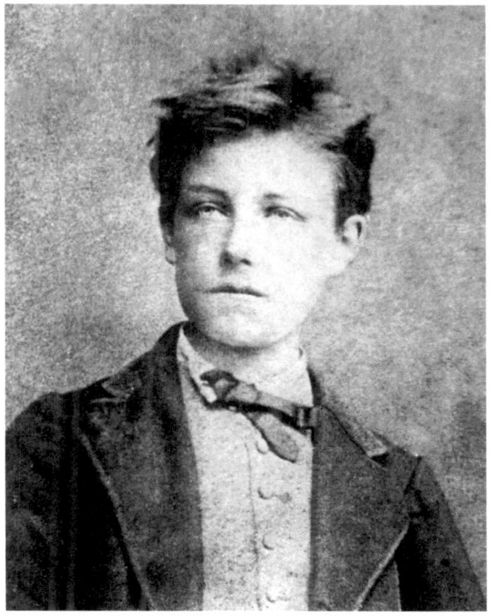

36. Étienne Carjat, *Arthur Rimbaud*, 1871. Photo: Wikimedia Commons.

Unfortunately, Wojnarowicz said little in the late '70s about the Rimbaud project beyond some notes for possible scenes in two "photo scripts."[13] And when he did talk about it later, Wojnarowicz became increasingly ambivalent about his relationship to the French poet. Already in 1983, Wojnarowicz told Sylvia Falcon of the *East Village Eye* that he had come to feel embarrassed by the connection. According to Falcon, he did "not share Rimbaud's boyish enthusiasm for evil."[14] Wojnarowicz flatly declared in 1990, "I didn't see myself as Rimbaud."[15] But in the same year he told David Hirsch that he imagined Rimbaud following "a vague biographical outline of what my past had been—the places I had hung out in as a kid, the places I starved in or haunted on some level."[16] In an autobiographical time line published in the catalogue of his *Tongues of Flame* retrospective, Wojnarowicz elaborated upon his intentions, explaining that in the *Arthur Rimbaud in New York* series he was "playing with ideas of compression of 'historical time and activity' and fusing the French poet's identity with modern new york urban activities mostly illegal in nature."[17]

Wojnarowicz's various statements about the series ten years after its creation are laden with nostalgia and melancholy. He describes "sifting" through the negatives of the series under the influence of a "heightening sense of mortality and the calendars of my past." Wojnarowicz's attempt to reconstruct his original motives for taking the pictures was influenced by an all-too-accurate premonition that, given the perilous state of his health, he did not have long to live. As he faced his mortality, the pictures became a kind of a travelogue of his past; as he put it, he was "capturing the elusive 'sites of attraction'; those places that suddenly and unexpectedly revive the smell and traces of former states of body and mind long ago left behind."[18] It is my contention that when the pictures were shot, however, they were less a retrospective than a projection of his current obsessions and ambitions for the future of his art.

One peculiar aspect of Wojnarowicz's statements about the series in 1990 is that he says nothing about his reasons for choosing Rimbaud in the first place, as if these were self-explanatory. To fill this gap, Carr joins Mysoon Rizk and Donald Kuspit, among others, in emphasizing the parallels in the two artists' biographies: "Both were deserted by their fathers and unhappy with their mothers. Both ran away as teenagers. Both were impoverished and unwilling to live by the rules. Both were queer. Both tried to wring visionary work out of suffering. David just didn't yet know the rest—that he would soon meet an older man and mentor who would change his life (as Paul Verlaine had changed Rimbaud's), and that he too would die at the age of thirty-seven."[19] I worry, however, that this emphasis on biographical connections risks turning the series into a form of self-portraiture, as if Rimbaud were a surrogate for Wojnarowicz himself. But as Wojnarowicz said, he did not see himself as Rimbaud. Instead, he was inspired by the poet's life and work. There is a difference between identification and inspiration. For Wojnarowicz, Rimbaud offered a model for how to turn his experience of an uprooted and marginal existence into art, how to convert the abject into an apocalyptic vision, what Rimbaud called "a season in hell." To be an artist means living as an outcast engaged in illicit activities. Such experiences feed the work. In a famous letter to Georges Izambard, Rimbaud proudly announced, "I am degrading myself as much as possible. Why? . . . I am working to make myself a seer. . . . It is a question of reaching the unknown by the derangement of all the senses." But this process of physical degradation does not yield a stable identity; the artist does not find himself in his sensations. In the same letter, Rimbaud declares, "It is wrong to say: I think. One ought to say: people think me. . . . I is someone else."[20] Rimbaud suggests that identity is projected outward onto others. There is no private, unified soul. The self is not interior at all, but a matter of public interactions and performances.

If Wojnarowicz said little about why he chose Rimbaud as a subject, one telling reference in an unsent letter to his sister, written before he began to craft his homage to Rimbaud, offers a manifesto of his ambitions at the time. Wojnarowicz may have had Rimbaud's famous seer letter in mind when he wrote down what he hoped would be an explanation of all he "had been heading towards in my life." He suggested that the way to find his own voice was to connect to his subconscious and his dreams. Like Rimbaud's, Wojnarowicz's path to being an inward seer involved "a separation of myself from the social system . . . to find that area in the vast cosmos both internally & externally where the true voice is to be found." He declared that "Rimbaud came close to it, he came so close but turned his back to it on its very steps, either out of fright from what he saw or because he was unprepared to meet it." In suggesting the possibility that Rimbaud did not go far enough, or failed to follow the logic of his own work, Wojnarowicz critiqued Rimbaud for a loss of courage, in much the same way that Rimbaud supposedly critiqued Verlaine. In terms of the radicalism of the French poet's use of language, the proposition that Wojnarowicz might outdo Rimbaud seems preposterous. But Wojnarowicz was not thinking about formal invention or poetic originality; he was trying to find his own voice through self-knowledge and truth telling. He longed for authenticity and connection. "i am a poet[,] one who hasnt found the true voice yet . . . i wont worry about total acceptance once i break thru the immediate binds around me which hold me back[.] what is really more important is that i at least give my life up to it."[21] From the beginning of the *Arthur Rimbaud* series, Wojnarowicz approaches his hero with ambivalence. He wants to follow him on the dangerous path of becoming a "seer," but he also suspects that Rimbaud *lost face*, as it were. The spectral figure of the photographs is part muse, goading Wojnarowicz and us on, and part prophet of failed ambitions—truly a dead poet.

Wojnarowicz's project might be said to literalize Rimbaud's famous but cryptic remark "I is someone else" by establishing his own identity through the image of the poet. But that image, made over into a cardboard mask, is flat and insubstantial, all surface. There is a peculiar discontinuity in the series between Rimbaud's unchanging expression and his disturbing surroundings and actions. Whether Rimbaud masturbates on a mattress, injects heroin into his vein, or rides the subway, he looks blankly at the viewer. Wojnarowicz's Rimbaud is distant and mute. In one picture, he "speaks," but only to talk about silence. Rimbaud is juxtaposed with the phrase "the silence of Marcel Duchamp is overrated," graffiti painted on the pier wall by Wojnarowicz himself (fig. 37). This quotation from Joseph Beuys refers to Duchamp's supposed retirement from making art in order to play chess, but in this context

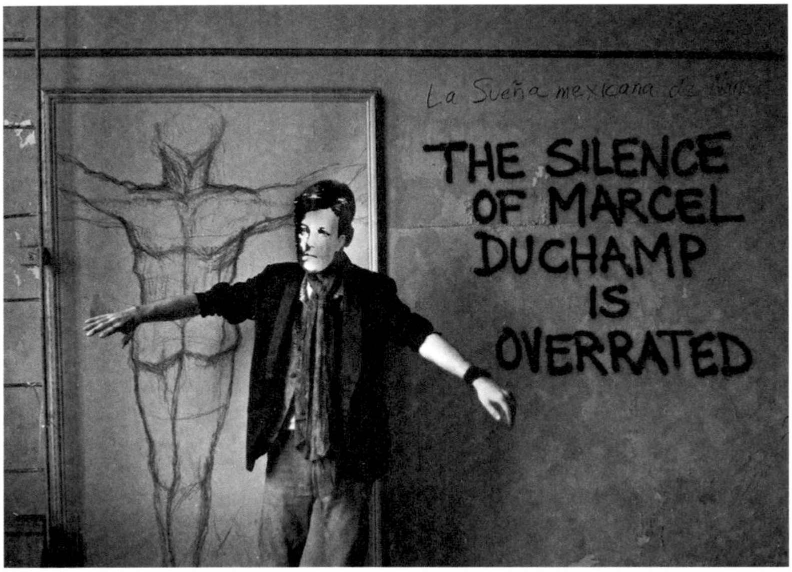

37. David Wojnarowicz, *Arthur Rimbaud in New York*, 1979–80. Photo courtesy of the Estate of David Wojnarowicz and P.P.O.W. Gallery, New York.

it also alludes to Rimbaud's abandonment of poetry while still a young man. Wojnarowicz might seem to castigate Rimbaud for his silence, and yet Wojnarowicz's Rimbaud is no jaded Duchamp; he is a martyr. His outstretched arms echo the naked figure on the wall and suggest Christ's crucifixion: being a seer exacts a terrible cost.

Cindy Sherman

At almost exactly the same time that Wojnarowicz was photographing the Rimbaud series, Cindy Sherman was creating her famous film stills. If Sherman did not literally put on a mask to create the pictures in which she used her own body as her subject, critics have interpreted the various outfits she wears as costumes, signaling that she is playing a role equivalent to the part of an actor in a film. Craig Owens writes, "Sherman's works are all self-portraits, but in them the artist invariably appears masked, disguised. . . . Sherman's women are not women but images of women, specular models of femininity projected by the media to encourage imitation, identification; they are, in other words, tropes, figures."[22] In the critical consensus that follows Owens's analysis, Sherman's self-portraits—unlike the treatment of Wojnarowicz's Rimbaud series—are almost never discussed in terms of her biography.

Sherman's *Untitled Film Still #24* (fig. 38) finds her in front of Pier 34 in 1978, a few years before Wojnarowicz and his friends turned this space into the makeshift studios and exhibition spaces I discuss later. Heavily made up, hair short and black, in a simple black top and pleated dirndl skirt, Sherman evokes a 1950s teenager posing for a quick snapshot. She reminds me a bit of Gaby Rodgers, who played the Pandora-like femme fatale in the film noir *Kiss Me Deadly*. However, the specificity of the location in New York City, with the Hudson and the Holland Tunnel exhaust tower in the background, interferes with that association. Perhaps Sherman was thinking about *On the Waterfront* (although in that film Eva Marie Saint's flowing hair was blond). As with Sherman's other film stills, this search for a specific origin never quite works. As Rosalind Krauss points out, although Sherman's film stills might evoke specific films, they are never precise reenactments of individual scenes; Krauss refers to "the simulacral nature of what they contain, the condition of being a copy *without* an original."[23] But I think this picture is particularly elusive in terms of its possible sources of inspiration and associations. An odd note is the concrete post in the corner with a tuft of grass—Hollywood publicity photographers definitely would have cropped that out, and they would have been sure to light the celebrity's face properly. What makes Sherman's photograph of the waterfront so difficult for me to make sense of is that I see it against the context of how the piers in the 1970s became largely all-male turf, a site of masculinity, which men, gay and straight, struggled to control or used to act out various fantasies. Of course, some women made art along the waterfront. Joan Jonas's 1972 performance piece *Delay Delay* (made into the short film *Songdelay* of 1973) is set in a vacant lot across from Pier 20, where Robert Whitman had begun his performance piece *Architecture*, and included the participation of Gordon Matta-Clark and Geoffrey Hendricks, among others. Also, as noted in chapter 2, Sherman's "Pictures Generation" colleague Louise Lawler created *Birdcalls*, warbling the names of male artists in response to the exclusion of women from Willoughby Sharp's Pier 18 project.[24] But the waterfront pieces by women like Sherman and Jonas don't seem to evoke discussions of the relationship between sexual identity and urbanism that have been the focus of scholarship on Wojnarowicz. Significantly, Sherman's self-portrait in front of Pier 34 and Jonas's *Delay Delay* both take place outside in full sunlight and thus resist a discourse that sees the dimly lit night streets and the dank passageways of the pier interiors as a metaphor for the states of unease and alienation that are such a staple of the Wojnarowicz discourse. An exception is Douglas Crimp's discussion of Jonas's *Songdelay* in

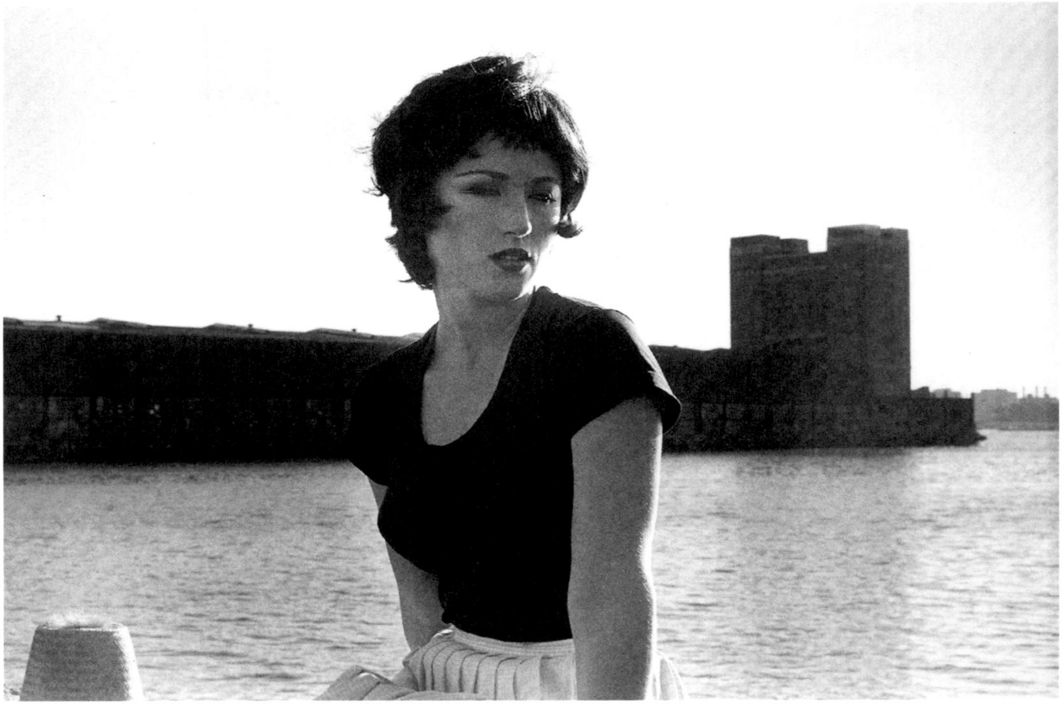

38. Cindy Sherman, *Untitled Film Still #24*, 1978. Photo courtesy of Metro Pictures, New York.

his memoir *Before Pictures*, in which he writes that its use of abrupt edits and disorienting viewpoints thwarts "our desire to know or possess the city beyond our immediate experience of it in the moment of use."[25] Certainly, themes of disorientation are woven through Wojnarowicz's account of the piers, but this is due in large measure to how the spaces in their darkness and ruin act on him. In contrast, Jonas filmed on a brightly lit day when it would have been easy to take in the location and make sense of our surroundings. It is her camera, rather than the location itself, that disorients us. The film undermines the very process of documenting the performance by highlighting how the lens and the microphone profoundly distort vision and sound. Crimp is particularly eloquent in the way he talks about how the film compresses space, so that it seems at one point that a warehouse building across the Hudson River in New Jersey appears to be directly behind the performer.

Although Crimp celebrates the way in which the film reinvigorates our sensory relationship to the city, I am struck by how different his approach to

Jonas's work, in its physicality and nostalgia, is from his view of Alvin Baltrop's erotic photographs. Baltrop's photographs do not figure directly in his discussion of his growing sense of identity as a queer man in the 1970s that so underlies his discussion of Baltrop and the piers. He does touch on the feeling of communal activity that permeates the piece—the way the performers collaborate to create rhythmic sounds and draw in space—but he does not talk about the potential queerness of the work. I think there is an argument to be made about how Jonas's vision of collaboration, with its emphasis on sensory presence and the joy of being in the world, might relate to Audre Lorde's discussion of the erotic, which I touch on in chapter 1. If not queer, the work was inherently feminist, and antimasculinist, in the way it brought men and women together to make a work of art under the direction of a woman.

Unlike the writing on Jonas's waterfront work, it is not unusual to discuss the erotic dimensions of Sherman's film stills, given their allusions to Hollywood romantic cinema. Yet the stills have not been given the kind of autobiographical readings that are a staple of the literature on Wojnarowicz. Sherman's film stills are literally self-portraits, but they are written about as if they were talismans of Roland Barthes's "Death of the Author." Paradoxically, Wojnarowicz's Rimbaud photographs, which have been assessed as autobiography, are not self-portraits at all in any conventional sense. Wojnarowicz is not the face we see in the images, nor is he the man beneath the mask (at least we assume that he's not in the photographs in which he pushed the shutter). Nevertheless, *Arthur Rimbaud in New York* has been written about as if it were a self-portrait in which Wojnarowicz merges his own identity with that of the French poet. This approach ignores one of the most interesting aspects of Wojnarowicz's use of the photocopied mask itself—the way it shifts the emphasis away from Rimbaud as a poet to his representation. Rimbaud's derangement of the senses becomes a different kind of derangement—the transformation and degrading of the image in the process of photographing a photograph that is itself a photographic copy. Is this another example of Krauss's "copy without an original"? Yes and no, because Rimbaud was a historical person who existed, and we have the ability to read his poetry directly. But central to Wojnarowicz's experience of the poet is his lack of access to that individual who lived in the past. This distorting and blurring of Rimbaud's face becomes an apt metaphor for the way in which Rimbaud has become myth, a construction of all of the representations of his life story and the ways in which his outrageous life supposedly relates to his poetry. If the mask of the poet's face can be read as self-portraiture, or at least as an attempt to get near the famous poet through imitation, it is every bit as much about the way the copy distances the hero, placing him always out of reach and several times removed.

To put it harshly, wearing a paper mask of Rimbaud does not make you into the poet. After all, Rimbaud is credited with having fundamentally transformed the course of French literature before he had reached the age of twenty. Victor Hugo called him the "infant Shakespeare"; perhaps no other artist besides Mozart was such a prodigy. By the time Rimbaud turned twenty-four, Wojnarowicz's age when he began the Rimbaud series, he had already abandoned poetry and the very talent of which Wojnarowicz was in awe. Indeed, on one level, *Arthur Rimbaud in New York* is about Wojnarowicz's inability to be Rimbaud and the difficulty of following in his footsteps. Emulation is not self-portraiture, and in this regard it is crucial to remember that the men who wore the mask of Rimbaud in the photographic series were not stand-ins for Wojnarowicz, who could easily have used a timer or shutter release and donned the mask himself. Thanks to Carr's brilliant detective work, we know that the men Wojnarowicz asked to assume the persona of Rimbaud were intensely close to him. Brian Butterick and Jean-Pierre Delage were lovers, and John Hall was a best friend. In this way, the Rimbaud series, or at least the process of making it, was a communal effort. However lonely the figure of Rimbaud appears to be in the final pictures, the work of creating those pictures was one of the first instances of Wojnarowicz's making collaborative art, forging the kind of bonds with such artists as Kiki Smith and Mike Bidlo that I touch on in chapter 6.

Although Wojnarowicz only started taking the photographs of the Rimbaud series when he returned from Paris in 1979, he had been planning to make some sort of visual work of art based on the poet's image for at least a year. A key trigger in the process was meeting the photographer Arthur Tress. Until Carr wrote her biography, Tress's role in Wojnarowicz's aesthetic formation had gone completely unnoticed, and even Carr does not make much of it. Yet Tress and Wojnarowicz were briefly lovers in April 1978, precisely the time that Wojnarowicz began to make complex visual art about his sexual identity, incorporating his literary heroes, including Rimbaud, Genet, and Burroughs. As Carr points out, Tress was one of the first successful artists Wojnarowicz met who made art explicitly about homoerotic desire. Undoubtedly, Tress shared with Wojnarowicz his many photographs of the piers, in which he posed male models in evocative poses. Although Tress's effect on Wojnarowicz's art and life never rivaled that of Peter Hujar, their relationship was nevertheless transformative at a time when the young artist was searching for new inspiration and aesthetic directions.

One evening in May 1978, Tress took Wojnarowicz on a tour of the train tracks and shipyards near Tress's studio, and the two artists had sex on a pier. This pier was more than two miles north of the so-called sex piers adjacent to the center of the gay neighborhood in the West Village, but its ruined condition mirrored the structures downtown that would soon become Wojnarowicz's favorite haunt. Tress's use of the abandoned waterfront buildings as his studio, where he found the evocative light and backdrops of many of his most memorable photographs, inspired Wojnarowicz to use similar piers as workspaces a few years later. The encounter with Tress that night was so intense that it provoked Wojnarowicz to write his first extensive memoir, in which the act of sex with another man fuses with the experience of the ruined waterfront. Carefully typed and pasted into his journal, the entry runs for three single-spaced pages and reads more like one of Wojnarowicz's published monologues than like a spontaneous series of recollections.

Wojnarowicz describes the experience as if Tress had led him out of the city to some strange foreign landscape. In an earlier waterfront memory, Wojnarowicz wrote about dangling his feet over the edge of the pier, "like Huck Finn from his eternal raft." The experience with Tress deepened and extended that fantasy so that the two became adventurers leaving civilization behind: "it was more like early river explorers we were trekking in the vast waste lands that no person had set foot on—there was the shriek of night birds and the wilderness covered everything softly we were looking for camp for the evening only I couldn't decide if we were men or women and if the landscape was desert exterior or mountainous or American or European or if Africa was the location or if the sky was always black and foggy mist." In this journal entry, Wojnarowicz captures the waterfront's paradoxical appeal. On one hand, it offers a return to childhood innocence, Huck and Jim on the raft alone together, floating down the Mississippi, seemingly escaping the oppression of an unjust society and the decorum of bourgeois respectability and female companionship. On the other, where such childhood fantasies are chaste, the masculine world of the piers is overtly sexual. The male bonding of childhood becomes male coupling. What remains constant, however, is a freedom from responsibility. The piers function for Wojnarowicz as what Foucault calls a heterotopia: an in-between space of freedom where the normal rules of society no longer apply. In his journals, Wojnarowicz compares leaving the piers with Tress to returning from some exotic land filled with wild beasts:

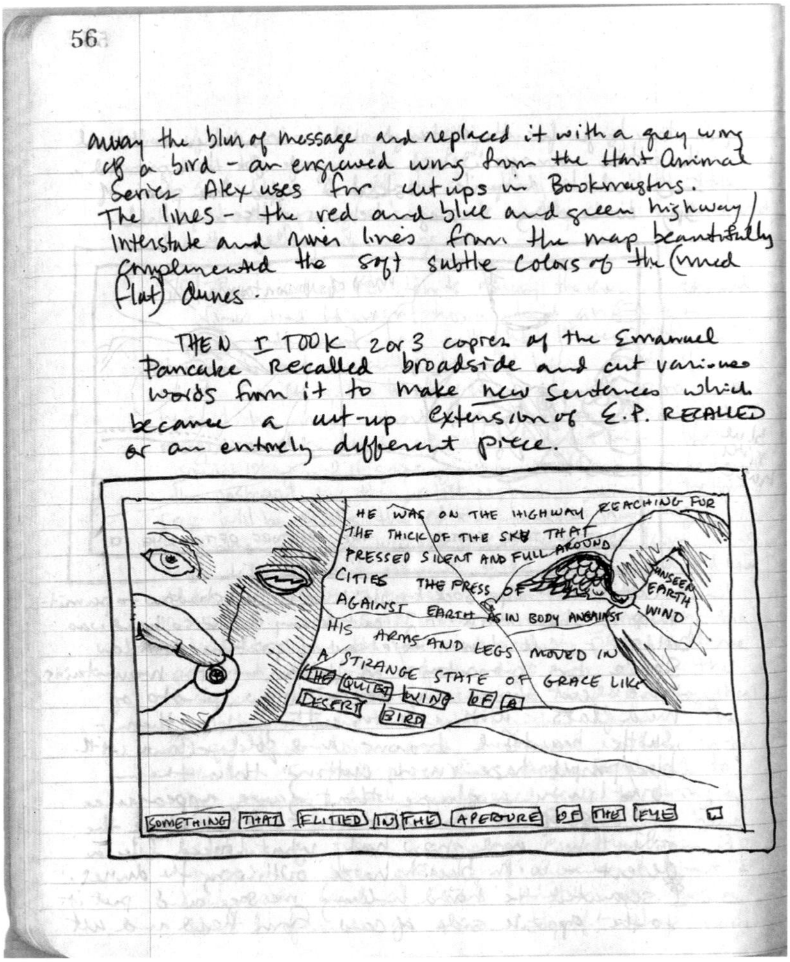

39. David Wojnarowicz, unpublished journal page, 8 May 1978. David Wojnarowicz Papers, Fales Library, New York University. Photo courtesy of the Estate of David Wojnarowicz and P.P.O.W. Gallery, New York.

"the desert winds and the river that eased from the unknown and stretched into some fantastic unlit landscape filled with all the wilds of any cultures fear and excitement and the wild animals roamed in the brush along the boats unseen dipping into the current and everything came into a sad but exciting perspective as we stood up and brushed ourselves off and put away the pipe and slowly made our way back into the wasteland of factory and apartment house." Leaving behind the magical piers for the now-dull streets of the city, Wojnarowicz and Tress are "wayward criminals" encircled "in this self-made prison" that is the routine of daily existence.

Besides sharing a transformative experience on the piers, Tress encouraged Wojnarowicz's growing interest in making visual art, suggesting that he contribute a collage to an exhibition of artists' postcards. Thrilled by the opportunity, Wojnarowicz began to think of ways to incorporate a picture of Rimbaud, found in a thrift shop book of "poesies," into the collage. As with the later *Arthur Rimbaud in New York* series, he planned to transpose the poet outside his own time—not the present of New York City but some sort of comic book future. Wojnarowicz wrote in his journal about his "plans for Arthur Rimbaud to be wearing sunglasses and be firing a ray gun which instead of rays would have a line of prose or poetry emitting from its nozzle." When the photograph of Rimbaud proved too large for the postcard format, Wojnarowicz instead fashioned a collage from a photograph "of a spy concealing messages behind [a] false eye ball." Wojnarowicz included in his journal a detailed sketch of this card, inscribed with the words "Something that flitted in the aperture of the eye" (fig. 39). The drawing shows the spy holding the fake eyeball in his hand, while in the empty socket Wojnarowicz drew his "trademark—the A. Rimbaud lightning streak." Although Rimbaud's image was eliminated from the initial project, Wojnarowicz nevertheless alluded to the poet through the lightning bolt of inspiration and the work's overall theme of inward vision.[26]

Shortly after ending his affair with Tress, and his early struggle to find a way to incorporate an image of Rimbaud into some sort of visual collage, Wojnarowicz spent several months in Paris visiting his sister. There he tried self-consciously to retrace the poet's path through the city. At some point, Wojnarowicz may have seen on the streets of Paris the guerrilla art placards of Ernest Pignon-Ernest, in which the very same Carjat photograph of Rimbaud is superimposed onto the figure of a man in a leather jacket, making it seem as if the ghost of the radical poet was appearing in the very streets where Wojnarowicz sought him. Wojnarowicz never acknowledged Pignon-Ernest's work, however. Did he repress the influence, or is it possibly a coincidence? Would Wojnarowicz, under the spell of Rimbaud's injunction to make everything new, allow himself to be so dependent on another artist's work? Instead, Carr reports, Wojnarowicz was initially disappointed that Paris did not live up to Rimbaud's dark, decadent imagery, or what Wojnarowicz called "the underworld," but eventually he found a gay leather scene and the red-light district of the Pigalle, though these had less to do with Rimbaud than with the kind of night life Wojnarowicz knew in New York. He thought about illustrating Rimbaud's *Illuminations* and made pen drawings of the poet masturbating (fig. 40) in much the same pose he was to put John Hall in the *Arthur Rimbaud in New York* photograph (fig. 41) (and later in his image of Yukio Mishima on

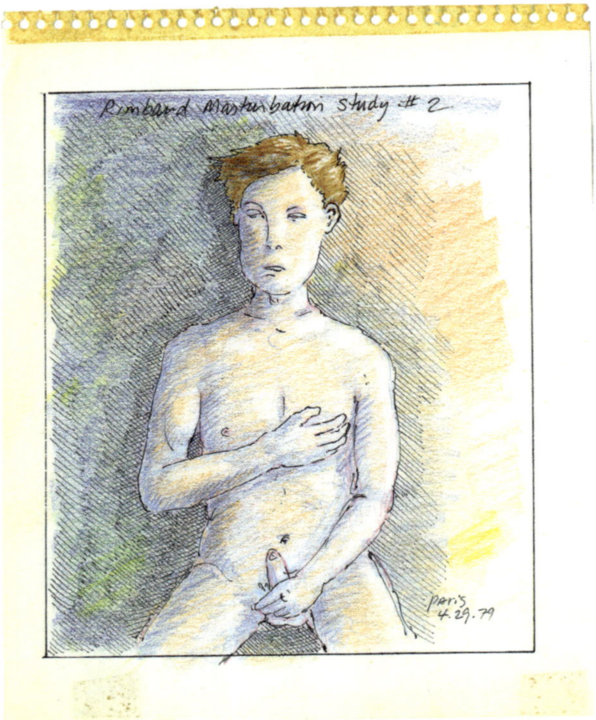

40. David Wojnarowicz, *Rimbaud Masturbation Study #2*, 1979. David Wojnarowicz Papers, Fales Library, New York University. Photo courtesy of the Estate of David Wojnarowicz and P.P.O.W. Gallery, New York.

the wall of Pier 34). By transferring Rimbaud's resurrection to New York, Wojnarowicz inverted his original pilgrimage of hero worship. Instead of Wojnarowicz following the great poet, the poet followed Wojnarowicz.

When Wojnarowicz began making his series of photographs, Rimbaud's reputation was at its zenith. Admired by post–World War II writers and musicians like Bob Dylan, Allen Ginsberg, Henry Miller, Tennessee Williams, and Patti Smith, Rimbaud's poetry and life story became almost a countercultural rite of passage for artists in the 1960s and '70s. Patti Smith, the punk rock star and poet so admired by Wojnarowicz, found solace in Rimbaud's poetry in her teens. His flight from his mother's home as a teenager to write poetry in Paris inspired her to escape the suburbs for New York City without so much as bus fare. Smith remembers in her memoir, *Just Kids*, "Rimbaud held the keys to a mystical language that I devoured even as I could not fully decipher it. My unrequited love for him was as real to me as anything I had experienced. . . . He became my archangel, delivering me from the mundane horrors of factory

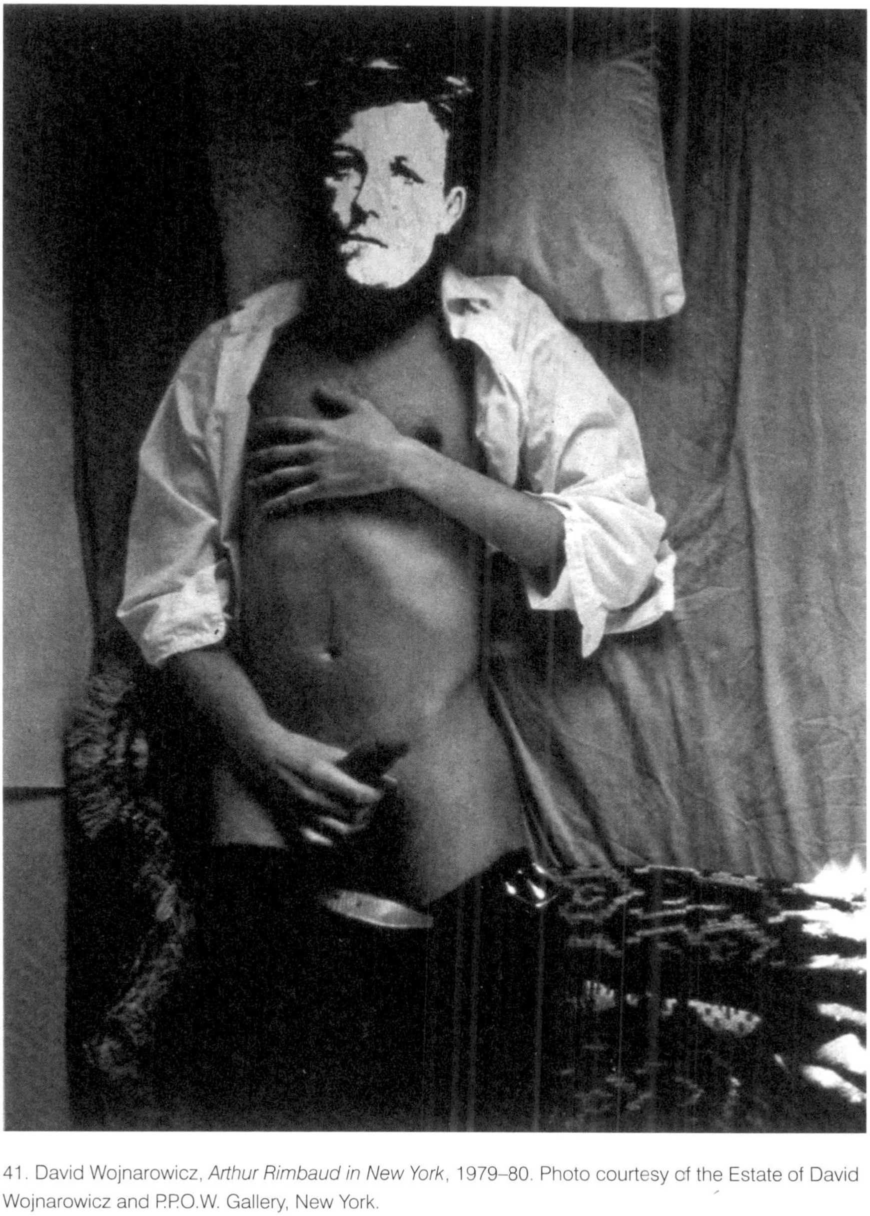

41. David Wojnarowicz, *Arthur Rimbaud in New York*, 1979–80. Photo courtesy of the Estate of David Wojnarowicz and P.P.O.W. Gallery, New York.

life. His hands had chiseled a manual of heaven and I held them fast. The knowledge of him added swagger to my step and this could not be stripped away. I tossed my copy of *Illuminations* in a plaid suitcase. We would escape together."[27]

Rimbaud appealed particularly to queer artists of all stripes. It is hard to think of two gay writers more different in temperament and style than Dennis Cooper and Edmund White, but both recalled the ways in which Rimbaud's work transformed their adolescence. White's short book on Rimbaud begins with a memory of discovering the poet while still in boarding school, an experience that was crucial to the painful process of coming to terms with his sexual identity. The lack of inhibition in the young Rimbaud's pursuit of Verlaine and in his writings about sexual acts with men liberated White; at sixteen, he was the same age Rimbaud had been when he first set out for Paris to escape the boredom of provincial family life: "I identified completely with Rimbaud's desires to be free, to be published, to be sexual, to go to Paris. All I lacked was his courage."[28] Cooper devoted an entire issue of his poetry journal *Little Caesar* to an elaborate homage to Rimbaud, complete with an introduction—handwritten as if scrawled by a teenage boy—confessing his failed attempt to model himself after the dead poet: "I wanted to look like him and made a pathetic attempt—short hair in a long hair era—a fool. I tried to follow him on drugs. I wrote stupid long visions—'The Drunken Concorde,' etc. Went nowhere. Then I was nineteen, then into my twenties writing and here I am twenty-five. No Rimbaud. I give up, and I don't."[29] The memories of Smith, White, and Cooper shared with Wojnarowicz's photographic series not only the longing to emulate Rimbaud but the fantasy that he was a living, breathing presence in their lives; Smith's "unrequited love for him was as real" as anything she had ever experienced. And yet, as much as they modeled themselves after Rimbaud, the poet proved inimitable. Beyond the difficulty of trying to make art as radical as Rimbaud's, or to mimic his violent and self-destructive actions, was Rimbaud's imperative to break with the past and make everything new. How do you imitate an artist who insists that the artist's task is to copy no one?

Cooper's solution was to mock his own hero worship in *Little Caesar* by juxtaposing popular and high art forms. Serious poems with Rimbaudian themes by the likes of the art critic René Ricard were juxtaposed with a Rimbaud-themed crossword puzzle, in much the same way that *TV Guide* would include a puzzle about sitcom stars. Like *People* magazine, Cooper included pictures of celebrities whom he considered Rimbaudian rebels, from James Dean to Johnny Rotten. The potential sentimentality of an image of

Rimbaud's tombstone, or an account of a visit to his birthplace, was undermined by an amusing Rimbaud comic strip, or by pictures of teen stars clipped from fan magazines, as if the poet were merely the nineteenth-century version of a rock star like Jim Morrison or, worse, a pop star like Shaun Cassidy. Such camp gestures were Cooper's way of distancing himself from his hero—or, as he put it, of giving up trying to be Rimbaud by rejecting the hierarchies between modernist poetry and vernacular cultural forms.

Cooper's passion for Rimbaud was clearly not sated by editing a special issue of *Little Caesar*. In 1980, when he heard about Wojnarowicz's similar attempt at homage and emulation, Cooper offered him extensive space in the journal. If we include the spread that appeared in the *SoHo News* announcing the upcoming publication in *Little Caesar*, Wojnarowicz had by this time printed and published eighteen unique photographs from the series. A number of these pictures were not published by Wojnarowicz in 1990 or later by his estate. Because these publications were produced shortly after Wojnarowicz took the photographs, they are arguably closer to his initial intentions than his exhibition produced a decade later. All but ignored in the critical reception of the artist, the double spread published in the center of the 18–24 June 1980 issue of the *SoHo News Weekly* (fig. 42) is particularly intriguing because it fuses Wojnarowicz's words and images in a montage format that resists a linear narrative. The spread is built around four photographs, two of which he never included in an edition. The largest photograph in the spread shows the Rimbaud figure pointing a gun at an enormous graffiti image of Jesus Christ. The iconoclasm of Wojnarowicz's photograph is echoed by the text running down the left side of the photograph, which declares, "I still don't believe in systems of order, policemen or borders." On the right side of the spread, a photograph depicts Rimbaud standing in front of an image of a man shooting up heroin, spray-painted by Wojnarowicz on the wall of one of the rooms in Pier 46. Just below, we see Rimbaud posing along the beach with the Coney Island amusement park in the background. Running along the bottom of the spread, like a film loop, is the repeated image of Rimbaud in one of the pier warehouses holding a cigarette in his bandaged right hand. The bandage alludes to Verlaine's famous act of shooting the poet in the wrist. Given that this picture is repeated eight times, it is surprising that it was not included in *Little Caesar* or the edition of the prints a decade later. After it was published in the *SoHo News Weekly*, did someone tell Wojnarowicz that it was actually Rimbaud's *left* wrist that had gotten shot? We will never know, but a decade later, when Wojnarowicz rethought the series, he shifted the focus away from

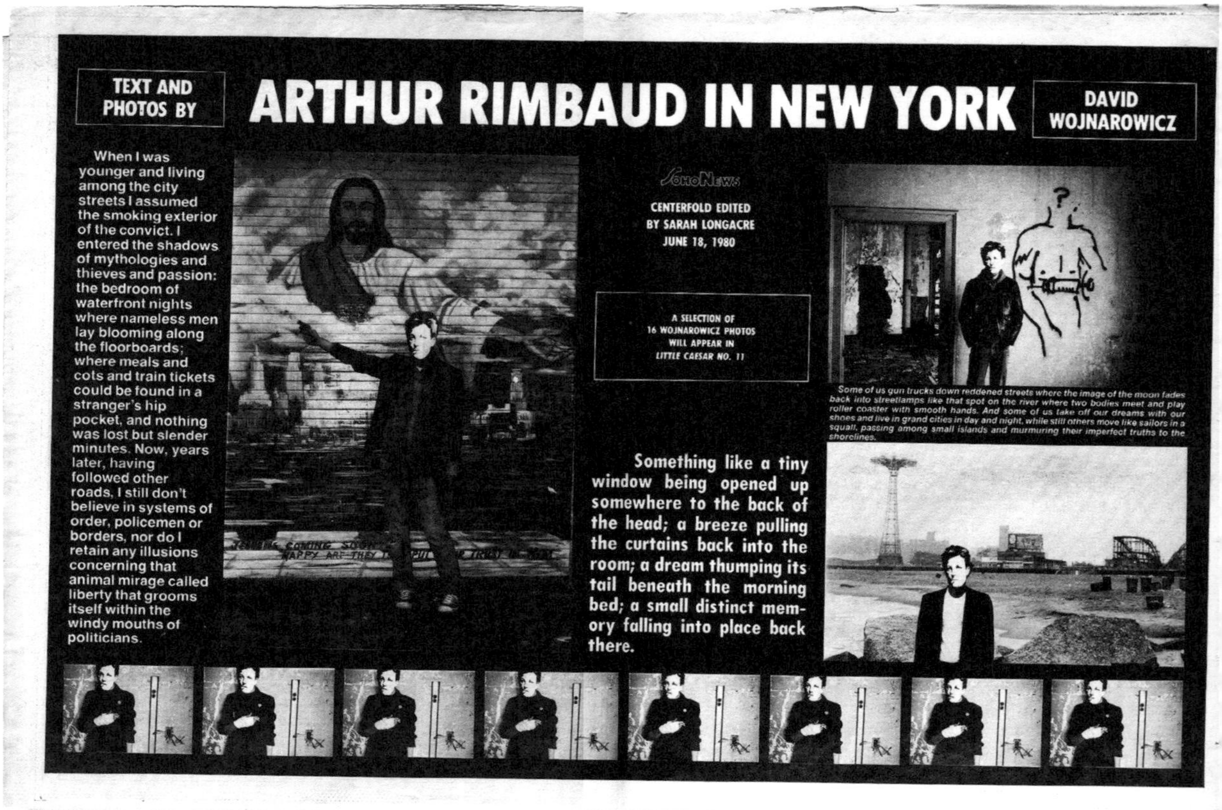

TEXT AND PHOTOS BY

ARTHUR RIMBAUD IN NEW YORK

DAVID WOJNAROWICZ

When I was younger and living among the city streets I assumed the smoking exterior of the convict. I entered the shadows of mythologies and thieves and passion: the bedroom of waterfront nights where nameless men lay blooming along the floorboards; where meals and cots and train tickets could be found in a stranger's hip pocket, and nothing was lost but slender minutes. Now, years later, having followed other roads, I still don't believe in systems of order, policemen or borders, nor do I retain any illusions concerning that animal mirage called liberty that grooms itself within the windy mouths of politicians.

SoHo News

CENTERFOLD EDITED BY SARAH LONGACRE JUNE 18, 1980

A SELECTION OF 16 WOJNAROWICZ PHOTOS WILL APPEAR IN *LITTLE CAESAR NO. 11*

Something like a tiny window being opened up somewhere to the back of the head; a breeze pulling the curtains back into the room; a dream thumping its tail beneath the morning bed; a small distinct memory falling into place back there.

Some of us gun trucks down reddened streets where the image of the moon fades back into streetlamps like that spot on the river where two bodies meet and play roller coaster with smooth hands. And some of us take off our dreams with our shoes and live in grand cities in day and night, while still others move like sailors in a squall, passing among small islands and murmuring their imperfect truths to the shorelines.

42. David Wojnarowicz, "Arthur Rimbaud in New York," *SoHo News Weekly*, 18–24 June 1980. David Wojnarowicz Papers, Fales Library, New York University. Photo courtesy of the Estate of David Wojnarowicz and P.P.O.W. Gallery, New York.

this violent and defiant Rimbaud to a more passive and melancholic figure of loneliness, addiction, and death.

Depicting Rimbaud as a gun-wielding rebel or tough resonates with the legend of the poet on several levels. It reminds us of his violent fight with his lover Verlaine, even though it was Verlaine who shot Rimbaud, and alludes to Rimbaud's later career as a sometime gunrunner. In the *Little Caesar* series, the Rimbaud figure holds a gun while standing on the piers in front of a crude drawing of the poet that Wojnarowicz painted on a window (fig. 43). This picture follows a little-known photograph of the hero on a motorcycle, posed from the back so that Rimbaud's face can only be spied in the bike's mirror. The

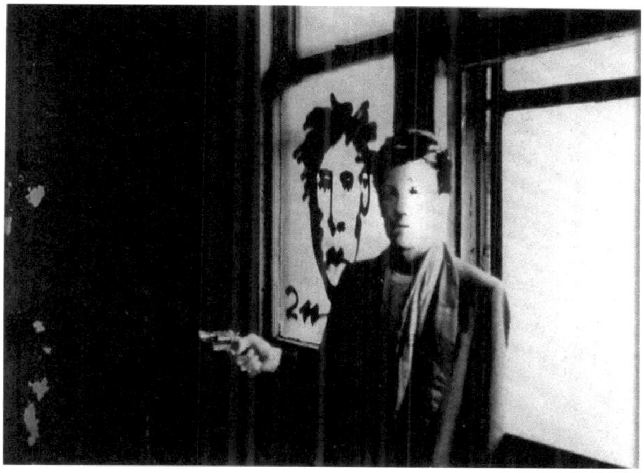

43. David Wojnarowicz, *Arthur Rimbaud in New York*, 1979–80. Photo courtesy of the Estate of David Wojnarowicz and P.P.O.W. Gallery, New York.

juxtaposition of Rimbaud with a gun and Rimbaud on a motorcycle creates an image of the poet as an alienated youth, akin to Marlon Brando in *The Wild Bunch* or James Dean in *Rebel Without a Cause*. Wojnarowicz also played with the theme of teenage disenchantment when he used a dime-store photo booth to take some photos of Rimbaud with a toy gun.

A decade later, Wojnarowicz reprinted the image of Rimbaud with a gun at the piers, but he moved it from early in the series, where it promised some sort of action of protest or anger, to a place near the end, where it seems a harbinger of death. The final three pictures in the reconstituted series concern heroin, culminating with the image of Rimbaud seemingly in the death throes of an overdose (fig. 44). Placing the gun image so close to images of heroin addiction and overdose suggests less an act of rebellion against the state or the church than a crime of desperation—the type of violence an addict might do to himself or others in pursuit of his next fix.

Given Wojnarowicz's fragile health in 1990, it may not be surprising that in choosing the twenty-five negatives that he did, and organizing them into some kind of narrative arc, he ended the series with the picture of Rimbaud in his death throes. Such drug use echoes the absinthe and opium addiction of so many in Rimbaud's avant-garde circles, including Verlaine. But was this how he imagined the series ending in 1980, before HIV/AIDS was even known? In two "photo scripts" he made around 1979, in which he noted possible settings for Rimbaud scenes, the overdose does not come at the end. Nor does the overdose end the portfolio of published pictures in *Little Caesar*. It is placed third from the end, followed by two more pictures on the pier, so that

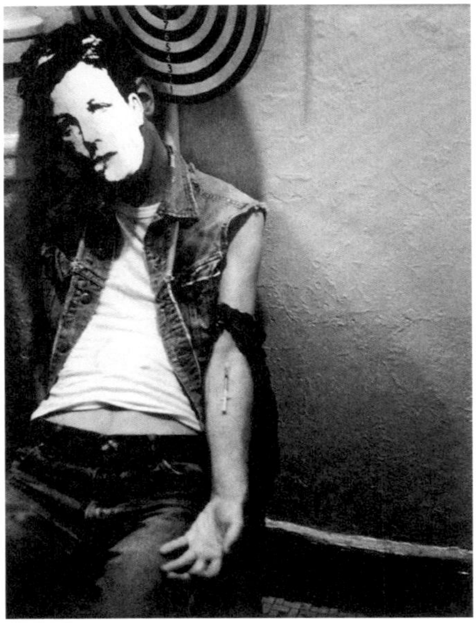

44. David Wojnarowicz, *Arthur Rimbaud in New York*, 1979–80. Photo courtesy of the Estate of David Wojnarowicz and P.P.O.W. Gallery, New York.

the poet seems to recover and go on to live another day. Having the series end with Rimbaud's death makes the series more reflective of Wojnarowicz's sense, in 1990, of his own impending death. I imagine that he would also have been thinking about the link between heroin addiction and AIDS, since drug users who used needles and homosexuals were among the high-risk groups for the disease. The melancholy ending not only makes the series more relevant to Wojnarowicz's illness; it makes its narrative structure conventional, predictable, and moralistic in its conclusion. At thirty-five, Wojnarowicz was a very different person from the artist of ten years earlier, more cognizant, perhaps, of the sacrifices and limitations involved in Rimbaud's famous call for the "derangement of all the senses" on the path to becoming a great poet or "seer."

Carr discusses at some length Wojnarowicz's use of heroin and other narcotics in his twenties, and his ambivalence about it. Concurrent with the Rimbaud series, Wojnarowicz's unfinished 8mm film *Heroin*, which was shot on the piers, includes an overdose, which he later claimed was a warning to friends who were becoming addicts. But he also created several images that romanticized the drug. In Paris in 1978, he posed in front of the Eiffel Tower pretending to shoot up. This picture was pasted into his journal under a dedication to his lover Brian Butterick, who was a user, and tagged with the two little lightning bolts that Wojnarowicz called "Rimbaud bolts," signs of inspiration and delight he associated with his favorite poet.[30] Back in New York, he repeated the pun of hypodermic needle and phallic tower in one of his 8mm film shots on the pier, this time using the Empire State Building as the spire.

Wojnarowicz's conflicting feelings about drugs may be clearest in the image of a man shooting up that he spray-painted on Pier 46 (fig. 35). Although the graffiti painting no longer exists, it lives on in countless photographs of the piers, perhaps most memorably in Wojnarowicz's own photograph from the Rimbaud series. A favorite of the artist, this photograph is one of only two that appear in the 1980 publications in the *SoHo News*, *Little Caesar*, and the edition that came later, in 1990. The original graffiti drawing, and the photograph based upon it, makes iconic Wojnarowicz's ambivalence about heroin and the potential for such narcotics to both inspire and confuse. In the wall drawing, the shirtless drug user aims the enormous hypodermic needle into his arm, which is tattooed with the Rimbaud lightning bolt. Heroin acts like a charge of electricity; it illuminates, to use that very Rimbaudian word. But where this figure's head should be is a giant question mark, as if asking whether such chemically induced stimulation can be trusted.

The nakedness of the muscular addict spray-painted on the wall, with his phallic needle, links drug addiction with sexual desire. Heroin users often report getting an erection when they shoot up, and the pricking of the skin with a needle is an obvious metaphor for the sexual intercourse that often took place on the pier, sometimes right in front of the drawing. In the context of the sexual theater that was the piers, the image is as much a metaphor for sexual desire as it is a picture about drug addiction. In Wojnarowicz's photograph, the needle points directly at Rimbaud, himself a figure of ambivalence as Verlaine's great muse and the cause of his destruction. The emotionless Rimbaud mask answers our gaze with no response or empathy; it functions like the great question mark in place of the addict's head. Ironically, having Rimbaud die of an overdose in the 1990 version of the series may be Wojnarowicz's least Rimbaudian gesture, in that it provides a predictable ending to the quest for drug-induced inspiration. Still, if this antiheroin conclusion seems like a nod to bourgeois morality, placing the overdose at the end makes the artist something of a martyr. Rimbaud's ultimate derangement of the senses becomes death itself.

Given Wojnarowicz's fascination with heroin in 1979, it may seem surprising that, according to Carr, the artist had not yet tried the drug, although several of his friends were users. But my point about the *Arthur Rimbaud in New York* series is that it is *not* autobiography, or not in any simple sense. Rather than merely catalogue Wojnarowicz's experiences as a young man living on the streets, it is more akin to an allegory of the coming into being of the type of artist Wojnarowicz wanted to be. Rather than see Rimbaud as a stand-in for Wojnarowicz, we should consider him the ultimate muse or guide, who, like Virgil for Dante, charts a path through the hell/paradise of the urban underground and ruined waterfront. Significantly, the journey Rimbaud takes us on doesn't just involve hanging out on the street like a male hustler. Early in the series as printed in *Little Caesar*, he interacts with enormous Dubuffet sculptures, and, according to his photo script, Wojnarowicz planned to photograph the Rimbaud character in front of a painting by Jackson Pollock. In other words, the path of illumination leads through aesthetic experience as well as sexual experimentation and physical degradation.

When Wojnarowicz exhibited the Rimbaud series at P.P.O.W., the pictures would have been seen free of any text other than a title and the artist's statement, which viewers could read or ignore. But one of the most striking aspects of the *SoHo News* spread is the way it juxtaposes Wojnarowicz's words and images on the page. Indeed, this is the most significant difference between how *Arthur Rimbaud in New York* was first seen and how it has come to be known since 1990, when the photographs were printed as a suite. Running to the left of the photograph of Rimbaud waving a gun in front of the image of Jesus, Wojnarowicz's words read:

> When I was younger and living among the city streets I assumed the smoking exterior of the convict. I entered the shadows of mythologies and thieves and passion: the bedroom of waterfront nights where nameless men lay blooming along the floorboards; where meals and cots and train tickets could be found in a stranger's hip pocket, and nothing was lost but slender minutes. Now, years later, having followed other roads, I still don't believe in systems of order, policemen or borders, nor do I retain any illusions concerning that animal mirage called liberty that grooms itself within the windy mouths of politicians.

It is unclear whether this is meant to be the voice of a jaded Rimbaud reminiscing about his early years on the streets or Wojnarowicz speaking of his own experience. Sandwiched between the photographs of Rimbaud on the pier and on Coney Island, the text alludes to the kind of sexual experiences Wojnarowicz was having along the waterfront: "where two bodies meet and play roller coaster with smooth hands." And yet in contrast to the way Wojnarowicz wrote explicitly about sex later, this description sounds remarkably discreet, as if the artist was not yet ready to reveal his or Rimbaud's homosexuality.

At the center of the spread is a paragraph proposing ideas that reflect Wojnarowicz's own ambitions: "Something like a tiny window being opened up somewhere to the back of the head; a breeze pulling the curtains back into the room; a dream thumping its tail beneath the morning bed; a small distinct memory falling into place back there." In this passage, Wojnarowicz returns to the idea he had explored in the collage he made for the postcard art exhibit: that true seeing was a process of looking within, "somewhere to the back of the head" or "back there." The idea that memory works like a window with the curtains pulled back relates to the final photograph in the *Little Caesar* series, in which Rimbaud stands by a window on the piers and light falls on his left eye (fig. 45). In text and image, the emphasis is on sight and the connection between seeing and inner vision.

In *Little Caesar*, Wojnarowicz's writing is severed from the photographs. Instead, his words make an appearance in the same issue with two monologues from his *Sounds in the Distance* that focus on what it is like to be a male hustler in San Francisco and New York. Although the second monologue, "Young Boy in Times Square 4:00 A.M. (New York City)," relates to the photographs of Rimbaud hanging out on the streets in front of movie theaters and a bar, it appears toward the front of the issue, with a gap of more than seventy pages between it and *Rimbaud in New York*, effectively discouraging such connections. Some text opens the Rimbaud series, but the words are not Wojnarowicz's. The introductory page consists of a fragment of Enid Starkie's popular biography of Rimbaud, partially obscured by the title "Rimbaud in New York" and Wojnarowicz's byline. Breaking up the text in this way might seem to undermine its significance, but the chosen fragment describes a telling event in the inauguration of the relationship between Rimbaud and Verlaine. When the young, disheveled Rimbaud is invited to a dinner party at Verlaine's home, his manners are atrocious, and he insults the other guests and Verlaine's wife. Starkie describes Rimbaud as giving "the impression of surliness and ill temper, but in truth he was more deeply sunk in misery and distress, more profoundly disappointed, than he had ever been in his life."[31] The sections that are blanked out have the effect of emphasizing the adjoining lines while at the same time creating a new disjointed sentence. The phrase "ill at ease and bewildered, and he" runs into the line "state of confusion, and he was never at the best of times a fluent conversationalist; now he lapsed into gloomy silence and remained tongue-tied, answering only in monosyllables the questions good naturedly put to him." This textual disjunction amplifies Rimbaud's alienated refusal to engage in conversation. Paradoxically, this child prodigy of poetry is "tongue-tied" and nearly silent. This, too, is the paradox of Wojnarowicz's photographic series, as it evokes the great poet not through his words but merely by reproducing an image of his face that, like the title of

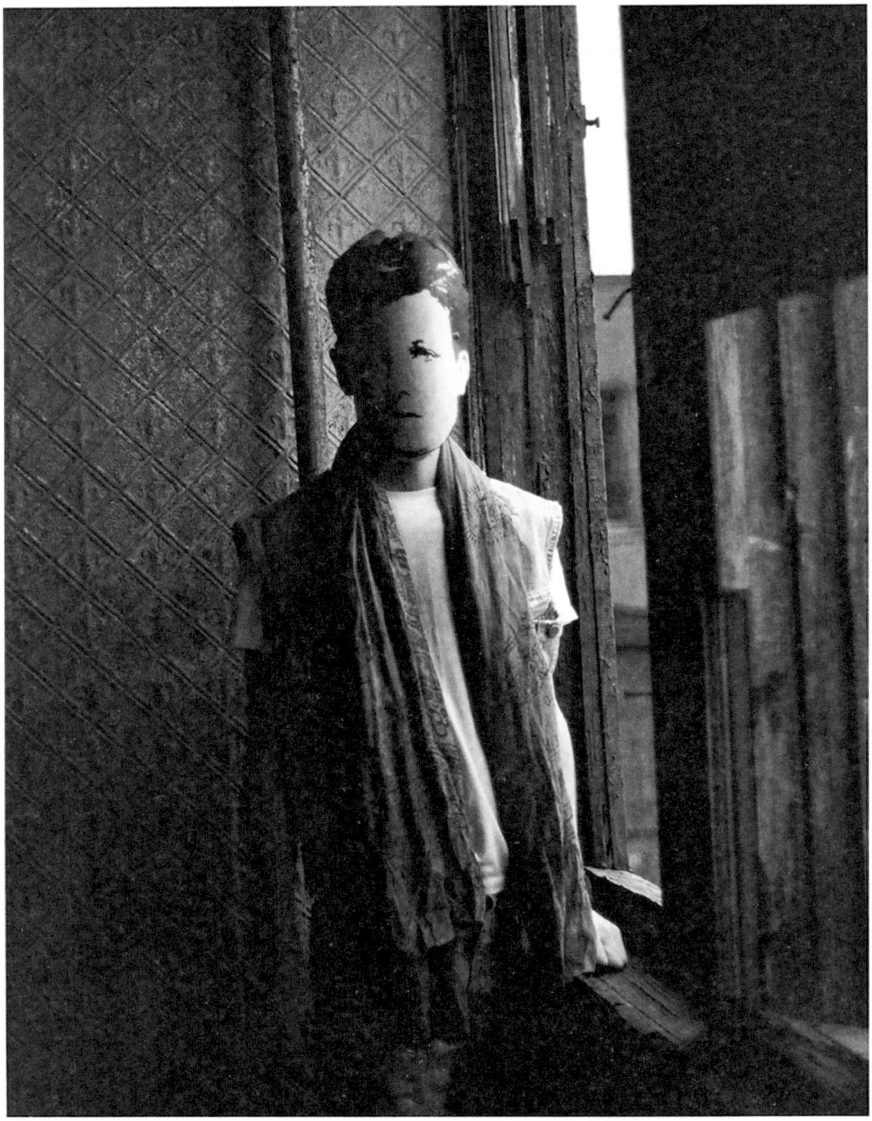

45. David Wojnarowicz, *Arthur Rimbaud in New York*, 1979–80. Photo courtesy of the Estate of David Wojnarowicz and P.P.O.W. Gallery, New York.

the series in *Little Caesar*, masks what is beneath. The face of Rimbaud never changes in the series, thus becoming a stand-in for the poet's unwillingness to speak civilly or to conform to the expectations of those around him. And yet this very lack of emotion, exaggerated by the removal of details in photocopying, itself expresses depression, loneliness, and despair.

Rimbaud's journey through the city culminates in two crucial images in *Little Caesar*. Rimbaud masturbates on a mattress on the pier and then, with a turn of the page, in an almost mirrorlike pose, shoots up heroin. Masturbation and overdose involve the poet pleasuring himself; both are pathetic, as if he has lost all respect in some desperate attempt at fulfillment. Is this what it looks like to undergo the "derangement of all the senses" that Rimbaud advocated? But drugs don't kill the poet after all. In the penultimate picture, he wanders among the ruins of the piers, very much alive. It is the modern city that is collapsing around him; the artist, or at least his poetic vision, survives. The final image of the *Little Caesar* series, in which Rimbaud's left eye is illuminated, reinforces this emphasis on the redemption of sight. Rather than end the series with death, the implication is that the artist has become the seer he prophesied and that there is more to see.

One of the treasures of the Wojnarowicz collection housed in New York University's Fales Library is the original mask that was used in the Rimbaud series (fig. 46). I am fascinated by this object, particularly the strangeness of how it looks from the inside: the tiny holes that pierce the eyes and the broken rubber bands that originally held it to the face. There is something deeply unnerving about it on its own, apart from its various manifestations in the Rimbaud series. I cannot help thinking about Jason's mask in *Halloween*, a film that premiered in 1978, the year Wojnarowicz was considering making some sort of art based on the image of Rimbaud. The association between American pop psycho-killer and French avant-garde poet may seem far-fetched (I think Wojnarowicz, who acted in and made his own low-budget horror films, would enjoy the association) until we realize that both have become mythic figures of adolescent rage. But whereas we can imagine the hard plastic skin of Jason's mask affording the antihero some measure of protection, the paper Rimbaud face is flimsy. Indeed, to put on such a paper mask would, I think, make the wearer feel vulnerable, as if the cloak of anonymity or charade could be torn and the personality underneath revealed.

Above all, the masked figure transmits an overwhelming sense of loneliness. In none of the pictures that Wojnarowicz published does Rimbaud interact with another person. It was only after he died that Wojnarowicz's

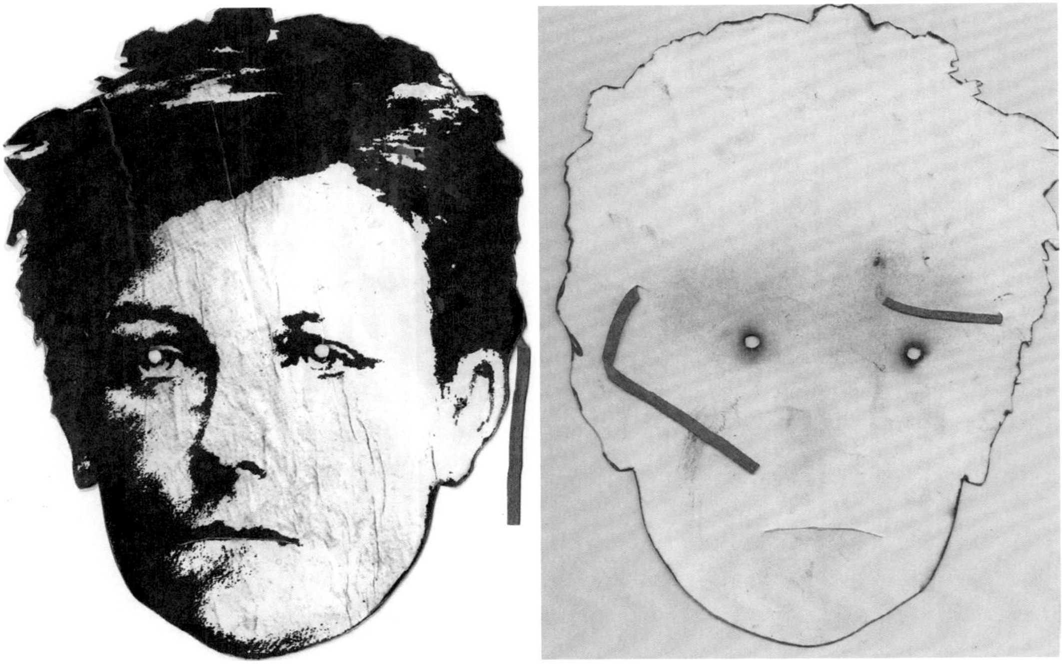

46. David Wojnarowicz, *Rimbaud Mask*, 1978–79. David Wojnarowicz Papers, Fales Library, New York University. Photo courtesy of the Estate of David Wojnarowicz and P.P.O.W. Gallery, New York.

estate chose to print the image in which a man, his back to us, makes love to Rimbaud on a bed (fig. 47). But even in this image, Rimbaud's flattened photocopied face expresses indifference, as if even in an embrace he is untouched by another human being. Surrounded by people in Times Square or riding a crowded subway, Rimbaud seems essentially alone. Surely loneliness is one of the dominant themes of Wojnarowicz's writings, particularly in the period that spawned the Rimbaud series. But whereas the poet Rimbaud went to extraordinary lengths to alienate potential friends and supporters, Wojnarowicz was intensely social and often went out of his way to collaborate with other artists. If what we might today call Wojnarowicz's "anger-management problems" made him at times difficult to get along with, they did not stop him from developing long-term relationships with a large circle of friends and lovers. Wojnarowicz was particularly loyal to his mentor, the legendarily misanthropic Peter Hujar, whom he cared for as Hujar succumbed to HIV/AIDS. As the epidemic developed and Wojnarowicz's work became a target of right-wing attacks and censorship, Wojnarowicz's visual art and writings focused

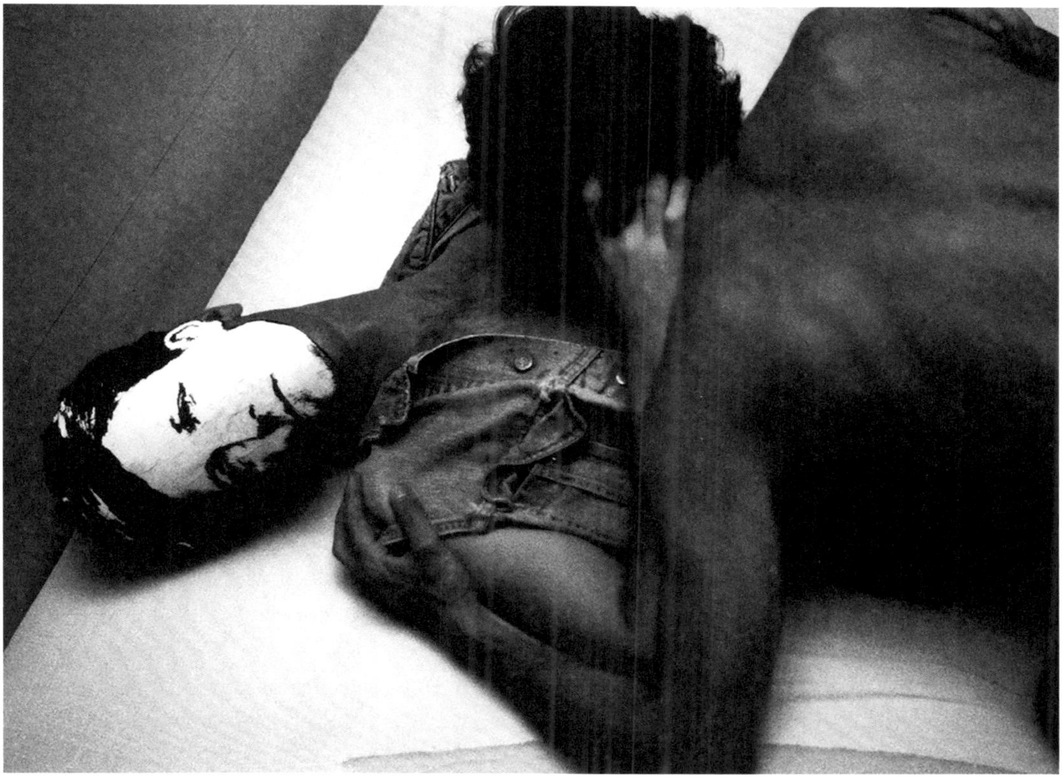

47. David Wojnarowicz, *Arthur Rimbaud in New York*, 1979–80. Photo courtesy of the Estate of David Wojnarowicz and P.P.O.W. Gallery, New York.

on questions of social justice and homophobia in ways that I think would have been anathema to Rimbaud's peculiar form of radicalism, which was so dependent on negation and on rejection of all forms of bourgeois moralism. Ironically, the more one studies Wojnarowicz's personal life and his commitment to social justice, the less Rimbaud makes sense as a model. Perhaps this is another reason for Wojnarowicz's decision to end the 1990 Rimbaud series pessimistically, with an overdose. In the end, the Rimbaudian path of sensory derangement and abandoning poetry was not Wojnarowicz's path, even though he too was facing his mortality. Emulation in *Arthur Rimbaud in New York* turns into a refusal to imitate, which, in a final twist, might be the quality of the project most true to the spirit of Rimbaud.

Chapter 5

The Pickup Machine

Posted like silent sentinels all around the town, stand thousands of mortal men fixed in ocean reveries. Some leaning against the spiles; some seated upon the pier heads. . . . But these are all landsmen; of weekdays pent up in lath and plaster—tied to counters, nailed to benches, clinched to desks. How then is this? Are the green fields gone? What do they here?
—Herman Melville, *Moby-Dick*

If the homosexual pick-up machine, which is infinitely more direct and less guilt-induced than the complex system of "civilised loves" . . . were to take off the Oedipal cloak of morality under which it is forced to hide, we would see that its mechanical scattering corresponds to the mode of existence of desire itself.
—Guy Hocquenghem, *Homosexual Desire*

The piers of the 1970s and '80s exist now largely as images seen through the lens of a camera. To understand the complex nexus of people, places, and histories that the piers represent is to study hundreds of photographs, most of which were not made to be exhibited in an art museum or gallery. Of course, many photographers with the highest aesthetic ambitions, like Alvin Baltrop, Shelley Seccombe, and Arthur Tress, created remarkable pictures of the piers, but so did amateurs like Frank Hallam and Leonard Fink. Hallam proudly admitted that some of his best pictures were taken holding his camera at waist level so that he wasn't even looking through the viewfinder. He didn't want his subjects to know that he was taking their picture. At times, his process was more akin to hunting game than to carefully composing a shot.[1] As is so often the case in the history of photography, the attempt to make a self-consciously aesthetic image may result in pictures that seem arty and overly romantic, while the supposed neophyte, driven by an intense passion for the subject, discovers something new. But inexperience or lack of skill did not guarantee interesting images, either. The vast majority of pictures of the piers, whether by professional photographers or amateurs, lack the peculiar qualities of eroticism, danger, and liberation that for me are so intrinsic to the experience of the waterfront.

Why were so many photographers drawn to the piers? Hallam talked about the brazen nudity and public sex: "They just sort of liberated the piers."[2] The activist and writer Arnie Kantrowitz echoes Hallam's sentiment: "The feeling, the openness, the fresh air and you're out there and after a while it becomes a habit like an addiction and that's mainly what it became is an addiction. It was like a drug. It was a drug."[3] Along with the sense of freedom and erotic allure was the foreboding that this freedom wouldn't last. The camera was the means of recording the waterfront scene for posterity, to prove that it really did happen. Baltrop said that he originally began to photograph the piers for voyeuristic reasons, but he "soon grew determined to preserve the frightening, mad, unbelievable, violent, and beautiful things that were going on at that time."[4] Shelley Seccombe also was keenly aware that the area was in transition. Photographs by Baltrop, Fink, Hallam, and Seccombe, among others, create a visual diary of the waterfront's transformation over several years. In contrast, Shunk and Kender in the 1970s, and Peter Hujar and Andreas Sterzing in the 1980s, came to the waterfront primarily to document a specific art project, yet their work also conveys the idea of a place in flux, where the normal rules of behavior have been suspended.

Despite the stated intentions of several pier photographers to record the scene before it disappeared, they did not approach their subjects methodically, like a historian or anthropologist, nor did they necessarily do a good job of documenting their own work. Too often, an early death from HIV/AIDS left the task of titling and dating their pictures to those left behind. The headings on the folders of Fink's archive at the LGBT Community Center National History Archive are short and inaccurate. Wojnarowicz's contact sheets are incompletely annotated; Baltrop did not date or title many of his photographs. Ironically, it was Hallam who, with no pretense of professional status, was the most consistent in writing down the pier number and dates on his slides.

One of the advantages of looking at the work of the pier photographers as a group is the guidance gained in creating chronologies and specific contexts for pictures that are missing dates and locations. Because Baltrop, Fink, and Hallam often photographed the same locations around the same time, we can use the information on Hallam's slides to help date and give specific pier numbers to Baltrop's photographs, for instance. This allows future scholars not only to date Baltrop's work more precisely but also to think of his pier pictures not as a single unit but as an evolution occurring over a period of more than a decade.

Dating the pier photographs accurately is not a trivial matter. At the MoMA PS1 *Greater New York* exhibition in 2015, I overheard a staff member describing Baltrop's photographs to a visitor. He claimed that they documented the height of the AIDS epidemic. But from Hallam's notations on his slides and my own pier research, I knew that most of these pictures were taken before the disease had been discovered. If there is one point I want this book to drive home, it is that photographs of sex on the piers from the 1970s are not pictures of men ignoring or defying the codes of "safe sex" that emerged in New York's gay communities as a response to the AIDS crisis. It may be impossible to untangle the associations between sex, disease, and death. But if we are to bring the history of AIDS into the interpretation of photographs of sex in the 1970s at all, it should be to remember a time before the epidemic, when public sex between men was considered a liberating act.

If the pier pictures are not about men getting infected with disease as they pleasure themselves, many of the photographs do focus on the death of a once grand transportation hub. Sometimes the ruined pier buildings are shown isolated from outside, as in Sterzing's picture of the façade of Pier 34 in the process of being torn down (fig. 48), revealing Wojnarowicz's *Gagging Cow* mural on the second floor. Or there is Baltrop's picture of Pier 48, with its roof and supporting girders in full collapse, as if the city had just withstood an earthquake. Amid this ruin, in full daylight and seemingly oblivious to the possibility that the burned-out dock will give out underneath, two men fuck doggy style.

In other pictures, the pier buildings are contrasted with the modern city, as in Seccombe's 1980 image of Pier 46 on fire against the backdrop of the World Trade Center (fig. 49). This picture emphasizes the enormous gulf between the wealth and modernity of the financial district and the dilapidation of the waterfront. Now, post-9/11, the fires on the pier portend the fate of the twin towers. In another memorable Seccombe photograph, a boy of about twelve balances precariously on a girder amid the collapsed scaffolding of a charred pier roof

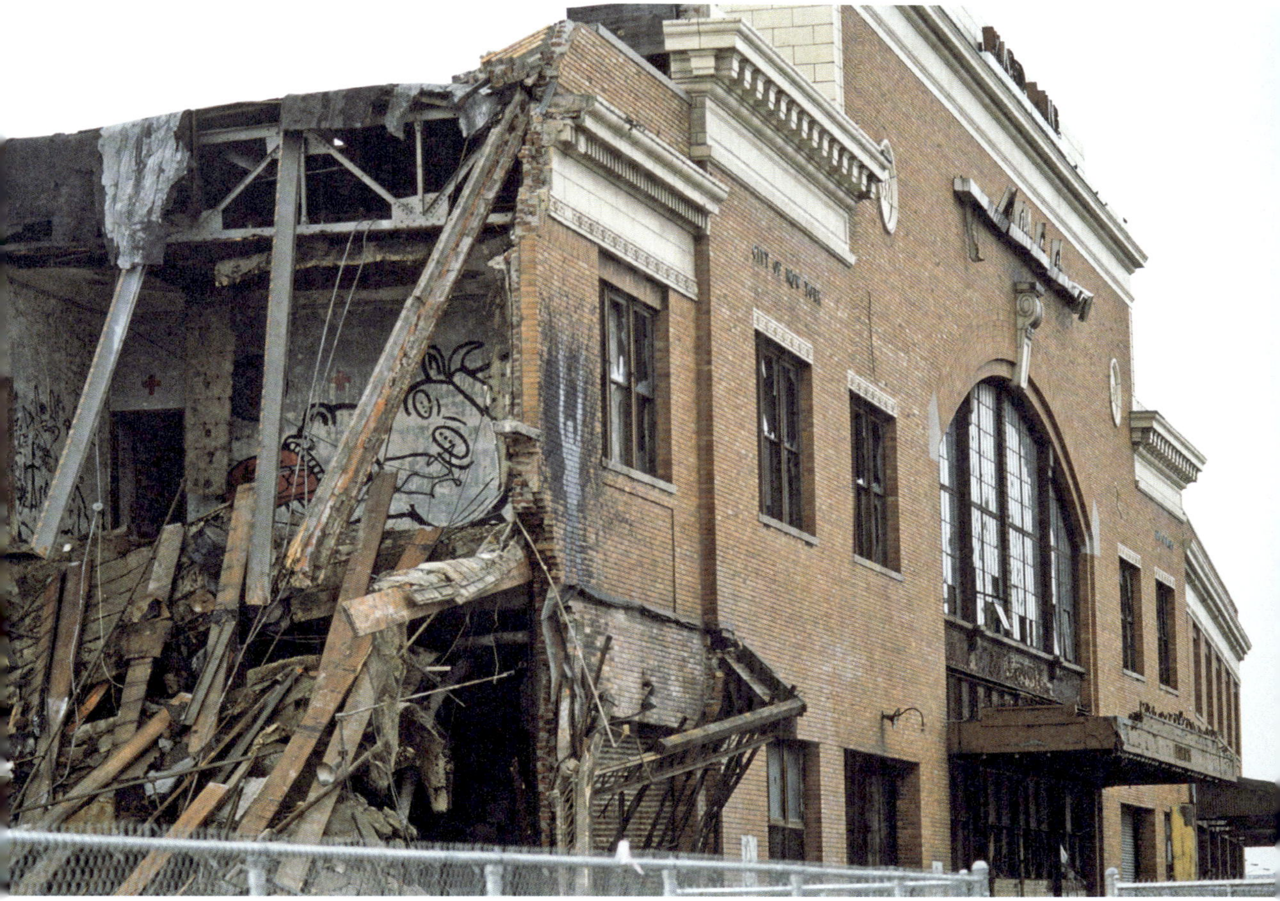

48. Andreas Sterzing, *Pier 34 Coming Down*, 1984. © Andreas Sterzing.

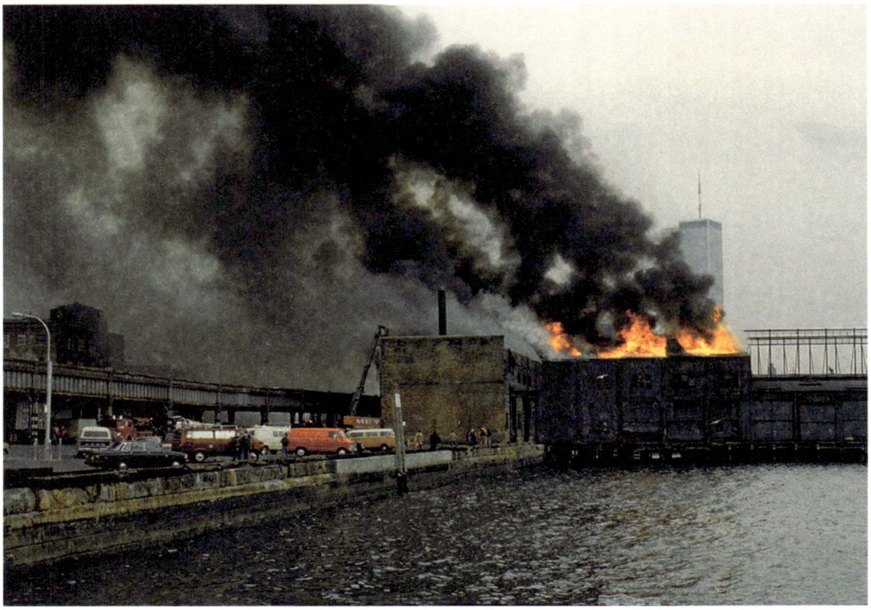

49. Shelley Seccombe, *Black Smoke from Pier 46, with World Trade Center in the Distance*, 1980. © Shelley Seccombe.

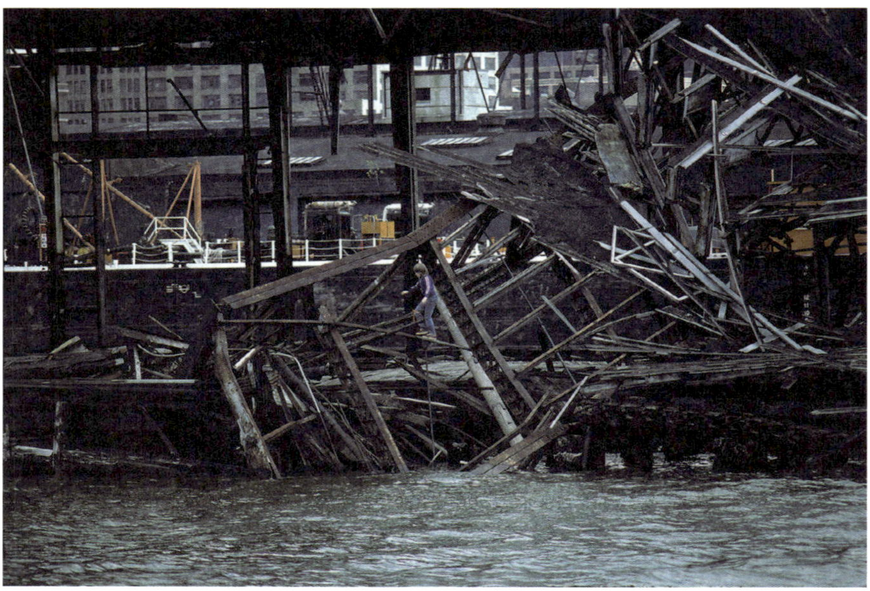

50. Shelley Seccombe, *Boy Climbs the Beams on Pier 48 Ruins*, 1977. © Shelley Seccombe.

(fig. 50). Behind him is the cityscape, its commercial and residential buildings intact, reminding us that such dangerous child's play was not happening on some abandoned lot in the so-called slums (as if that would make it all right) but in the heavily populated and affluent West Village. Seccombe writes, "the twisted steel attracted many neighborhood kids, who nonchalantly scrambled over this ad hoc jungle gym, with nary a mishap." For Seccombe, the contrast between the deteriorating buildings and the way people managed to use the burned-out spaces for their enjoyment was what made the piers so fascinating.

Shelley Seccombe

Unlike the male pier photographers discussed in this chapter, Shelley Seccombe does not identify as queer. She came to photograph the waterfront in the 1970s, when she and her husband, the sculptor David Seccombe, moved to Westbeth, an artists' housing complex across from the piers. In part because she photographed mostly in color and was less engaged in the psychic lives of the people experiencing the piers, her pictures lack the anxious film-noir character of Baltrop's or Fink's work. Nevertheless, her photographs of children wandering on the docks convey the near anarchy of the bankrupt city and its inability to police its public spaces. Seccombe herself claimed that she was drawn to the piers for "their photographic quality; the elegant decaying structures with their peeling paint made an appealing backdrop for the sometimes wacky activities on the dock. . . . What kept me coming back and haunting the piers for years was the spontaneous appearance of those unwitting actors, and the majesty of their stage." For Seccombe, the gay men sunbathing or cruising the ruins for sex were part of the larger spectacle of New York in the 1970s, a scene in which the river continued to be a worksite. In the Westbeth complex, she had many gay friends and neighbors, among them Harry Shunk, but she also made it her business to get to know the tugboat captains and crews, who allowed her to photograph the waterfront from the vantage point of their crafts. Seccombe was as interested in capturing the "signals of the deckhands sent to the captain, putting scows in order for delivery to their destination," as she was in the sex workers who hung out along West Street.[5] Reminiscing with her about the queer scene some three decades later, I felt her empathy for the LGBTQ community, and her feelings of being an outsider among the gay men cruising the waterfront. Ironically, perhaps, her being an outsider to the queer subculture gives her waterfront work a quality of inclusiveness. Her point of view is often panoramic, as if she were intent on taking in the totality

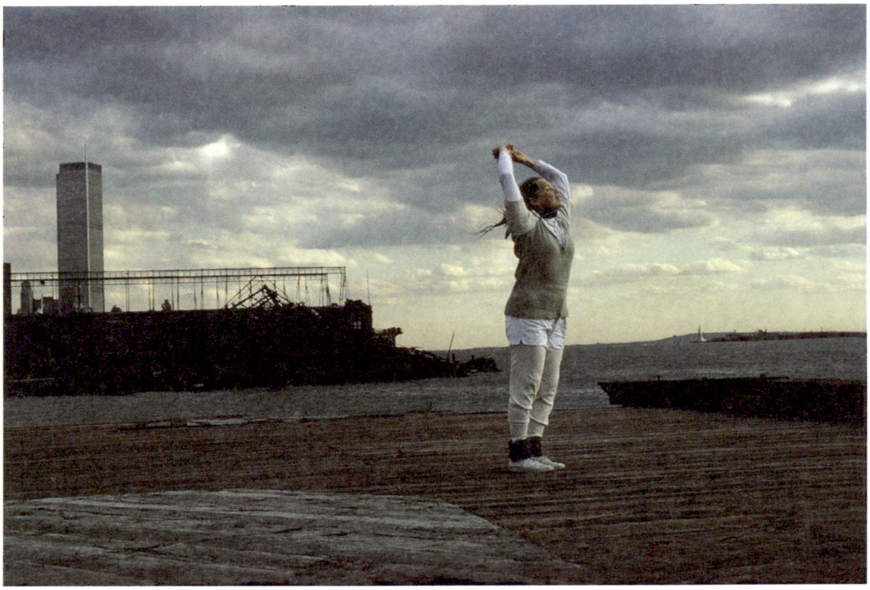

51. Shelley Seccombe, *Exercise on the Pier (49)*, 1978. © Shelley Seccombe.

of the waterfront experience. In many of her pictures, straight couples enjoy the docks alongside same-sex couples. Significantly, one of her most liberating images is not of a nude man but of a woman exercising at the end of Pier 49 (fig. 51). Raising her arms above her head in a stretch that seems to take in all the energy of the darkening clouds and the flowing river beyond, this female athlete seems every bit as free and autonomous as one of Baltrop's nude men.

Seccombe did not flinch from photographing nude sunbathers at the end of Pier 46 or in front of one of Gordon Matta-Clark's cuts. But in contrast to the work of so many of her male counterparts, she rarely frames her subjects through the structures, as if voyeuristically watching them from the shadows. Her emphasis is not on longing or surreptitious desire but on the freedom of so much public nudity and its place in a new spirit of liberation. A witness to many of the fires that turned the waterfront buildings into ruins and the resulting sense of anarchy, Seccombe's sensibility is far less apocalyptic than that of her male colleagues. Could all this crazy activity on the waterfront, the pantheistic nudity and romantic coupling inspired by the river, herald a utopian community of freedom and tolerance? Fittingly, she calls her book of pier pictures *Lost Waterfront: The Decline and Rebirth of Manhattan's Western*

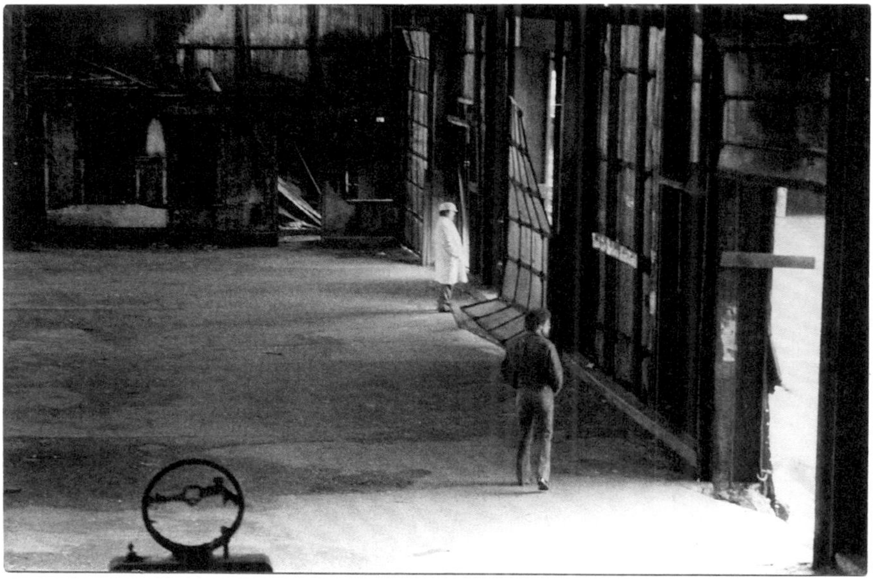

52. Alvin Baltrop, *The Piers*, n.d. (1975–86). Photograph used courtesy of The Alvin Baltrop Trust, © 2010, The Alvin Baltrop Trust and Galerie Buchholz. All rights reserved.

Shore, as if her subject were a beautiful beachscape. The captioning alongside a picture of a man and woman embracing at sunset reads, "especially in summer . . . the pier seems a benign place. Couples gaze at the afterglow from a beautiful sunset, stroll in the moonlight, sit on the edge of the river as boats glide silently by."[6] This bucolic description ignores the message of another Seccombe picture (fig. 7), in which sex workers stand in front of a spray-painted warning: "Teenagers and adults responsible for terrorizing people—breaking Pier and probably they set the fire—daytime muggers now working in teams."

Of course, it was precisely the fires that turned the pier sheds into the subject of Seccombe's pastoral reveries. Like Seccombe, Baltrop, Fink, and Hallam were not immune to the charms of a beautiful sunset over a collapsing structure, but what made the pier special for these gay photographers was the spectacle of men seeking and finding sex with other men. Indeed, admiring the view might be only a ploy in the hunt for a blow job. From the vantage point of a catwalk or stairway, Baltrop photographed two men looking out at the river: we can guess that what they wanted was sex. One of the figures is dressed in a white butcher's coat; he was probably taking a quick break from his job at the nearby meat market for some sort of hookup (fig. 52). In another

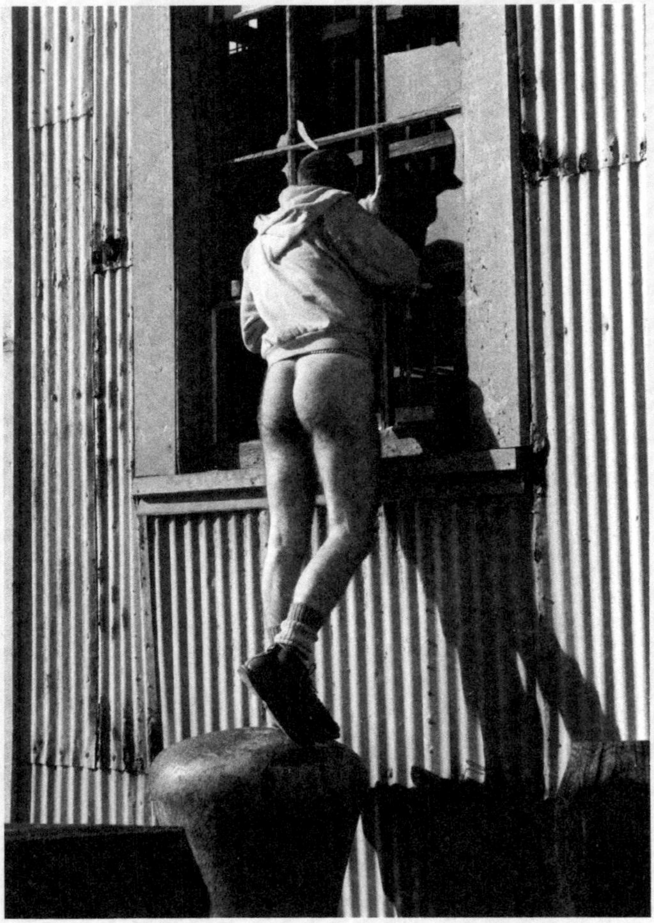

53. Alvin Baltrop, *The Piers*, n.d. (1975–86). Photograph used courtesy of The Alvin Baltrop Trust, © 2010, The Alvin Baltrop Trust and Galerie Buchholz.

iconic Baltrop photograph, we see a man, naked from the waist down and standing on a bollard, peering through a window into the pier building (fig. 53). The window, rather than an opening through which to view the river, is a means of voyeurism. The tumbledown structures, their walls pocked with cracks and holes, provide endless opportunities for such spying. Hallam often took his pictures from the vantage point of a darkened space, as if he and his camera were hidden from his subjects. Fink also took many similarly furtive images of men cruising the pier shed's long corridors and interconnecting rooms in search of sex and companionship. In such pictures of male cruising, the camera plays a double role. It allows the viewer to feel like a voyeur spying on an illegal, clandestine activity unfolding in a public space. At the same time, it makes the viewer a fellow cruiser. Interestingly, Hallam claimed that he never had sex on the piers because he was too busy taking photographs; also, he did not want to risk having his camera stolen while he was having sex. Nevertheless, Hallam was himself cruising the cruisers, hoping to capture them unaware as they sought and found sex.

Frank Hallam

Born in Indianapolis, Hallam came to New York City in 1958 and began taking slides of the piers in the early 1970s. Besides being an accomplished photographer, he published, under the pseudonym Frank Holland, several short stories and an autobiographical novel called *Debut: Chicago, 1952.* Hallam's use of a pseudonym speaks to the paradoxical nature of both his photography and his writing. He devoted his work to representing queer life in the most direct and explicit terms, yet his identity was forged by the closet. In his private journals, rich with the minutiae of such everyday events as unclogging a bath drain or paying his mother's property taxes, Hallam rarely said anything about the pier sex that his camera was so explicitly documenting. On a typical weekend day spent photographing on the piers, he writes simply that he sunbathed and took some pictures. Although his trips to the waterfront often followed Sunday mass, Hallam says nothing about the tensions and incongruities of being a practicing Catholic one moment and a gay man cruising the piers the next.[7] And although his novel is autobiographical, its most vivid passages are devoted to his observations of those around him. In the foreword to *Debut: Chicago*, which explores the underground gay bar culture of an American metropolis, he talks about how he "welcomed conversation with all sorts of people in those gay bars." Just as he later denied having sex on the piers, he claimed that he wasn't "interested in them sexually. . . . But conversation wouldn't hurt. And understanding them might help me understand my own self." He chose the word "debut" carefully. Hallam's "coming out" was not a public declaration of his sexuality to a heterosexual world, or even of having sex with another man, but was more akin to the "debutante tradition of entering a new social group."[8]

Although I came to know many of the artists whose work I discuss in this book, my relationship to Frank Hallam stands out. I not only studied his work closely; I got to know him and collaborated with him on printing and

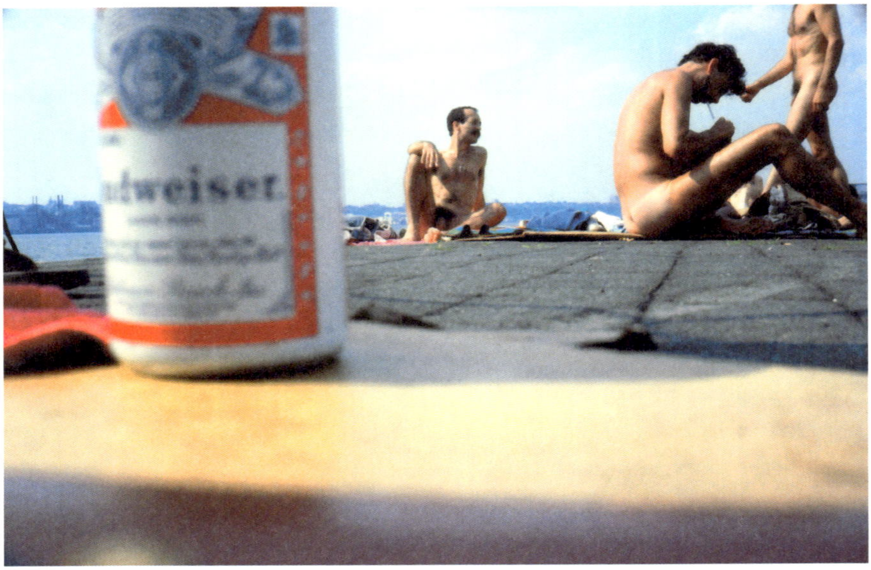

54. Frank Hallam, *Sunners and Bud Can, Pier 46*, 1979. Private collection.

preserving some of his pictures. In person, Hallam was quite reticent, shy about talking about himself or the hundreds of pictures he took of the piers and other aspects of gay life, such as the Gay Pride Parades and the queer scene at Riis Park. He was already in his eighties when I met him, and his health was fragile. Initially, he was reluctant to invite me to his tiny apartment on 14th Street, which was nothing more than a single room in what used to be a single-room-occupancy building but had been converted to a gay hotel. He seemed very much alone, but the more I got to know him, the more I realized that he had built his social life around the bar culture he had entered in the early 1950s. For many, the bar scene and other gay institutions—the piers, porn theaters, bathhouses—were merely places to find sex, but as Hallam explains in his novel, for some they were sanctuaries of friendship and community. During the short time I knew Hallam, he loved meeting me at Julius's, the oldest gay bar in New York City, where he would proudly introduce me to his buddies as the art historian who was interested in his photographs.

When thinking about Hallam's work, it is crucial to remember that he shot color slides that he rarely turned into prints (it was only at the end of his life that we worked together to make such prints). When Hallam showed his work, it was usually as a slide presentation at a gay community center rather than in a gallery setting. Like his novel, Hallam's pictures were assembled in a narrative that unfolds over time and tells a story about the past. Significantly, Hallam left his work not to a museum but to an archive of gay history. He saw his pictures not as art but as a process of remembering.

Hallam was open about the fact that he never asked his subjects for permission to photograph them. That he took images of naked men unobserved gives some of his pictures a furtive quality (fig. 54). I came to relate to Hallam's own shyness, which imbues his photographs with an artless directness and presence, as if what we are seeing is unmediated by any aesthetic project. In pier pictures by other photographers, we sometimes sense subjects performing for the camera, but even when Hallam's subject is the blatant exhibitionism of a nude gymnast, it comes across as a spontaneous action at a specific moment. It was Hallam's ability to observe the waterfront world so keenly that resulted in his most significant picture in terms of art history—his shot of the destruction of Matta-Clark's *Day's End*. Although Hallam did not know he was photographing a major work of art, he noticed that something extraordinary was happening. Poignantly, in framing the picture through the wire fencing, Hallam echoed the way that Matta-Clark filmed *Day's End*, as if through a porthole. The voyeurism of Hallam's photographs connects with this essential aspect of Matta-Clark's art and the truth that what we see through our eyes is itself a holing through of space.

Alvin Baltrop

Born in 1948, Baltrop was almost a generation younger than Hallam when he started photographing the piers, and apparently far more comfortable about his sexual identity. Black, openly bisexual, and a navy medic from 1969 to 1972, he began to photograph the waterfront after studying at the School of Visual Arts. Working as a part-time mover, Baltrop purchased a van that he often parked next to the river and lived in. From 1975 to 1985, he took hundreds of pictures of the waterfront buildings and the newly emerging queer subcultures that used these spaces for sex and nude sunbathing. Baltrop's attempts to exhibit his work were often frustrated by homophobia and racism, both in and outside the gay community. It was only after he died that his work gained renown, thanks to the advocacy of his protégé and executor, the artist Randall Wilcox, and art historian Douglas Crimp.[9]

Although most of Baltrop's photographs appear to have been taken during the day, many have a film-noir quality. He delighted in photographing men

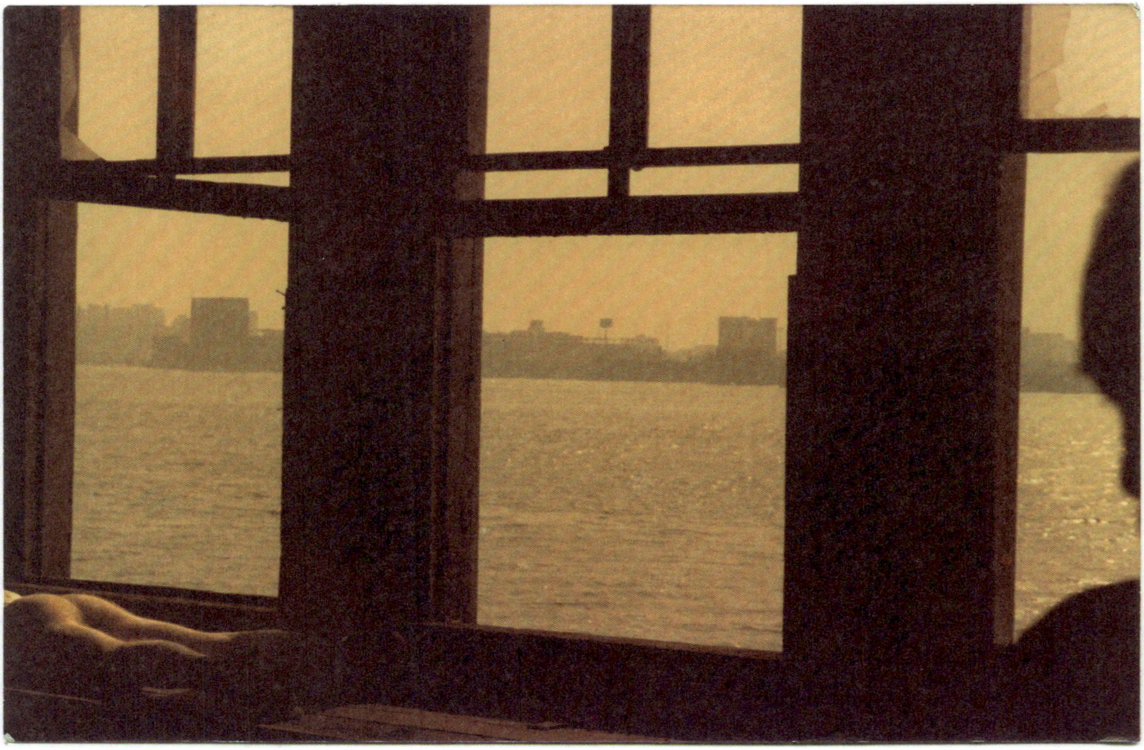

55. Alvin Baltrop, *The Piers*, n.d. (1975–86). Photograph used courtesy of The Alvin Baltrop Trust, © 2010, The Alvin Baltrop Trust and Galerie Buchholz. All rights reserved.

having sex out in the open, but for me some of his most powerful images are more surreptitious and disturbing. For example, in one picture we see just the buttocks of a man lying on the floor in front of a series of enormous open windows—his head and torso have been cut out of the frame (fig. 55). In the right corner of the picture we see the shadowy profile of a man entering the space, as if approaching the naked figure unawares. Without the context of the piers' gay culture, we might think that the naked man was dead, his nudity speaking less of freedom than of vulnerability. Both Baltrop and Fink photographed men engaging in various S/M scenarios. In one Fink picture (fig. 56), a bearded man smiles broadly as he whips his willing victim amid the rubble of the dock building. If the scene shocks, it is not because we believe that anyone is at risk of physical harm. By contrast, Baltrop's picture of a young straitjacketed man dangling upside down (fig. 57) is frightening because the

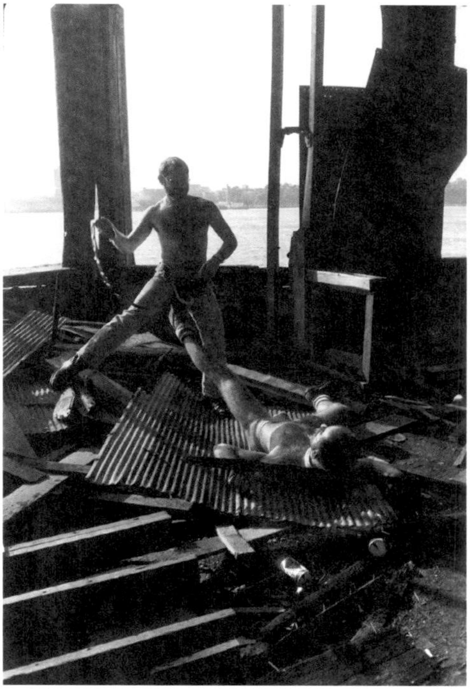

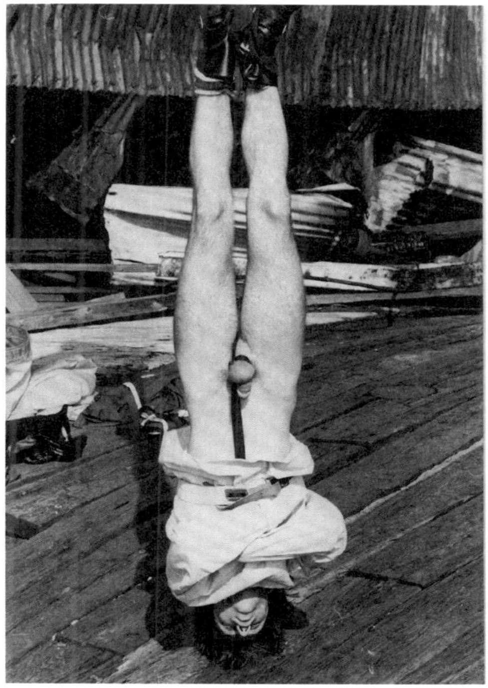

56. Leonard Fink, *Two Men*, ca. 1978. Collection of the LGBT Community Center National History Archive. Photo: LGBT Community Center National History Archive.

57. Alvin Baltrop, *The Piers*, n.d. (1975–86). Photograph used courtesy of The Alvin Baltrop Trust, © 2010, The Alvin Baltrop Trust and Galerie Buchholz. All rights reserved.

radically cropped image provides no context. The boy's eyes are closed and his face is expressionless; he could have been lynched.

No picture expresses the danger of the waterfront more explicitly than Baltrop's image of the police pulling a dead body out of the river (fig. 58). I tried to learn whether the victim was ever identified, but my search of newspaper databases revealed only that such events were all too common in the 1970s. Without knowledge of the specific circumstances, our fantasies roam wild. Was he a victim of organized crime? A suicide? Or could he have been a mugged and murdered gay cruiser? Baltrop's work self-consciously depicts the waterfront not as a utopia but as a place of "sporadic joys": "The casual sex and nonchalant narcotizing, the creation of artwork and music, sunbathing, dancing, merrymaking and the like habitually gave way to muggings, callous yet detached violence, rape, suicide, and in some instances, murder."[10] Baltrop's

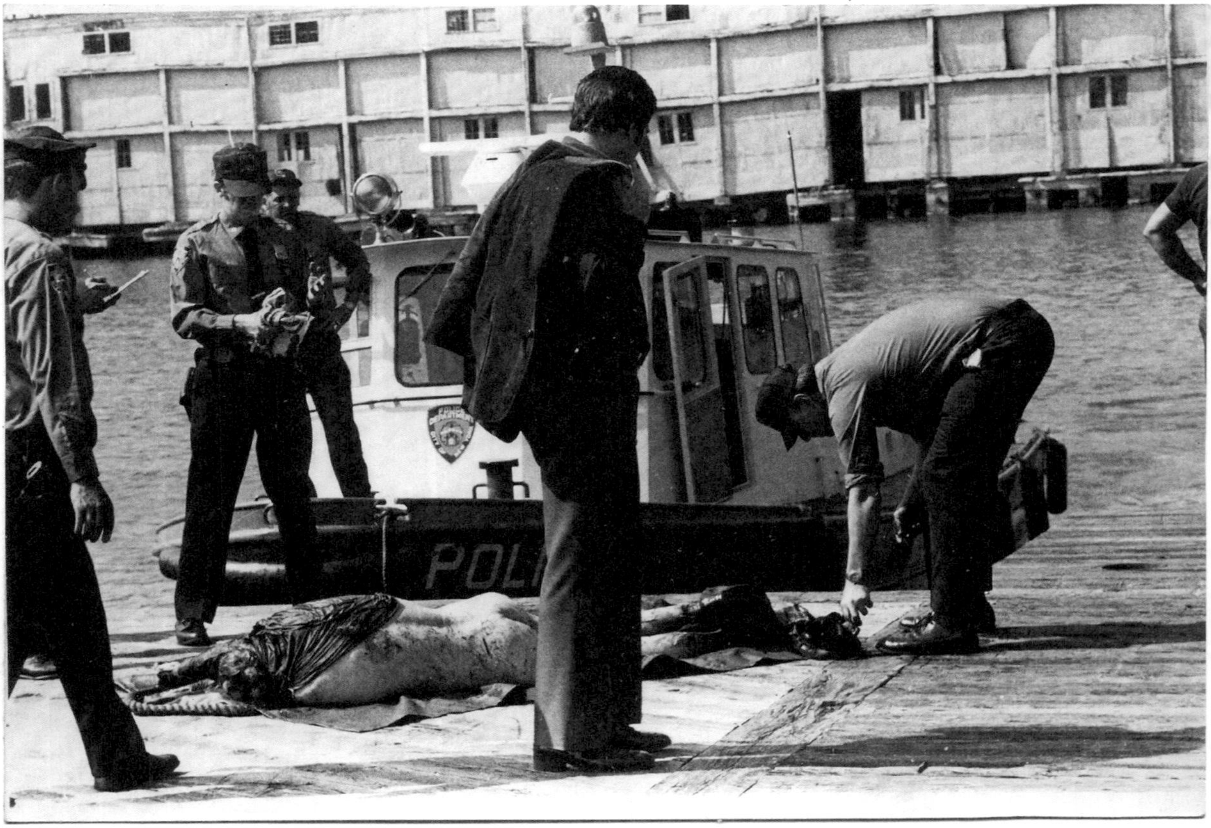

58. Alvin Baltrop, *The Piers*, n.d. (1975–86). Photograph used courtesy of The Alvin Baltrop Trust, © 2010, The Alvin Baltrop Trust and Galerie Buchholz. All rights reserved.

photographic record depicts the piers as a place where liberation and comradeship are undercut by violence and decay. To be naked, to kiss brazenly on the docks, as one couple does in a Baltrop photograph, creates an exhilarating sense of freedom precisely because of the risks involved. The body fished out of the water is only an extreme example of the horrors visited on gay people and queer youth of color in particular. Many of Baltrop's subjects were working-class, unemployed young men, some of them probably homeless. Fink, however, was a relatively affluent lawyer. He and many of his friends in the gay community experienced the piers as part of a nexus of entertainment that included bathhouses, sex clubs, and porn theaters. The waterfront provided fun and danger for a few hours, and then they could return to the safety of their homes and day jobs. But for Baltrop, who for a time lived in a van parked along the river, the waterfront was more like a second home. Looking at photographs of so many naked bodies sprawled out on the docks on a summer day, we might think we were witnessing the radical democratization of men. We can be sure that some of the waterfront pleasure seekers experienced it that way, but Baltrop was always keenly aware of the inequalities embedded in queer life and in the gay civil rights movement.

Leonard Fink

As different as their sensibilities were, both Baltrop and Hallam shared a sense that what they were seeing on the piers would not last and needed to be recorded. But recording the scene turned these photographers into men who watched rather than participated directly. It is significant that neither made a determined effort to photograph himself on the piers. Leonard Fink, by contrast, took many pictures of himself posing on the waterfront in various states of undress. A close contemporary of Hallam, Fink was also an amateur photographer who took most of his pictures of the waterfront, and of the gay scene in the West Village, on the weekends. But unlike Hallam, Fink was not shy, at least not when he performed for the camera. Sometime in the summer of 1979, for example, he took a picture of himself stripped down to a black jock strap, athletic socks, and sneakers, standing in the doorway of the abandoned shipping building on Pier 46 (fig. 59). His hypermasculine stance—feet planted squarely on the floor, arms outstretched to touch the door frame—might seem unwelcoming, barring entry to the row of identical interior rooms extending behind him like so many folders in a filing cabinet. But in a companion photograph, probably from the same shoot, he turns

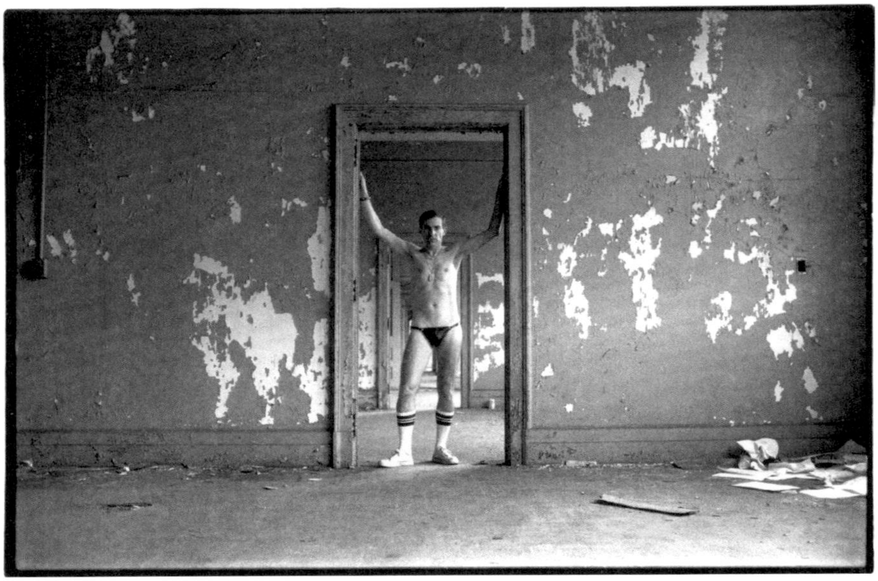

59. Leonard Fink, *Self-Portrait, Standing in Doorway (Front), Pier 46*, ca. 1978. Collection of the LGBT Community Center National History Archive.

around in the doorway and almost aggressively offers the viewer his naked buttocks (fig. 60).[11]

In a series of related pictures taken on Pier 46 and its neighboring collapsing structures, Fink, possibly with the help of an unseen friend, poses for the camera in various stages of undress and engaged in sex with other men, as if he has thrown off the inhibitions and shame rooted in prohibitions against homosexuality and public nudity (fig. 61). Yet the explicitness of Fink's photographs needs to be considered in the context of his extreme circumspection about allowing them to be seen.[12] Fink appears to have lived a double life. On weekdays he worked as a lawyer for the New York City Transit Authority. His family supposedly had no idea that he was gay until he was dying of HIV/AIDS in 1993. As far as we know, he never exhibited any of his work publicly or published any of his photos. He did turn some of his favorite pictures into homemade holiday greeting cards, but only a few individuals received these sexually explicit greetings.

That Fink photographed himself in outrageously exposed positions—in several pictures he went so far as to show himself getting fucked—while keeping his erotic work hidden from all but a handful of friends reminds us how

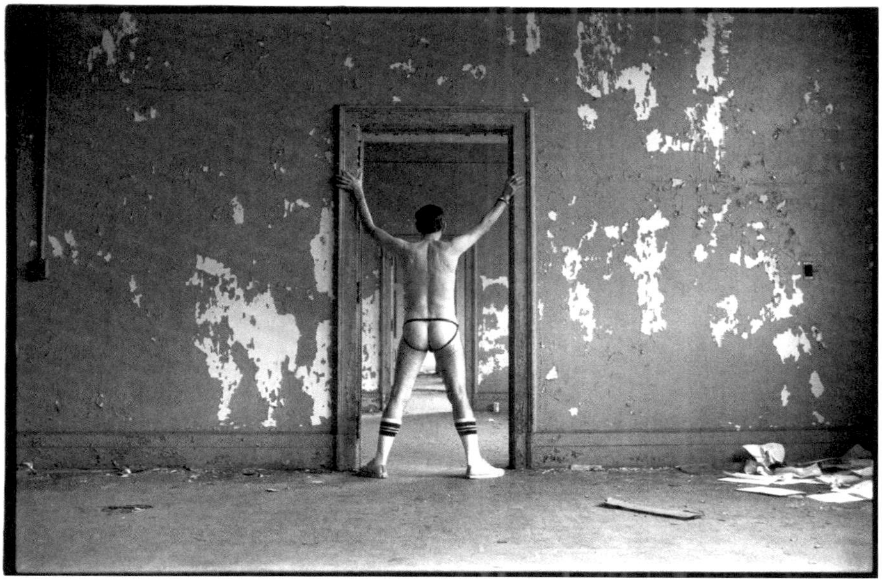

60. Leonard Fink, *Self-Portrait, Standing in Doorway (Back), Pier 46*, ca. 1978. Collection of the LGBT Community Center National History Archive.

powerfully the trope of the closet operated in the 1970s and '80s, and of its role as the central metaphor of the gay rights movement. The imperative to come out of the closet is a frequent theme of banners and posters in many of Fink's photographs of Pride marches, starting with the very first such march, in 1970. Fink also took hundreds of pictures of men congregating outside gay bars on Christopher Street, which would have been unthinkable in the pre-Stonewall period.

In this context, it may seem the height of hypocrisy that Fink, the unofficial "mayor of Christopher Street," according to one of his close friends, was in the closet to his family and work associates.[13] But I believe that we need to resist the tendency to read gay photography, whether self-portraits or pictures of others, as autobiographical expressions of the artist's identity and erotic desires. I would emphasize instead that Fink's pictures invent personae and project fantasies about the world, imaginary constructions distinct from what little we know of Fink's biography. The carnivalesque atmosphere of freedom from bourgeois morality and pride in being queer that pervades Fink's pictures is not the product of Fink's merely recording what he saw; his work creates a kind of fantasy space of liberation and community. In pictures that often

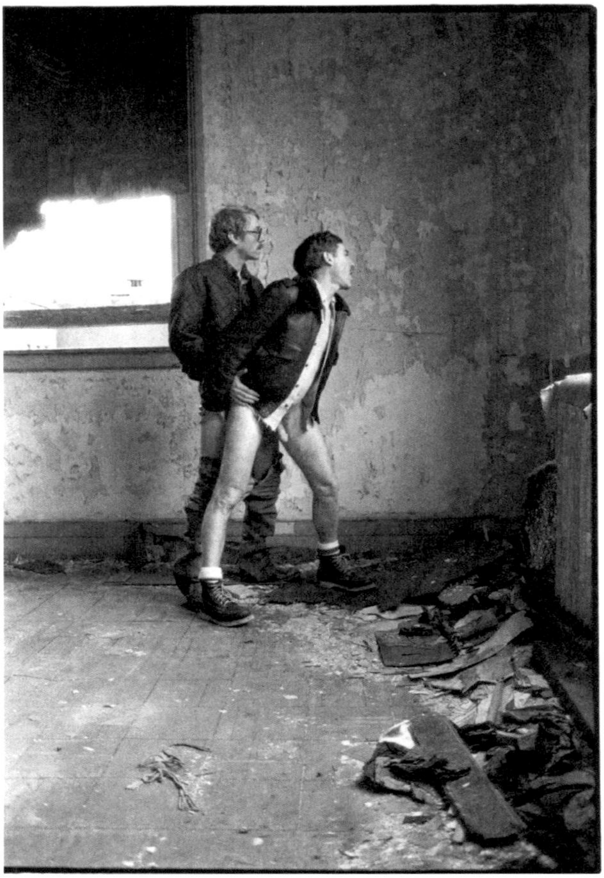

61. Leonard Fink, *Getting Fucked, Pier 46*, ca. 1979. Collection of the LGBT Community Center National History Archive.

appear more open than the realities they represent, Fink's work extends the quasi-private bar culture that he knew and loved to the streets and the waterfront. Fink's pictures of the marches, the bars, and the waterfront are linked by the theme that LGBTQ people in the 1970s and '80s were beginning to take over public spaces and to use those spaces to act in ways that had always before been kept private. The message of sexual and bodily liberation, celebrated in a gay march once a year, was reinforced every hot summer afternoon that men lay naked for tourists to see from the boats that circled Manhattan. But it was nowhere more intense than in the picture of Fink posing proudly shirtless, in tight minishorts, straddling his motorcycle on the ramp to the West Side Elevated Highway as a handsome young man watches admiringly in the background (fig. 62). The exhilaration of parking his motorcycle in the middle

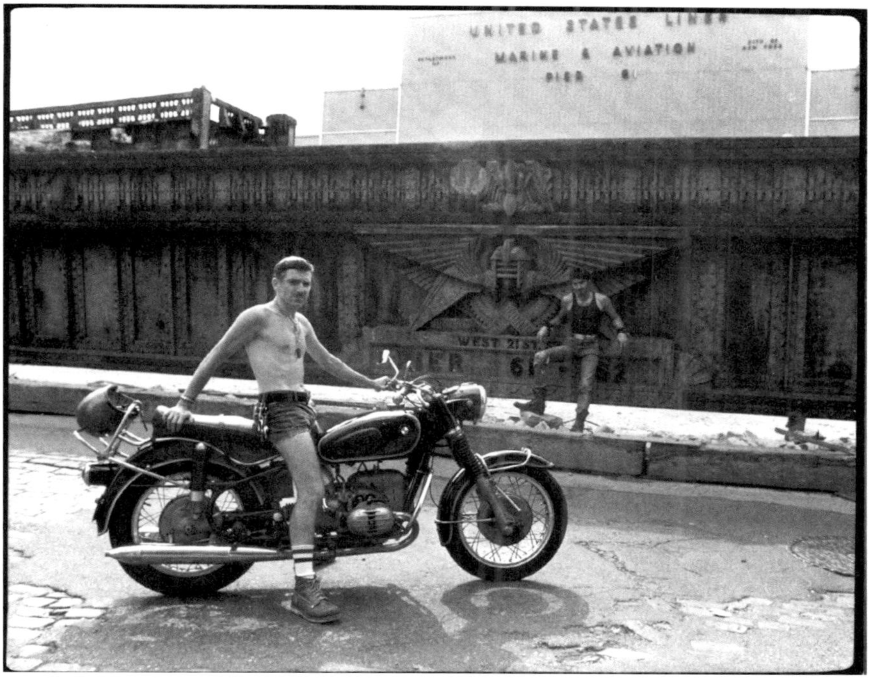

62. Leonard Fink, *Self-Portrait on West Side Highway Ramp*, ca. 1978. Collection of the LGBT Community Center National History Archive.

of a multilane freeway ramp without fear of being run over by speeding cars (themselves symbols of American culture and aspiration) is a potent metaphor for Fink's larger themes of sexual liberation and the rejection of middle-class decorum. The breakdown of the city's infrastructure presented an opportunity to test new social structures and new ways of being *out* in the world. Fink's reported hatred of his job gives his pictures of the city's crumbling transportation system another layer of meaning. Fink's piers, which no longer serve shipping, and his highway, which no longer carries cars, are unproductive, at least in terms of the economic system that underlay his profession of defending the city from lawsuits. What irony that a man who spent his working hours handling accident claims against the city would spend his leisure time risking life and limb to explore dangerous municipal ruins.

Perhaps the picture that best sums up Fink's apparent frustration with his day job is the photograph of a giant phallus that the graffiti artist Tava painted on the ramp of the West Side Highway in 1976 (fig. 63). Like Fink's photographs,

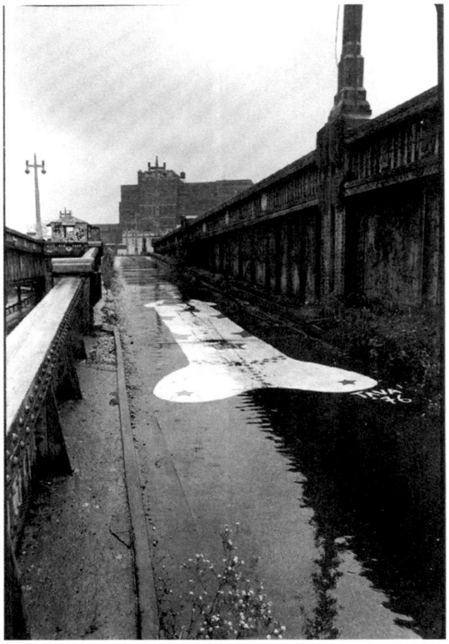

63. Leonard Fink, *Tava Phallus*, ca. 1977. Collection of the LGBT Community Center National History Archive.

Tava's obscenity is not merely a "fuck you" to the city and to traditional values but also an attempt to appropriate public space for queer uses. It shares a certain exuberance with Fink's iconic image *The Kiss* (fig. 64), in which Fink himself locks lips with a friend on the piers, outside in the bright sunlight for all to see, defying indecency laws and celebrating love.

Unfortunately, the limits of Fink's utopian vision are also crystalized in Tava's rude image. If such a picture defies those who would constrain or censure sexual desire, it also excludes women. Indeed, with the notable exception of Fink's pictures of gay marches, women and transgender people play little part in Fink's utopia, and even when he does photograph women in Gay Pride celebrations, he seems more invested in the idea that they might be the mothers of gay men than in the possibility that they might sustain lesbian relationships and a community apart from men. He also photographed the transgender activists Marsha P. Johnson and Sylvia Riviera, but not on the piers, and in ways that emphasized their role in the spectacle of the Gay Pride marches, rather than connecting with them in their private life as part of his own community of friends. Certainly, Fink's willingness to be hypermasculine while allowing himself to be fucked on the piers presents a challenge to patriarchy, but his overall vision of gay community is separatist. Still, in repeatedly offering his anus for penetration, Fink undermines the phallic regime that Tava's over-the-top penis either celebrates or parodies. This is particularly true of Fink's extraordinary image of himself standing on the catwalk of Pier 46, arms akimbo, back to us, ass exposed (fig. 65). The telescoped quality of the picture emphasizes Fink's gaze into the distance, perhaps recalling the act of peering through a viewfinder and taking a picture. The structure on which he stands, its sequence of triangles within triangles

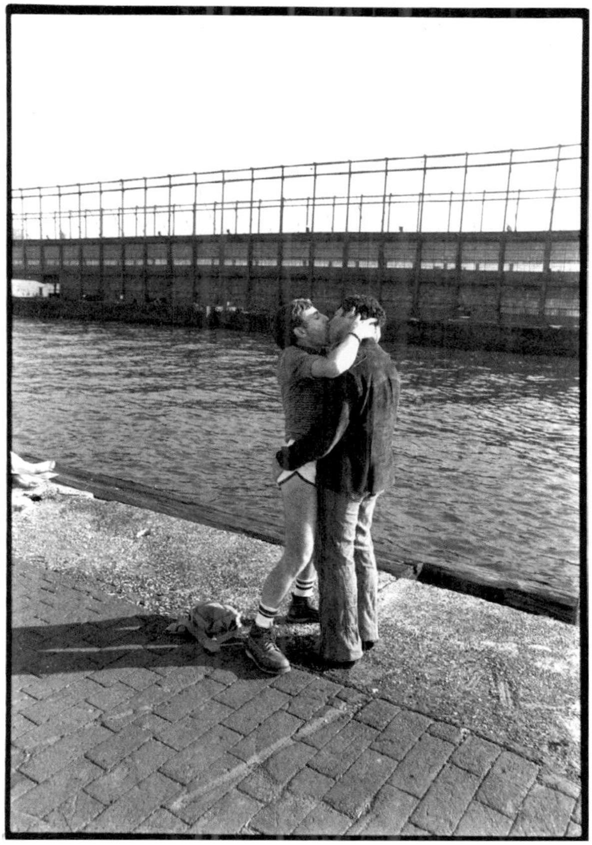

64. Leonard Fink, *The Kiss*, 1979. Collection of the LGBT Community Center National History Archive.

penetrating space and forming a narrow, tubelike bridge that leads the eye forward, is also an apt metaphor for the anal canal as a site not of abjection but of pleasure, discovery, and even power. As Fink opens himself up for penetration and exposure, he also takes command over all that he surveys, refusing what Hocquenghem claims is the Oedipal imperative to privatize and sublimate anal desire. Hocquenghem, as if with Fink in mind, suggests how such an exaltation of anal eroticism might undermine the phallic regime: "to reinvest the anus collectively and libidinally would involve a proportional weakening of the great phallic signifier, which dominates us constantly both in the small-scale hierarchies of the family and in the great social hierarchies. The least acceptable desiring operation (precisely because it is the most desublimating one) is that which is directed at the anus."[14]

Fink's waterfront pictures enact many complex roles, but at their core is an essential message: Fink wasn't just a voyeur. He might enjoy watching, but he

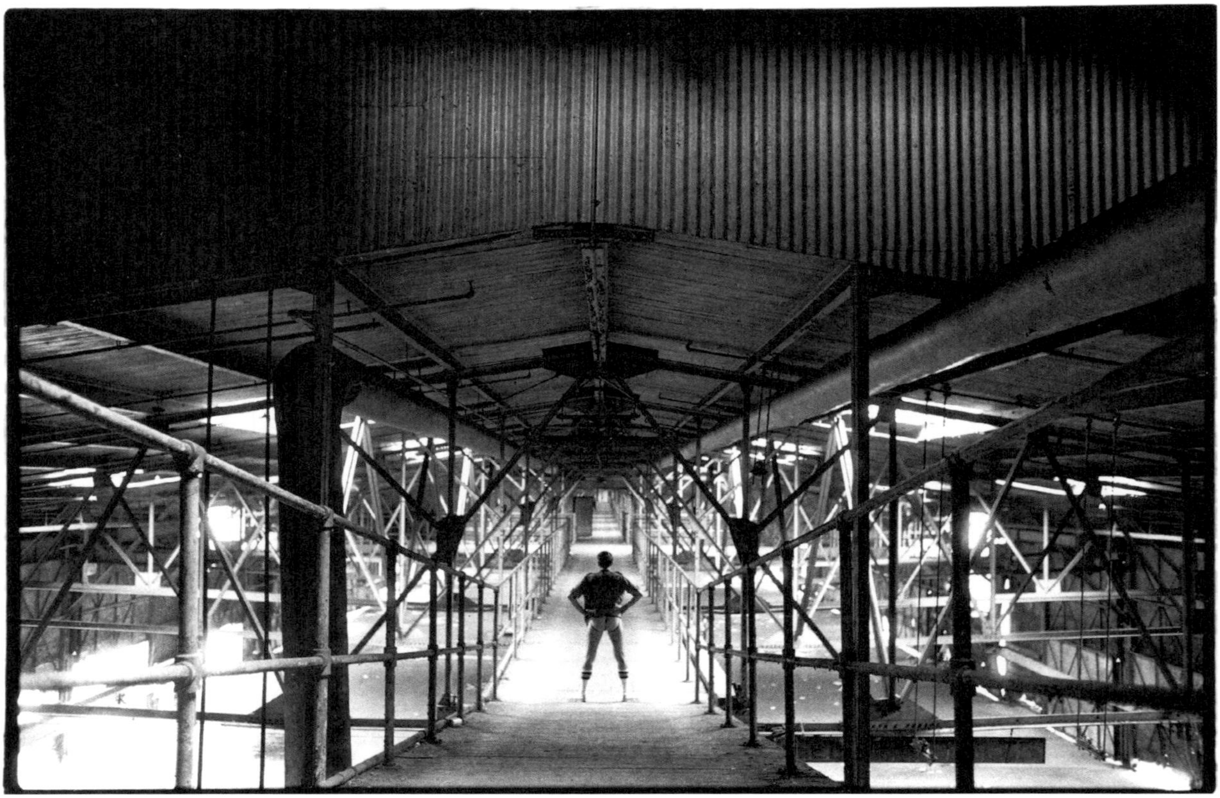

65. Leonard Fink, *Self-Portrait, Catwalk, Pier 46*, 1979. Collection of the LGBT Community Center National History Archive.

was also there to have sex and to make trouble. Significantly, Fink doesn't just show men fucking; he creates a picture of himself kissing another man out in the open, in full view of the river and street traffic. This act of self-picturing needs to be considered in the context of the tradition of documentary photography representing LGBTQ people. If such empathetic photographers as Brassaï, Robert Frank, and Diane Arbus identified with queer people as nonconformists, they were nonetheless always depicted in their work as outsiders or "freaks," to use a favorite term of Arbus's. Fink may have been unaware of his predecessors, but that he repeatedly inserted himself into the scene sets him apart from the othering of the subject that is such a staple of the documentary tradition. Even if Baltrop and Hallam didn't share Fink's urge for self-exposure, they shared with him a sense of being part of the community they were recording. We need to remember also that the initial audience for most of the pictures taken on the piers was not the art world but the type of gay men who visited the piers.

In their search for subjects along the waterfront, the pier photographers often found one another. In the previous chapter, I discussed at length Fink's photograph of David Wojnarowicz. Another chance encounter took place in 1981, when Stanley Stellar ran into his friend and colleague Peter Hujar during a photo shoot on Pier 46. Stellar was photographing J. D. Slater, one of the most famous porn stars of the day. Undoubtedly inspired by Slater's exhibitionism, Hujar asked Stellar to photograph him having sex in the background of a picture of Slater leaning against a doorway alongside a wall of Keith Haring graffiti (fig. 66). The picture's startling juxtaposition of an act of fellatio, a beautiful male body, and a signature Haring work is only intensified when we learn that it also includes the image of Hujar, one of the great photographers of the twentieth century. Later that day, in an act of mutual trust and respect, Stellar lent Hujar his camera, and both photographers used it to take portraits of each other.

Stellar told me that he believed Hujar was reluctant to take pictures of sexual acts because he did not want his pictures to be confused with pornography.[15] It is true that, for all the eroticism of many of Hujar's photographs of men, many of them nude, he did not shoot for the gay weeklies and skin magazines that employed both Stellar and Tress. Indeed, some of Hujar's most beautiful pier pictures were not of people at all but of the art made on the walls of Pier 34, which I discuss in the next chapter. Still, the fact that Hujar urged Stellar to photograph him getting his dick sucked, or making an obscene gesture in front of a giant phallus painted on the wall of Pier 46, is proof that

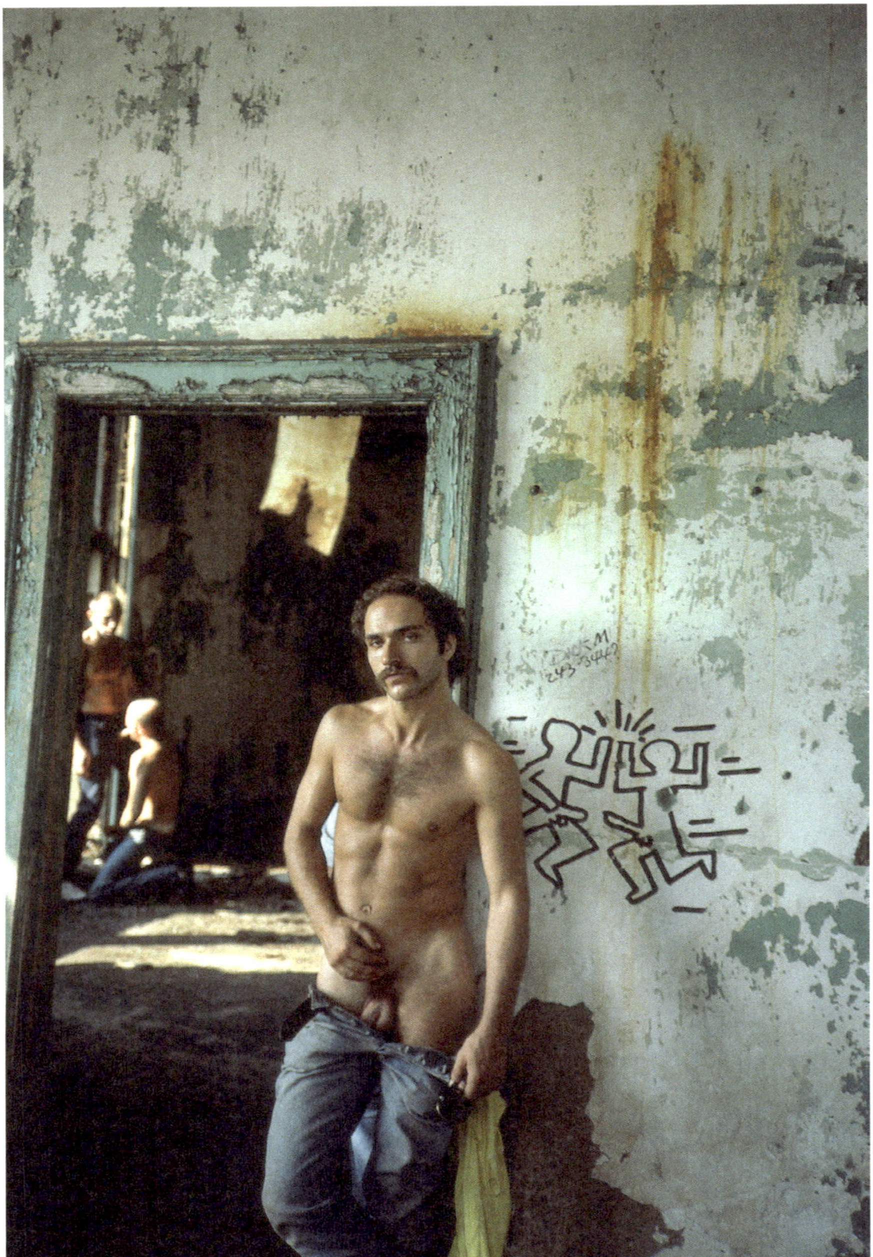

66. Stanley Stellar, *Peter Gets His Dick Sucked*, 1981. © stanleySTELLAR.

he was no prude. He respected Stellar's work and wanted to collaborate with him. No doubt, given the homophobia of much of the established art world, he worried that his work would be marginalized or seen as prurient. But his reluctance to photograph sex on the piers may also have had something to do with wanting to be part of the erotic life of the place, rather than make art about it. The fleeting nature of a sex act was anathema to Hujar's aesthetic, which strived for timelessness and classicism. Many of Hujar's most famous pictures are in the abstracted space of the studio, and although he used natural light, the time of day and the season are unclear. In contrast, the best pier photographs capture a specific moment and place. Even when Hujar photographed the long corridors of a burned-out pier building, we sense silence and abandonment, as if we are seeing some ancient ruin. The transience of the pier experience, which explained so much of its allure for photographers, was less fertile ground for Hujar, and, I might add, for his nemesis, Robert Mapplethorpe, whose best work was also done in the studio.

Another fortuitous moment in which two pier artists crossed paths occurred when Hallam was on Pier 46 in 1982 during the filming of *Pompeii New York*. This experimental movie by Ivan Galietti includes a cameo performance by Wojnarowicz and a musical performance by singer/accordionist Phoebe Legere; it was Galietti's response to the way the waterfront, with Tava's murals of naked men and other graffiti, reminded him of the remains of ancient Pompeii in his native Italy. It tells the story of a young man who stalks his male lover through the abandoned piers as he cruises for sex. Thinking Galietti was filming some sort of porno, Hallam took slides of him and his crew performing various sexual acts for the camera. (The two artists met and learned about each other's work only years later.)

Hallam may have thought that he was inconspicuous as he photographed such peculiar events. Years later, he discovered in the archive that Fink had been taking pictures of him. Hallam remembers seeing Fink on the piers, but neither knew the other.[16]

Arthur Tress and Stanley Stellar

This idea of the chance encounter between two men drawn together by similar desires is central to the quintessential pier photograph, Arthur Tress's *Dockside Interview* (1977; fig. 67). The location is probably Pier 48, near the foot of Christopher Street—but it could be any of the so-called sex piers that lined the West Village. Taken from the inside looking out, the photograph depicts only the lower half of two figures, one fully clothed, one completely naked, in some sort of encounter. A third of the composition is taken up by the black band of the half-opened gate, which slices the figures in half, rendering them faceless and anonymous. The picture is constructed around a series of stark contrasts—inside/outside, black/white, light/darkness, and public/private—that echo its central motif of naked and clothed. The title suggests that these two men on the edge of the pier are having some sort of conversation; however, "interview" implies not so much a dialogue as a one-sided series of questions and answers that might yield a life story. The idea that Tress would depict two men having this sort of intense dialogue on one of the sex piers is ironic, given what he told me during just such an interview that I conducted with him in search of information about photographs like this one. Tress insisted that sex on the piers "was all very impersonal. When you were having sex with them you never looked at them in the face." Nevertheless, Tress was "always curious about people." He would try to strike up conversations: "I would say, 'oh, what are you doing down here?' I would want to get to know these people and that was the last thing they wanted."[17] The hands in the pockets that accentuate the clothed figure's crotch suggest the content of their conversation, if indeed any words were actually being exchanged. And so the dockside interview in question might not be about personal revelations, but a kind of sizing up.

Tress's claim that cruising on the pier was "furtive" and "oppressive" goes against the notion that the waterfront scene was a kind of laboratory for sexual freedom, which we encounter in the writings of so many of the artists discussed in books like Delany's and Wojnarowicz's. The photograph *Dockside Interview* is compelling because of the way it seems to invite contradictory responses about the nature of the sex scene on the piers, and what it might mean for the larger culture. The very idea that a man could be completely naked, out in public, in full sunlight, suggests liberation, and yet in Tress's photograph his face is obliterated. Despite the picture's obvious exhibitionism, and the way these figures seem to be crossing the boundaries of acceptable behavior, they also could be seen as hiding, meeting surreptitiously. The concept of the closet, that central if deeply problematic metaphor for the plight of the unliberated homosexual, still hangs over this image. If these men are shockingly "out" in the brazenness of their sexual encounter, they are also still "in," because the piers were exactly the kind of remote and secretive site frequented by a man who hid his sexuality from his straight friends and colleagues. Even more suggestive of the closet is the position of the photographer himself, lurking in the shadows and spying on the figures though the space behind the gate.

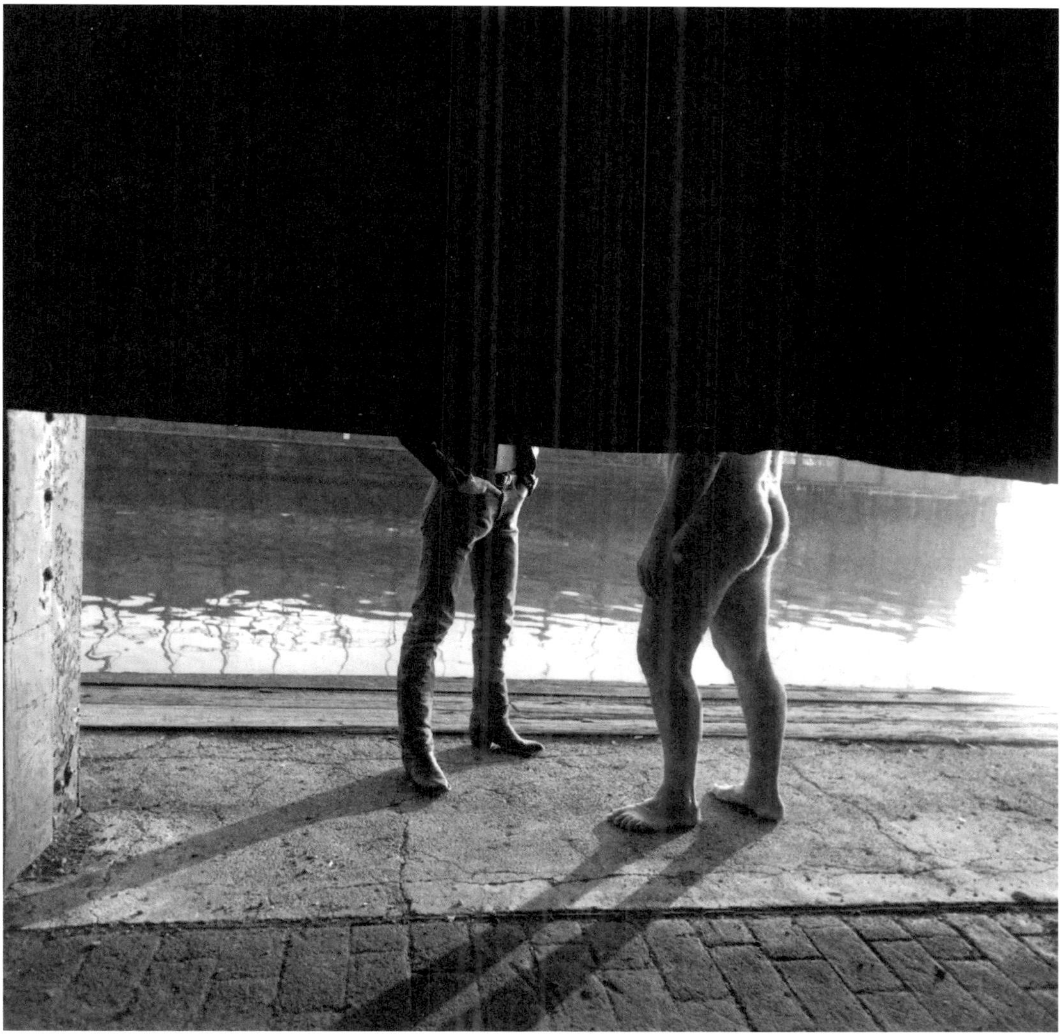

67. Arthur Tress, *Dockside Interview, New York*, 1977. © Arthur Tress.

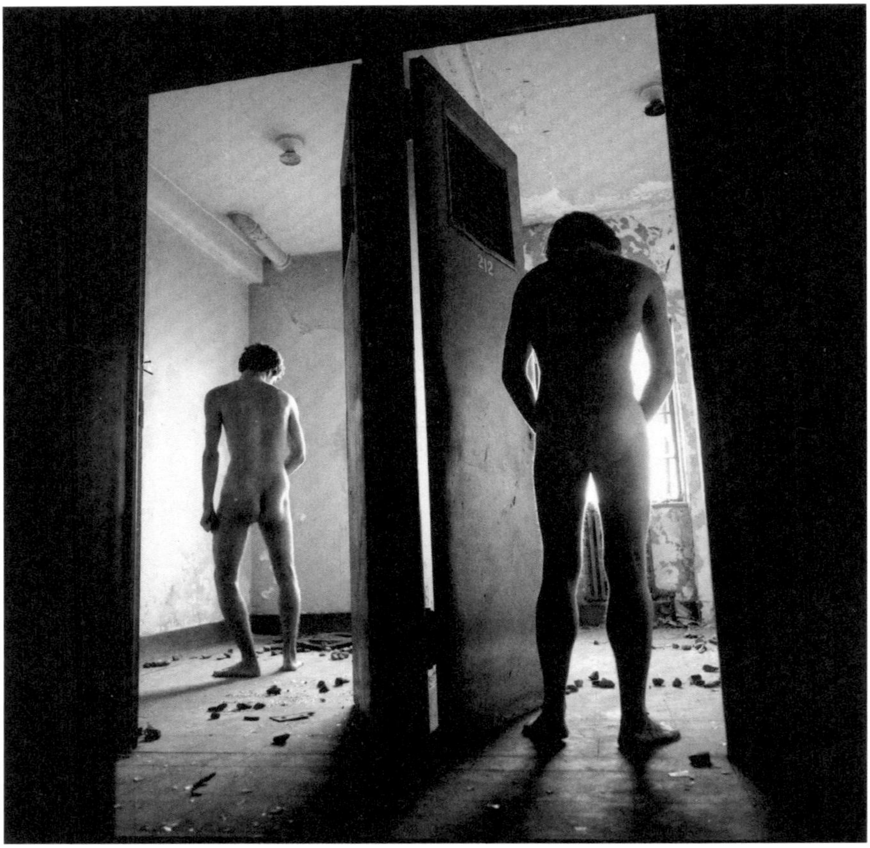

68. Arthur Tress, *Two Men, Two Rooms, N.Y.*, 1977. © Arthur Tress.

The photographer's point of view becomes our point of view, and we become implicated in the voyeurism and lurking.

Another photograph by Tress, *Two Men, Two Rooms* of 1977 (fig. 68), emphasizes what he calls the furtive nature of the sex, while evoking the theme of the closet. It shows two completely naked men with their backs to us standing in the doorways of adjoining rooms. Their posture and hand position suggests that they are both masturbating, but they don't seem to be looking at anyone. As in *Dockside Interview*, their faces are hidden, but here desire isn't even an exchange between the two men, nor is the photographer able to fully see them pleasuring themselves.

The ambivalence about what to think of the kind of sex men were having on the piers, which I sense in Tress's photographic tableaux, is dealt with

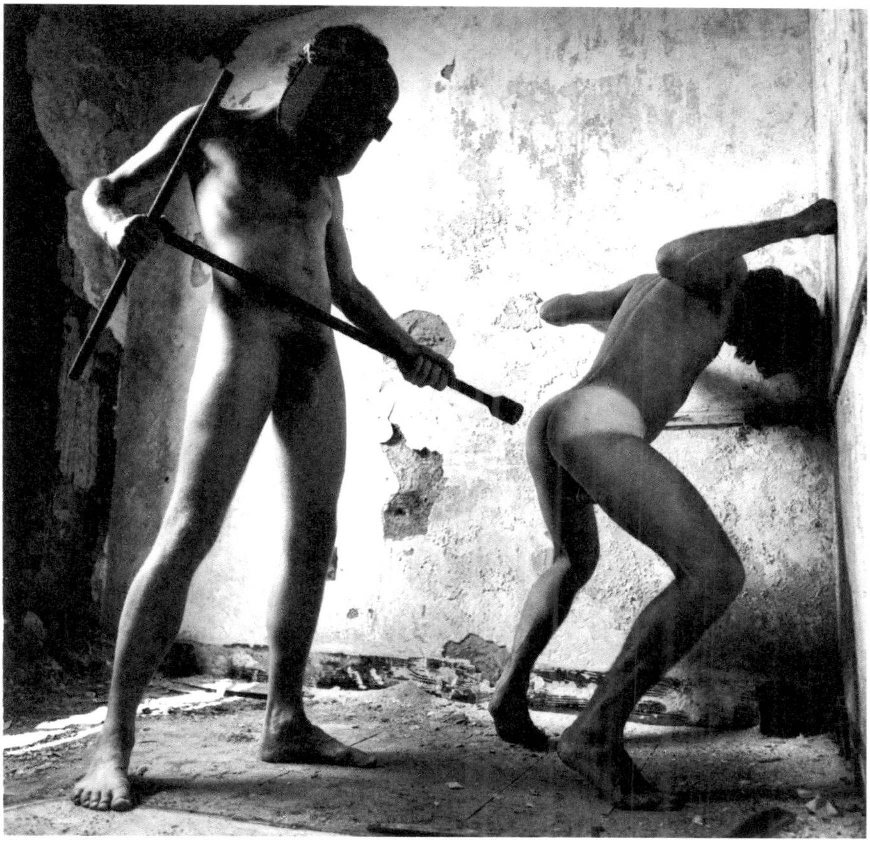

69. Arthur Tress, *Untitled*, 1978. © Arthur Tress.

directly by Hocquenghem in his contemporaneous book, *Homosexual Desire*. Hocquenghem acknowledges that gay men themselves are often ashamed of the "scattering," that is, "the fact that homosexuals have a multitude of love affairs, each of which may last only a moment." Still, he wants us to turn such shame on its head and embrace cruising: "Instead of translating this scattering of love-energy as the inability to find a center, we could see it as a system in action, the system in which polyvocal desire is plugged in on a non-exclusive basis. . . . The homosexual condition is experienced as unhappy because its mechanical scattering is translated as absence and substitution. We could say that on the contrary homosexual love is immensely superior, precisely because everything is possible at any moment: organs look for each other and plug in, unaware of the law of exclusive disjunction."[18] It is amusing to juxtapose this

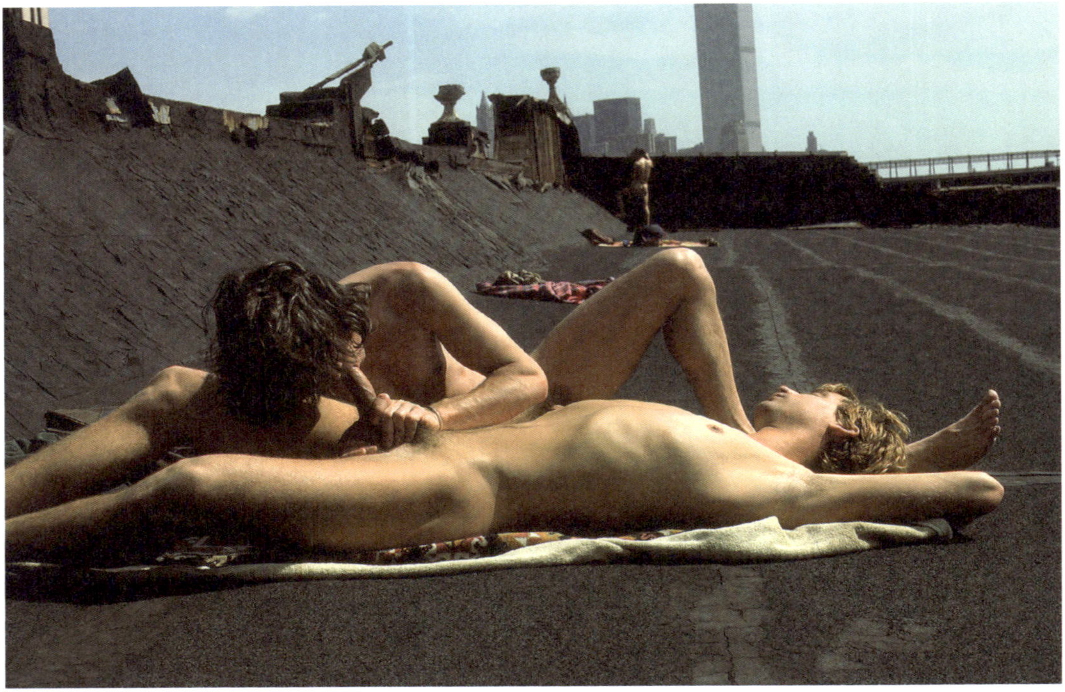

70. Stanley Stellar, *May 1st*, 1977.

passage with Tress's photograph of a naked man wearing a welder's shield, about to "plug in" an enormous riveting tool into the ass of a young man who bends down obligingly to receive his "rod" (fig. 69). This photograph is one of a series in which Tress substitutes various cognates, such as a cardboard gun, for an erect penis. On another level, in parodying the phallocentric nature of so much gay pornography, Tress shifts attention to the anus and the pleasures of sodomy, which Hocquenghem insists is the real threat that homosexual desire poses to the patriarchy.

Stellar, Tress's contemporary, remembered the sex scene on the piers with far less ambivalence than Tress: "I just loved it. It didn't have to be me out in three in the morning, feeling scared, on a scummy street in the West Village. I could be in the light, under the sunlight. Feeling the warmth on my head, on my face, letting him feel that, and all the world. . . . It was exhilaration and freedom finally. And if you don't like it, or some guy goes by in a truck and yells something, well, fuck you back. Fuck you!"[19] This sensation of liberation infuses Stellar's photographs, like *May 1st* (1977; fig. 70), in which two men have sex completely naked on the roof of one the pier buildings. The way the young man lolls back, illuminated by the warm sun, as his companion sucks his dick speaks not only of pleasure but also of a newfound sense of belonging in the world. The anonymity of the characters in Tress's *Dockside Interview*, and its voyeuristic point of view, its harsh, cold contrasts of shadows and light, is replaced with a vision of sex between men that is warm and open. Unlike *Dockside Interview* there is no barrier between Stellar and his subjects; they are happy to be pictured, and being *seen* only heightens their pleasure.

In many ways, Tress and Stellar are polar opposites. Born in 1940, a generation older than Stellar, Tress as an artist comes out of a surrealist tradition in which photographic realism is used to suggest dreamlike states. The nakedness and erotic actions of Tress's pier photographs often make us feel privy to some sort of hallucination in which men, suddenly naked in public, act out their most repressed desires. Stellar's pictures might equally be the product of posing his subjects, but he strives to capture the erotic freedom of a particular moment. Tress's work holds on to the idea that desire is fantasy, something we might dream about, while Stellar's images show that something has happened, something that, by implication, could also happen to us. Although Tress and Stellar approached the piers differently, they both relied on gay magazines for their livelihood, and this context has some bearing on their nudes. For example, many of Tress's pictures were destined for *Mandate*, a magazine that focused on gay social life and included what Tress called "tasteful nudes." Periodicals like *Mandate* were delivered via the U.S. mail; thus, given federal obscenity laws, erect penises could not be shown. Stellar, by contrast, published pictures in what he jokingly called "the sleazy porn magazines" and thus was freer to explore explicit sex. But the format of their work says nothing about either Tress's or Stellar's ambitions—both considered their homoerotic photography art.

Despite the gay liberation movement, the market for male nude photography was severely limited in the late 1970s and early '80s. The exception was the work of Robert Mapplethorpe. As Stellar observed, "it was the great age of Mapplethorpe, Mapplethorpe, Mapplethorpe, everything was Mapplethorpe." How and why Mapplethorpe achieved such mainstream success is a complex story, but at the risk of oversimplification, I believe the answer lies in the way his work both shocks and flatters. Its conservative and elegant form always tempers its thematically radical nature. In 1976, Mapplethorpe did venture out onto one of the West Village piers to take some pictures. The result, *Dennis on the Pier*, in which a naked man is seen from a distance lying somewhat awkwardly in an odalisque-like pose amid some wooden planks, is contrived. It lacks Mapplethorpe's signature use of dramatic light and classical composition. No wonder Mapplethorpe never published the image.

For the most part, Mapplethorpe shot his photos, whether portraits or sex acts, as if they were still lifes. His flowers, faces, and genitals tend to be photographed up close, under studio lights, within a tightly contained space with shallow depth of field. By contrast, Tress, Stellar, and most of the other photographers discussed in this chapter relied on available light in their pier work. Whereas the subjects of Mapplethorpe's best pictures seem to exist only in the abstracted space of the picture plane, Tress's figures relate with the ruins around them; they are not passive objects of the photographer's gaze. Stellar, too, uses existing waterfront structures to create an active tension between his nude figures and their environment. If Mapplethorpe was always on the hunt for extreme sex acts and the kind of erotically desirable men who practiced them, Stellar was much more interested in location. He was "looking at the buildings and the doorways and the sidewalks and skyscrapers and the roofs and seeing beauty in that." Nakedness in the midst of the ruins created a frisson, a thrill: "putting a person in it, but not just a person like in all the other photos of the world, but a nude person." For all the shock of Mapplethorpe's most explicit images, he was still usually recording an act that was occurring within the privacy and safety of his studio, or in some other controlled location. The pier photographers' sexual subjects were out in the world, exposed to the camera and anyone else who happened to be out that day in that essentially public space.

Yet the visibility created by the available sunlight has its limitations. Whether in Acconci's *Untitled Project for Pier 17*, Whitman's *Architecture*, or Wojnarowicz's diaries, the piers were often at their most evocative when the sun went down. Shooting with available light made night pictures difficult. Also, few photographers were willing to risk nocturnal forays into the waterfront sheds. It was perilous enough to walk among the broken planks in the daytime. How much more dangerous was it to be there at two in the morning, in complete darkness, when there was the constant danger of inadvertently falling into the water or being grabbed from behind by muggers? Setting off the flash would only send the pier denizens scurrying like frightened bats. But there are some notable exceptions to the rule that pier photography was a sunlit affair. Baltrop took some pictures at night, and in the mid-1980s so did Efrain Gonzalez, whose best work falls outside the scope of this book. But

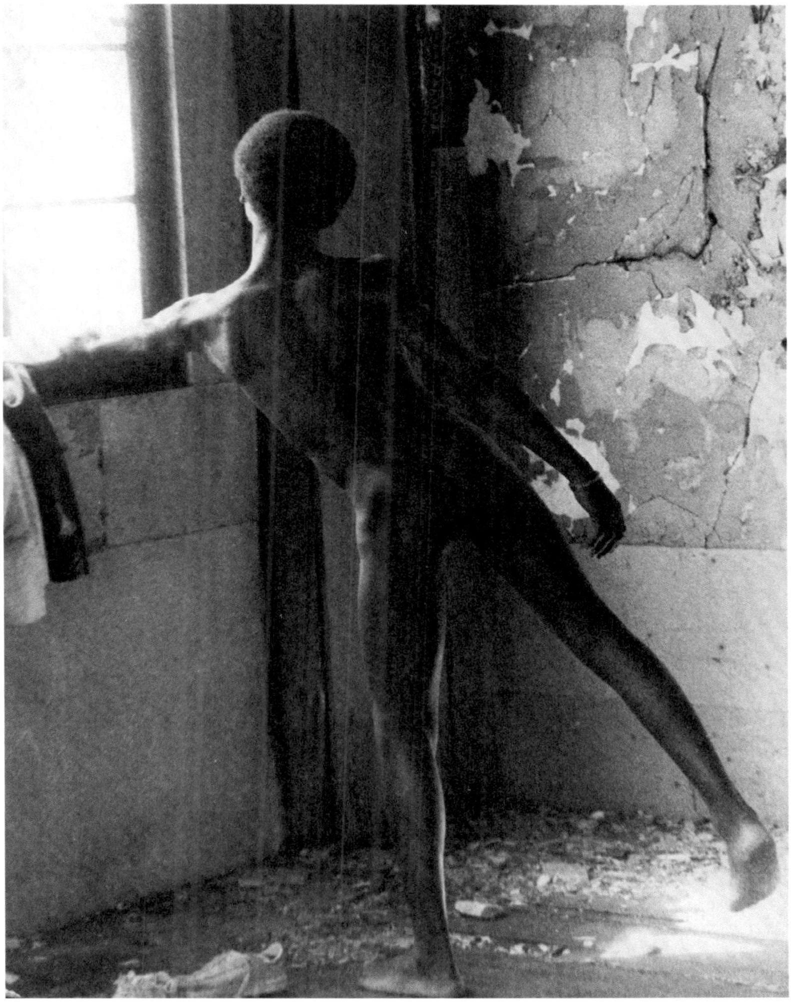

71. Alvin Baltrop, *The Piers*, n.d. (1975–86). Photograph used courtesy of The Alvin Baltrop Trust, © 2010, The Alvin Baltrop Trust and Galerie Buchholz. All rights reserved.

these nocturnal pictures tended to be taken out on the sidewalks, under the bright street lights, and not in the pier sheds where men were having sex.

In 2016, I was asked by the Whitney Museum of American Art to record a brief description for an audio guide of an Alvin Baltrop photograph in the Whitney's permanent collection. In this photograph (fig. 71), probably taken on Pier 46 sometime in the late 1970s, Baltrop focuses on a beautiful naked man stretching. When I first looked at the picture, I was disappointed that it was not more sexually explicit. The fact, too, that the young man is alone and

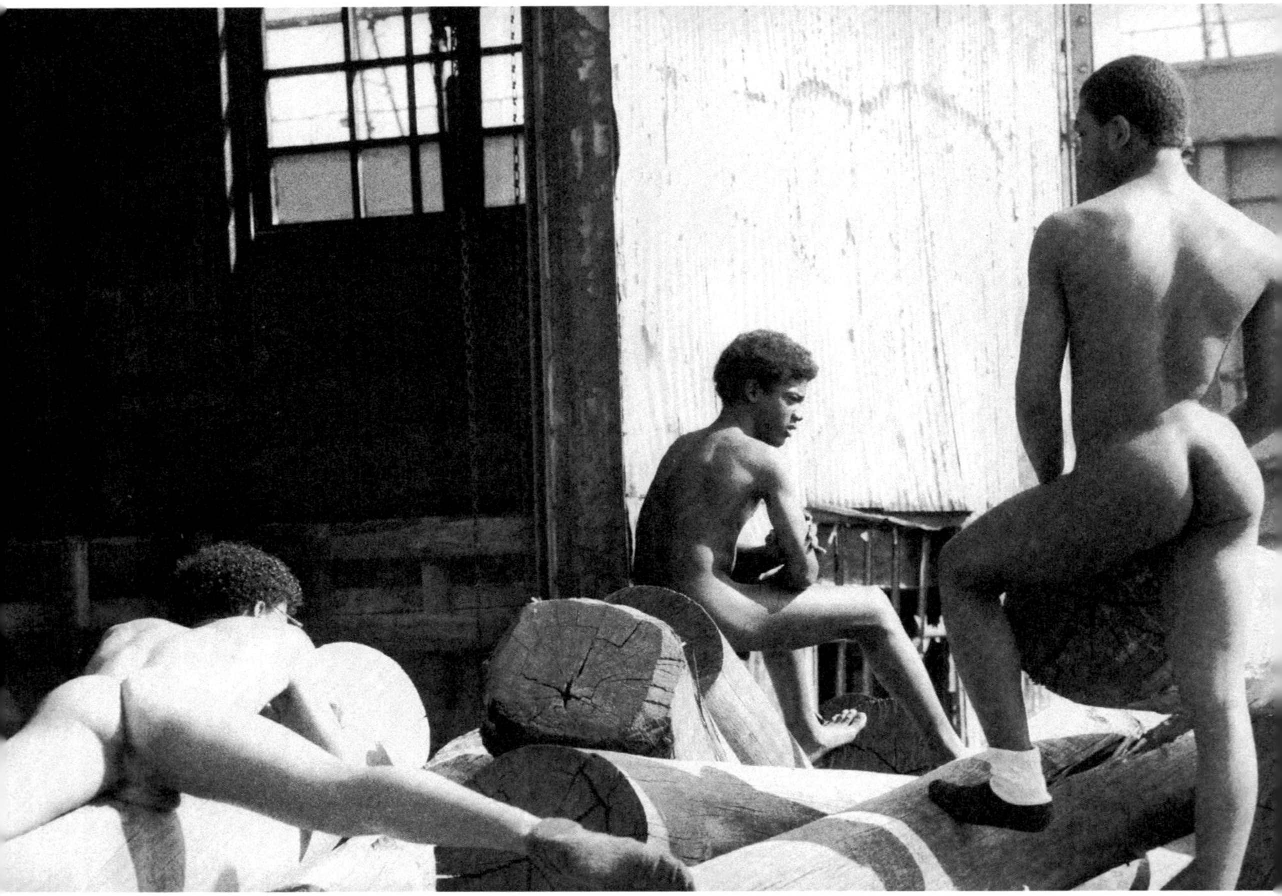

72. Alvin Baltrop, *The Piers*, n.d. (1975–86). Photograph used courtesy of The Alvin Baltrop Trust,

concentrating on his body mitigates against the feeling of comradeship that is one of the pleasures of many of Baltrop's best pictures. For example, there is a wonderful series in which three black teenagers hang out on a barge full of wooden logs (fig. 72). The boys clearly knew that Baltrop was photographing them, and their lack of inhibition about being admired by an older man speaks for the beauty of same-sex desire. There is an engaging sense of nonchalance in these young men—as if to say that being so naked in such a place is no big deal. Yet we know the risk they are taking, the physical danger, and the possibility of ostracism by family and friends.

If the Whitney's photograph lacks some of the daring of Baltrop's other photographs, it is still notable because of its subject's posture and what it says about Baltrop's own identity as an artist. The teen's lithe, muscular body and his pose on one foot suggest that he is a dancer, someone who is creative and thus a surrogate for Baltrop himself. Baltrop signaled the importance of this picture for his sense of identity by putting it at the top of a pile of pictures that accompanies his interview in the film *Gay Sex in the 70s*. Just like Baltrop, this young dancer was undoubtedly drawn to the abandoned building on the city's edge for its sublime beauty along the Hudson, and for the freedom it afforded to be brazenly naked in public, escaping bourgeois decorum. Taken before the advent of the AIDS epidemic, it speaks of a time in the 1970s when expressing the homoerotic in such an uninhibited way was emblematic of the so-called sexual revolution and the breaking down of political control and social repression. And yet the dancer's freedom exists amid urban poverty and neglect. His autonomy is precarious, a matter of being in a place where few other people would want to be, and it is unlikely to last.

The contrast of beauty and decay, joy and despair, is perhaps the most powerful and enduring trope of the pier photographs. How can people be having so much fun in such a world? Sigmund Freud, of course, would have no trouble reconciling this contradiction. Eros and Thanatos, life and death—each drive intensifies the other. More concretely, it is not hard to imagine how the decay and crumbling surroundings might heighten an ecstatic sensation of life for the men having sex. And yet one of the most moving pier pictures includes no people at all. I am thinking of Fink's picture of the fire-charred remains of the façade of the building at Pier 48 (fig. 73). Fink's obsessive photographing of the waterfront is poignant for me not because it affords a glimpse of some pre-HIV/AIDS paradise where gay men lived in a constant state of sexual bliss (I remember too well how frantic and frustrating the hunt for sex could be in the late 1970s), but because of the way it recorded the piers

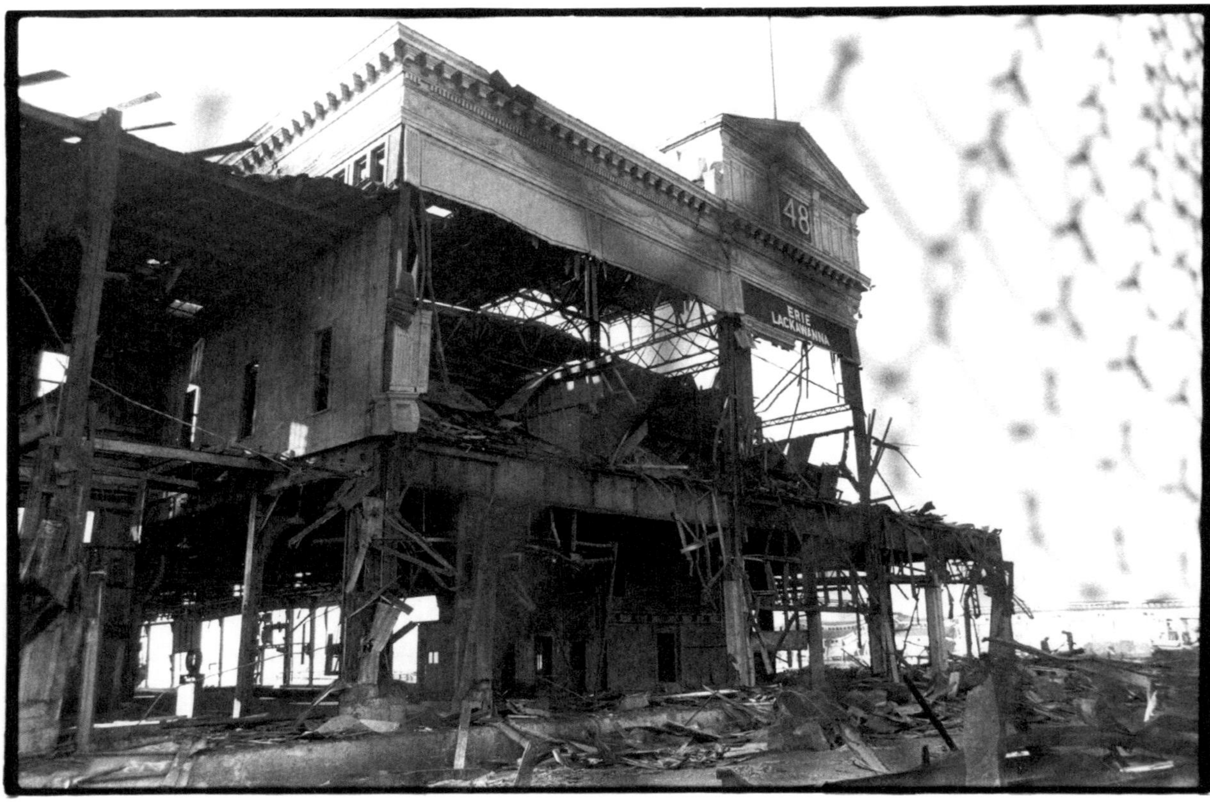

73. Leonard Fink, *Pier 48*, 1979. Collection of the LGBT Community Center National History Archive.

themselves, beautiful as objects and evocative of the long history of the waterfront that encompasses Herman Melville's day job as a customs inspector, the return of the survivors of the *Titanic*, and the labor disputes that inspired *On the Waterfront*. Given the extraordinary role of New York City architecture in so many of Fink's most memorable images, it should come as no surprise to find that he wanted to be an architect when he was growing up.

Although my actual memory of my time on the piers grows increasingly foggy, every year brings to light more photographs of that place and time. This very proliferation, rather than spurring my memories, fuses with them, so that I am no longer certain what I witnessed and what I saw in an archive or a magazine. You would think that spending so much time looking at so many pictures of collapsing structures and men copulating amid the ruins would leave me jaded, but the best of the pier photographs still seem, if not shocking, liberating and sometimes unnerving. They continue to reveal to me a secret place and time that only a few initiates experienced. Although I know from the photographs themselves that the West Village piers were often crowded with sunbathers, and that thousands of gay men cruised the warehouses, the piers still exist for me as deeply personal, even private, discoveries. I call the artists who made these pictures a pier group—but few knew the others or that they all shared a similar obsession. Each photographer, each artist, each participant or witness, thought he or she was discovering the piers as if for the first time, and they became a deeply personal subject. Inevitably, there are those who want to single out the achievement of one photographer over another, declaring which pictures are art and which are merely snapshots or pornography. But it is how the images speak to one another that moves me. I keep comparing them—not to decide which is better or more authentic, but to try to answer the same questions. Did such an extraordinary place really exist? Was I ever there?

Chapter 6

Something Possible Everywhere

AH–H– THE JOY OF TRANSGRESSION, THE SWEETNESS OF SIN—IT SOOTHES ME TO THE MARROW OF MY SOUL.
—Ignatz the Mouse

In one of Andreas Sterzing's most beautiful photographs of Pier 34 (fig. 74), Mike Bidlo and David Wojnarowicz sprawl out on grass that has mysteriously grown inside the waterfront building, their pose recalling the easy posture of the male figures in Édouard Manet's *Le Déjeuner sur l'herbe*. Wojnarowicz lolls back as Bidlo speaks to him. Both are oblivious to the thousands of commuters pouring into the financial district to the south and to the Holland Tunnel's endless stream of traffic, running just beneath the pier. Painted on the wall behind them is an enormous head outlined in black. Most probably just finished by their friend Luis Frangella, the drawing fuses with the cracked and stained plaster and seems ancient, like a fresco in Pompeii. Indeed, the dilapidated state of the building, with its rusted institutional light fixtures dangling from the ceiling, broken glass dividers, and crumbling floors, suggests that some sort of Pompeian disaster has recently occurred, emptying the space of all other inhabitants, though Bidlo and Wojnarowicz seem safe from any hint of impending disaster as they relax in this strange urban pastoral.

The city government built the enormous structure on Pier 34 in 1932, and its vast spaces were originally leased to the Clyde-Mallory Steamship Line and later to the New York and Cuba Mail Steamship Company, commonly known as the Ward Line.[1] Though the Ward Line went out of business in 1954, the company's name remained emblazoned on the terminal building's façade. In 1932, when this building joined the extensive network of shipping terminals around Manhattan, Bidlo and Wojnarowicz's lazy posture would have been unthinkable. In 2018, following this neighborhood's transformation into fashionable promenades and million-dollar condos—not to mention the heightened security at the entrances of the Holland Tunnel to guard against terrorist attacks—their ease would be equally unimaginable.

How did Bidlo and Wojnarowicz come to assume their pastoral pose in the middle of a city-owned building? By the time Sterzing took this photograph in the spring of 1983, dozens of friends and colleagues associated with the burgeoning East Village art scene had effectively seized control of the abandoned Ward Line terminal building. Although Bidlo was instrumental in reaching out to a broad network of artists, Wojnarowicz was the chief instigator of the Pier 34 experiment. As discussed in chapter 4, Wojnarowicz spent a good deal of time in the late 1970s wandering through the pier buildings lining the gay West Village. He was particularly fond of Pier 46, at the foot of Christopher Street. It was there that he made one of his first large-scale paintings, if we can call it that—the sprayed-painted graffiti of a man shooting up—and Pier 46 provided the setting for several of the *Arthur Rimbaud in New York* photographs. But as the West Village waterfront became increasingly popular—witness Hallam's image of dozens of naked sunbathers crammed onto the end of Pier 46 in the summer of 1982 (fig. 2)—Wojnarowicz sought solitude in the waterfront buildings farther downtown. The old Ward Line terminal at Pier 34 was all but empty: "I'd see a dog in the distance; it would just disappear into a room and I'd never be able to find it. Or I'd sit on the back balcony of one of these warehouses and just watch the river for part of the day. What I loved about them was that they were about as far away from civilization as I could walk, and I really loved that sense of detachment." In words that remind me of Vito Acconci's first anxious visit to the end of Pier 17 at 1:00 A.M., Wojnarowicz remembered staying "up at night in some of those places." "They were a little unsettling sometimes because you could hear certain noises that could sound very threatening coming closer and closer and nothing would appear and you'd wonder 'what the hell . . . ?'—whether you're hallucinating or whether there's something present. Sometimes you would feel the presence of another human in the dark and nobody would reveal themselves."[2]

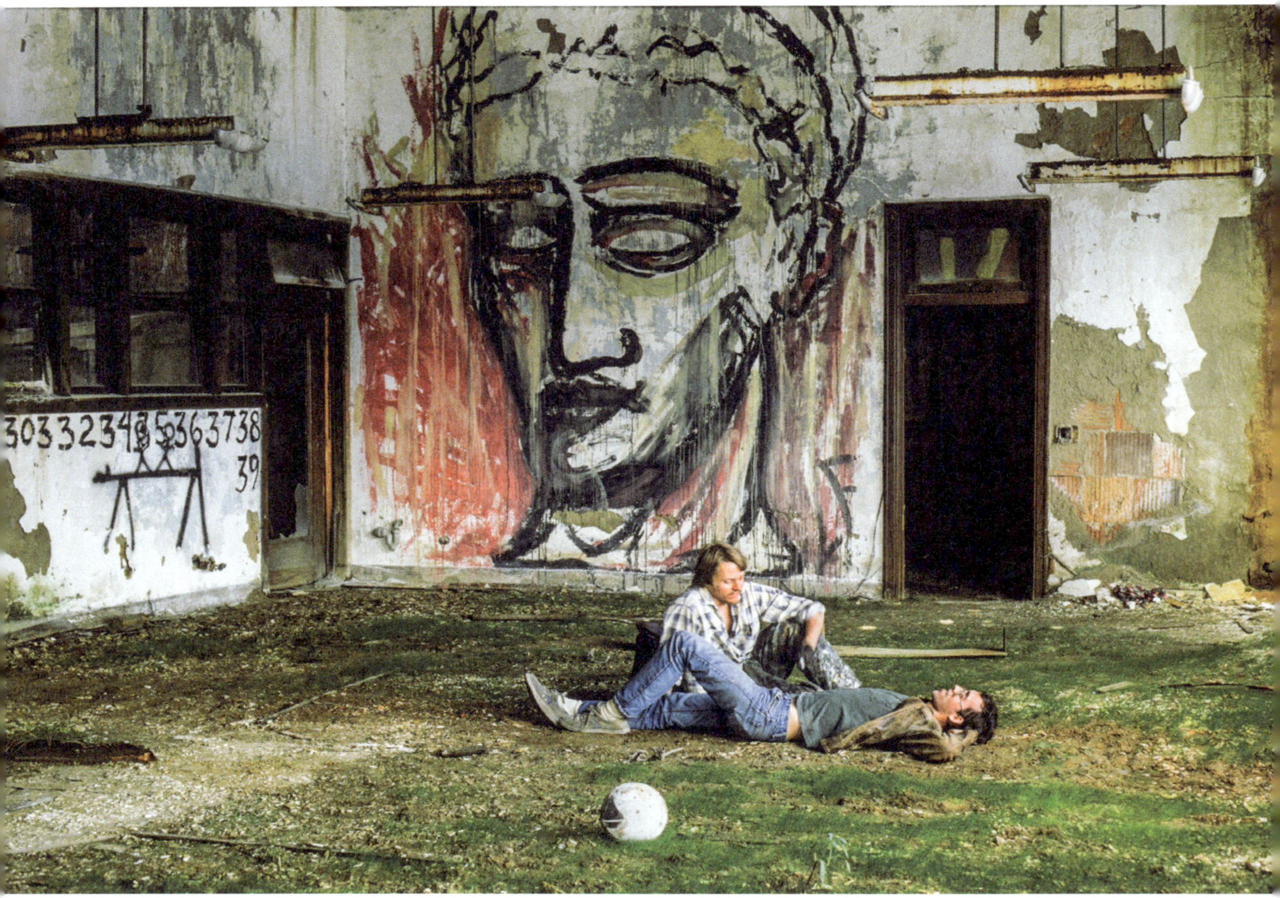

74. Andreas Sterzing, *David Wojnarowicz and Mike Bidlo*, 1983. © Andreas Sterzing. Reproduced with permission of P.P.O.W. Gallery, New York.

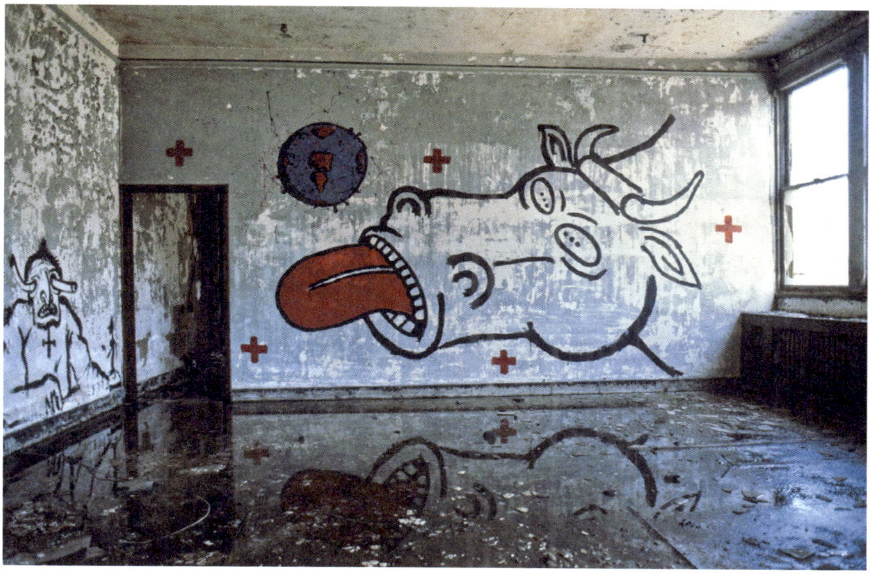

75. Andreas Sterzing, *David Wojnarowicz Mural*, 1983. © Andreas Sterzing. Reproduced with permission of P.P.O.W. Gallery, New York.

The chronology is uncertain, but probably in 1982, Wojnarowicz began to paint large-scale paintings on the walls of the abandoned second-floor offices of the pier buildings: a giant image of a gagging cow's head at Pier 34 (fig. 75) and a green toothy pterodactyl at Pier 28 (fig. 76). As Marion Scemama's photographs document, he also made large-scale images of a dog's head and bird man on Pier 28 that are less well known. This was an opportunity to experiment with painting on a large scale without worrying about the reaction of the art world. Working largely unobserved, he could make mistakes and take risks. Wojnarowicz traced his paintings of dinosaurs to a powerful dream, but the pterodactyl may also have been inspired by a comic book hero.[3] Wojnarowicz's friend and collaborator James Romberger, the graphic novel artist, told me that Wojnarowicz might have known about the pterodactyl supervillain Sauron, who had his debut in the popular *X-Men* series in 1969, just when Wojnarowicz was at a particularly rebellious moment in his adolescence.[4] Sauron is the alter ego of Karl Lykos, who is infected as a teenager by the bite of a mutant pterodactyl. The infection turns him into a flying creature with the ability to hypnotize and drain the life force out of other animals and people. In one iconic panel from the comic book, the flying supervillain

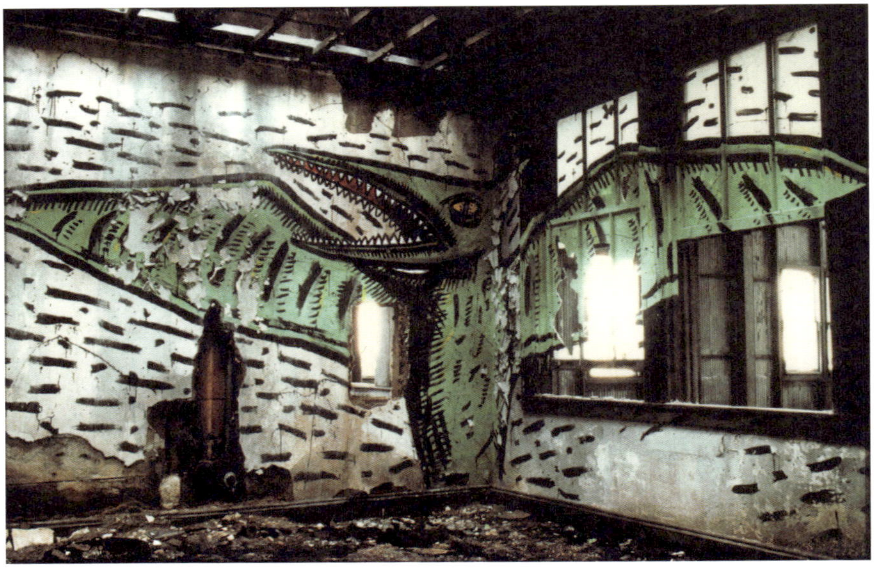

76. Marion Scemama, *David Wojnarowicz Mural, Pier 28*, 1983. © Marion Scemama. Reproduced with permission of P.P.O.W. Gallery, New York.

exclaims that he has chosen the path of evil, "an evil so great . . . so monumental that only one name in all the annals of literature will contain it! The name of Tolkien's ultimate villain . . . who was truly evil incarnate."[5]

Megalomania aside, Sauron's embrace of evil is not so different in spirit from Ignatz's wry musing, used as the epigraph for this chapter: "Ah-h-the joy of transgression, the sweetness of sin—it soothes me to the marrow of my soul."[6] Ignatz is the antihero of *Krazy Kat*, another comic strip that Wojnarowicz admired and that was the inspiration for a mural he painted a year later on Pier 34 (fig. 77). The brick-throwing Ignatz, like the pterodactyl, is the perfect alter ego for Wojnarowicz, always the outsider questioning the authority of the "one-tribe nation." The gun that goes "KRAK" on the left side of the mural is another potential image of rebellion. A few years later, Wojnarowicz posed with a toy machine gun as a mock terrorist for a *Life* magazine photographer.[7] Popular comic book rebels like Sauron, the pterodactyl supervillain, and Ignatz, the brick-throwing mouse, were aligned with Wojnarowicz's more exalted literary heroes, Burroughs, Rimbaud, and Genet. This mix of high and low artistic parents, all iconoclasts who refused to follow the rules, sustained "the fire in the belly" that drove his art, its humor, and even, in the case of Ignatz, its childlike sweetness.

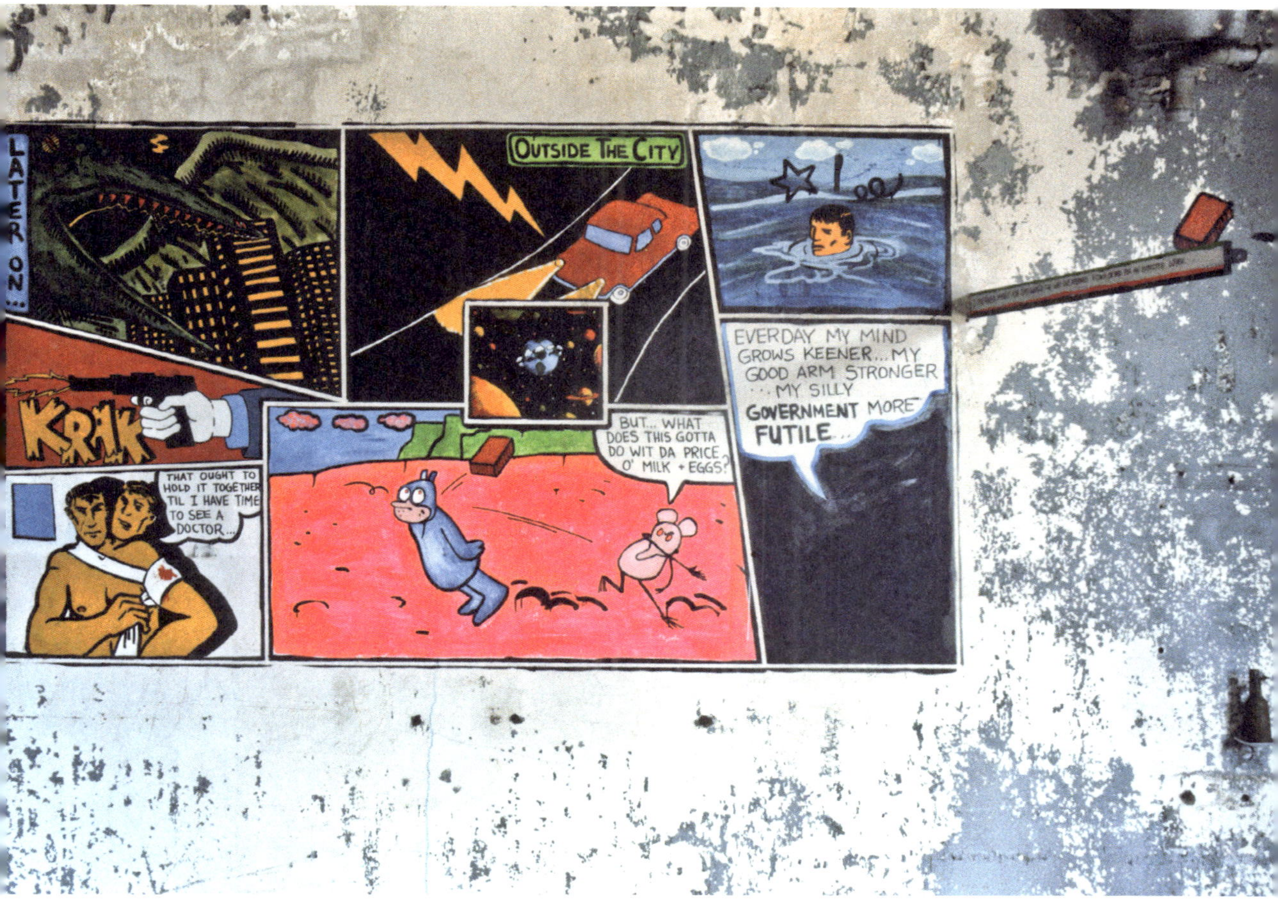

77. Andreas Sterzing, *David Wojnarowicz Mural*, 1983. © Andreas Sterzing. Reproduced with permission of P.P.O.W. Gallery, New York.

Given the tragedies and trauma that were central to Wojnarowicz's saga and self-mythology, it is sometimes hard to keep in mind the disarming nature of so much of his imagery, and how much he wanted to amuse us and himself. Kids love dinosaurs because they can be both scary and cute, and in the middle of the day, when Pier 28 was flooded with light, it would be hard to take Wojnarowicz's flying dinosaur too seriously. This brings another possible inspiration to mind, the puppet Pterri from *The Pee-Wee Herman Show*, which was first seen on television in 1981 on HBO. Barely bigger than a seagull, this miniature green flying dinosaur was a mischievous sidekick of Captain Carl in the HBO special, and later in the children's show *Pee-Wee's Playhouse*.[8] Whether one finds such beasts frightening or charming, there is an exhilarating freedom in the way Wojnarowicz's dinosaur opens his mouth in a silent scream, and spreads his wings across two sides of the room of Pier 28. Ingeniously, Wojnarowicz paints the dinosaur's left wing over the glass window, illuminating the figure from behind during the day and giving it a feeling of weightlessness. The artist echoed the animal's power to defy gravity when he leaped in front of the mural for Marion Scemama's camera (fig. 78), his arms merging with the pterodactyl's wings. This marvelous photograph was Wojnarowicz and Scemama's update of the Yves Klein/Shunk-Kender *Leap into the Void*. Like that picture, it served as a manifesto and as a harbinger of the rest of Wojnarowicz's career. It depicts the artist as rebel, full of unconstrained energy, like a mischievous child playing with imaginary dinosaurs.

Critics have cited Wojnarowicz's deep empathy for animals to argue that his flying dinosaur and cow are thematically linked. One extinct, the other waiting to be slaughtered, according to Mysoon Rizk, they represent the artist's "dominant sense of impending mortality."[9] Surely, in these early days of the AIDS epidemic (the first reports of the disease were published in 1981), Wojnarowicz's premonition that he might die young must have intensified. In general, Wojnarowicz saw animals as surrogates for human emotions of anxiety and joy, and as innocent victims of mankind's abuse of the natural world. I think Wojnarowicz also appreciated the way in which the wall drawings connected him to the supposed origins of art itself. He spoke of the pier structures as being like "caves"; painting these enormous beasts on the cracked plaster walls of the piers was profoundly elemental for him, akin to a Paleolithic shaman summoning spirits to keep demons at bay.[10] For me, the flying dinosaur and the gagged cow do relate, but not, as Rizk would have it, as equivalents. If the artist struggles with his inevitable mortality and the relentless oppression of society, he is also capable of great joy and defiance; above all, he is never a passive victim, never *cowed.*

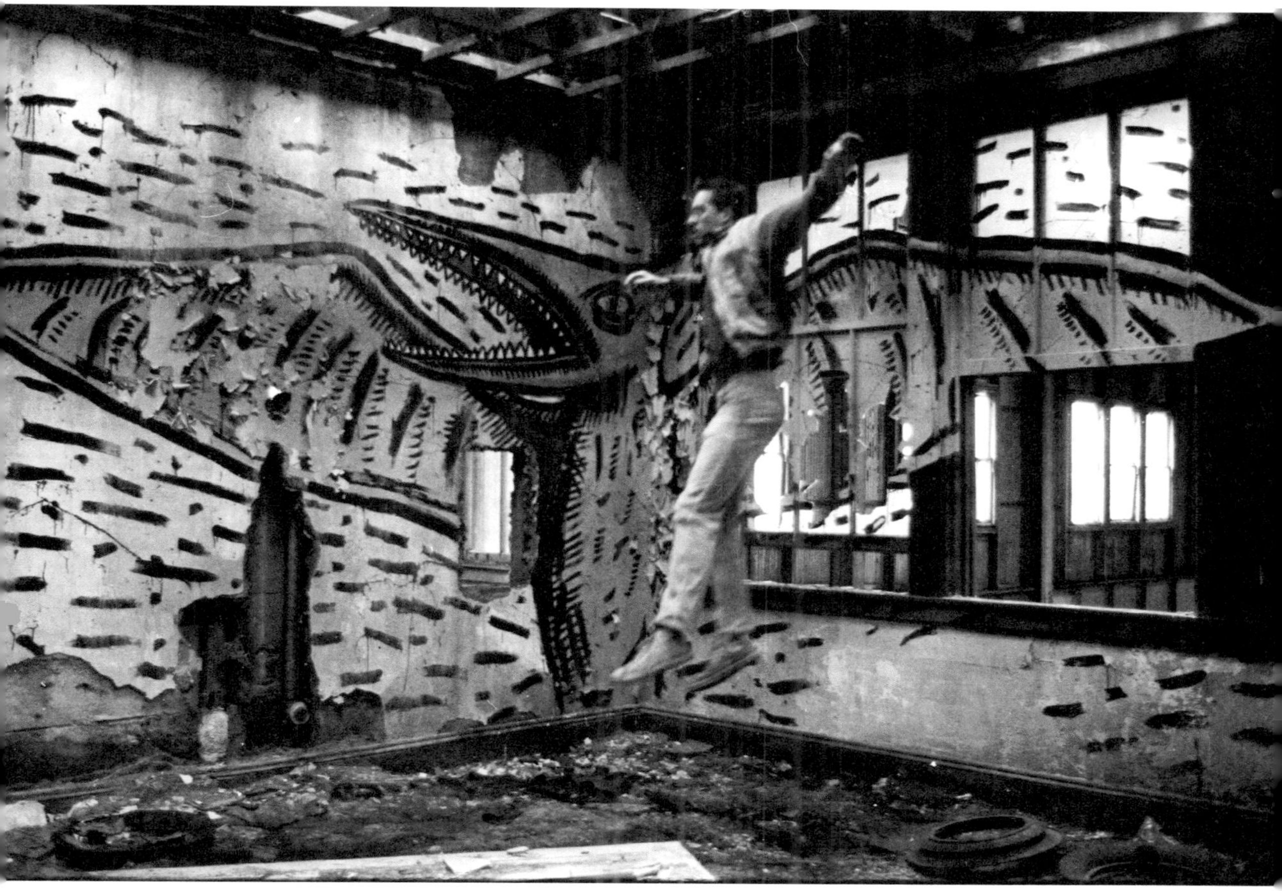

78. Marion Scemama, *David Wojnarowicz Jumping, Pier 28*, 1983. © Marion Scemama. Reproduced with permission of P.P.O.W. Gallery, New York.

Wojnarowicz's *Krazy Kat* mural on Pier 34 was quite different in format from the animal murals he painted before it. Here, Wojnarowicz not only borrowed the characters but imitated the comic strip layout, beginning with a cell in which another giant pterodactyl echoes the flying dinosaur at Pier 28. The clearest reference in the Pier 34 mural, however, is to George Herriman's *Krazy Kat* comic strip itself. Herriman died in 1944, and although his characters were resurrected in a poorly drawn and far less subversive television cartoon series in the 1960s, which Wojnarowicz might have known, I think it is more likely that he was introduced to this comic through his network of older friends, such as Hujar, since *Krazy Kat* has long been admired by cognoscenti who appreciated Herriman's expressionistic characters and surreal storylines. The strip's repeated theme of Ignatz mocking the authority of Offissa Pupp by throwing bricks at the love-besotted Krazy must have appealed to Wojnarowicz's anarchic tendencies.

Only two of the cells in the lower quadrant of the mural are derived directly from Herriman's strip; Wojnarowicz either appropriated the other images from different comics or made them up. In creating a new story out of bits of disparate sources, Wojnarowicz echoed one of his favorite authors, William Burroughs. Then in his late sixties, the notorious Beat writer of the once-banned *Naked Lunch* enjoyed cultlike status among Wojnarowicz's East Village contemporaries.[11] A forerunner of the queer sensibility that challenged binary modes of gender identity, Burroughs also challenged the rules of writing, assembling novels from fragments of other texts in a "cut-up" technique inspired by the artist-poet Brion Gysin. A mix of the intentional and the accidental, this repurposing produced new meanings and associations that reverberated with the original appropriated materials. Although Wojnarowicz did not literally use the cut-up method to create his mural, his comic strip, assembled from multiple sources to undermine the linearity of the strip's narrative form, relates to Burroughs's method, in which the beginning, middle, and end of various stories and even sentences are radically remixed and inverted so that the fragment turns into the whole and the whole becomes fragmented.

The sense that Wojnarowicz's mural is just such a fragment is reinforced by the words "Later On," which appear in the first cell, suggesting that we enter its story, or nonstory, in the middle. Given the comic strip form, we anticipate that each cell relates to the others in terms of a consistent set of characters and a narrative flow, but the various themes and viewpoints frustrate any attempt to create a coherent story. The cells shift from a pterodactyl looming over the city, to a bird's-eye view of a car racing along a highway, to a circular inset of the planets, to a man swimming, to a gun that goes KRAK, to a scene of a man bandaging a wounded buddy, and then, incongruously, to Ignatz hurling a brick at Krazy. Akin to montage, Wojnarowicz's method derives from cinema, and is more often used in comic books than in the surrealist collages that inspired Gysin and Burroughs. The montage of images works through adjacency—one thing next to another—rather than by layering one thing on top of another. In a sense, this relates to the overall Pier 34 experiment, where for the most part artists didn't so much collaborate with one another—although that happened too—as work next to one another on nearby walls and rooms. For example, Bidlo placed a painting that emulated Jackson Pollock on the wall next to Wojnarowicz's mural. When the work of artists overlapped on the pier, as when the *Krazy Kat* mural was tagged with graffiti, it tended to partially hide, rather than augment, the work underneath. But this too created new meanings, reverberating with the building's general air of desolation and ruin.

Despite the disjunctive nature of the different elements in Wojnarowicz's mural that frustrate or incite interpretation, the overall effect of the image is highly ordered. Instead of the big expressive lines of his earlier wall paintings of the pterodactyl and the gagging cow, which engage the space of their surroundings, the *Krazy Kat* mural stays within the frame of the strip. *Krazy Kat*'s bright colors and gridlike structure are so separate from its surroundings that on first viewing the mural must have resembled a pop art canvas hung on the wall of a museum rather than an image embedded in its environment. Wojnarowicz broke the frame of the mural, however, in two related gestures. First, in a nearby corner of the room he whimsically repeated a fragment of the image of Ignatz throwing the brick. The brick itself hovers to the right of the main mural, as if the mouse were aiming at the mural itself rather than at Krazy. The second gesture was more in the spirit of Burroughs's cut-ups. Wojnarowicz either attached or repurposed an existing window shade bracket that stuck out perpendicularly from the wall into the scheme of the mural. The painter Jean Foos salvaged this bracket, and thirty years later it remains one of the few things that survived the destruction of Pier 34. In an exhibition I organized for the Hunter Galleries in 2016, this object functioned like a reliquary, the only element in the show that had hung in the original space (fig. 79).

The importance of the bracket element to the mural is suggested by the fact that Wojnarowicz's mentor, Peter Hujar, photographed him at the very moment when the artist stood on a chair and began writing two sentences, one on each side (fig. 80):

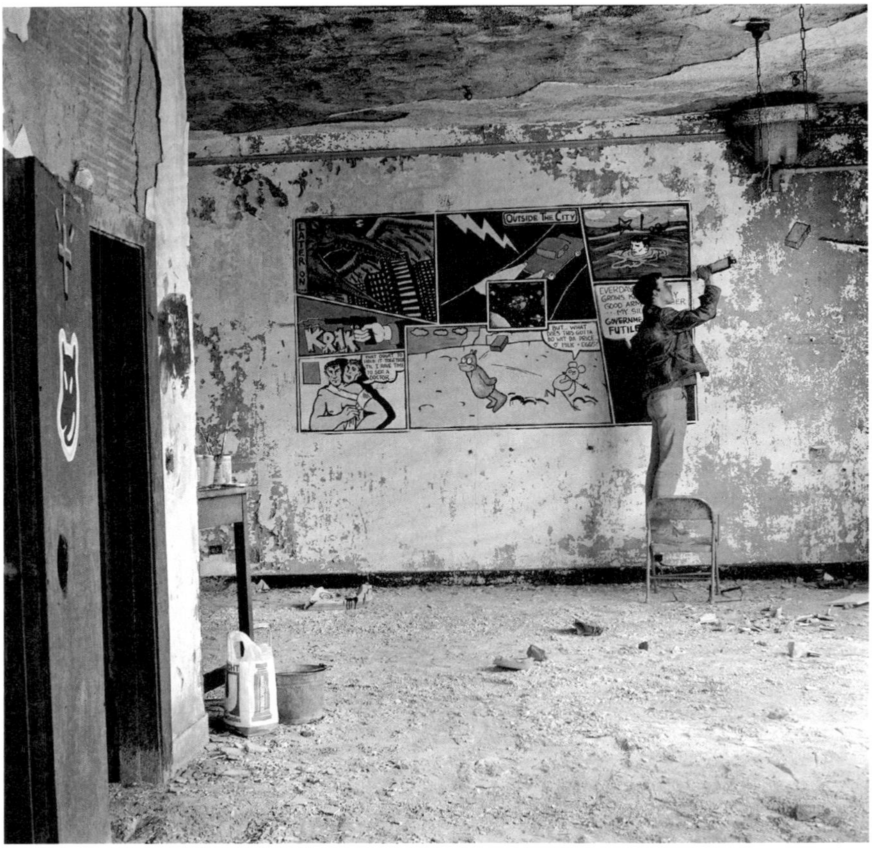

79. Peter Hujar, *Canal Street Piers: David Wojnarowicz Working on Krazy Kat Comic on Wall*, 1983. © 1987 The Peter Hujar Archive LLC; Courtesy Pace/MacGill Gallery, New York and Fraenkel Gallery, San Francisco. Reproduced with permission of P.P.O.W. Gallery, New York.

> *HE FLEW HIS PLANE STRAIGHT OUT OVER THE ATLANTIC TIL IT RAN OUT OF GAS. I PREPARED MYSELF FOR THIS WORLD THE WAY ONE PREPARES A COUCH OR BED FOR AN EXPECTED LOVER.*

Whether Wojnarowicz made these words up or stumbled upon them in one of the books he was reading "cut-up style," they resonate with what Cynthia Carr calls the mural's overall themes of "courage and catastrophe."[12] The allusion to an impending plane crash over the Atlantic relates to the panel of a man in the water in the upper right, which may have been sourced from a *Terry and the Pirates* strip in which Terry's mentor, Pat, falls from a cliff into the sea.[13] The

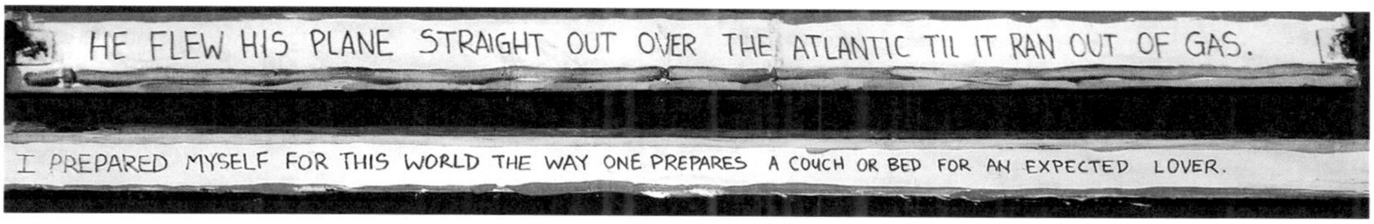

80. David Wojnarowicz, HE FLEW HIS PLANE . . . *(Window Shade Bracket Found at Pier 34)*, 1983. Photo © Jean Foos. Reproduced courtesy of the Estate of David Wojnarowicz and P.P.O.W Gallery, New York.

man in the water also relates to Wojnarowicz's memory of living and hustling on the streets as a teenager. According to the artist, he often used money he earned from sex with men to take a bus to swim in a country lake, literally and psychically cleansing his body.[14]

The other sentence on the bracket is harder to relate to the mural. But its message of self-preparation connects to the words that accompany the wounded man who is being bandaged by his friend in the lower left, and to the speech balloon that reads, "THAT OUGHT TO HOLD IT TOGETHER TIL I HAVE TIME TO SEE A DOCTOR." The inward and outward pressures on mind and body that threaten psychic disintegration are a constant theme of Wojnarowicz's writing, but so is the idea that making art sustains and holds the artist together. On another very general level, creating such whimsical and colorful art in an abandoned pier building that is itself so damaged and marginal is itself reparative. But I am intrigued by the connections between this ambiguous phrase and another text in the mural. Among the changes Wojnarowicz made from his *Krazy Kat* source (fig. 81) is his rewriting of the words Ignatz declares as he throws the brick. Instead of "EVERY DAY MY MIND GROWS KEENER. MY GOOD ARM STRONGER . . . MY SILLY ENEMIES MORE FUTILE," Ignatz says, incongruously, "BUT . . . WHAT DOES THIS GOTTA DO WIT DA PRICE O' MILK + EGGS?" Rather than simply remove Ignatz's original words, however, Wojnarowicz shifts them to a speech balloon in the final cell, so that it now reads, "EVER[Y] DAY MY MIND GROWS KEENER . . . MY GOOD ARM STRONGER . . . MY SILLY GOVERNMENT MORE FUTILE." In the context of the mural, this self-help mantra suggests that the man with the bandaged arm is recovering and, to paraphrase the statement on the window shade bracket, he is becoming prepared for a world where the government is silly and futile.

But perhaps I am working too hard to make sense of Wojnarowicz's Krazy comic strip. Maybe the key to the real subversion of the mural is Ignatz's rhetorical question, "But . . . what does this gotta do wit da price o' milk + eggs?"

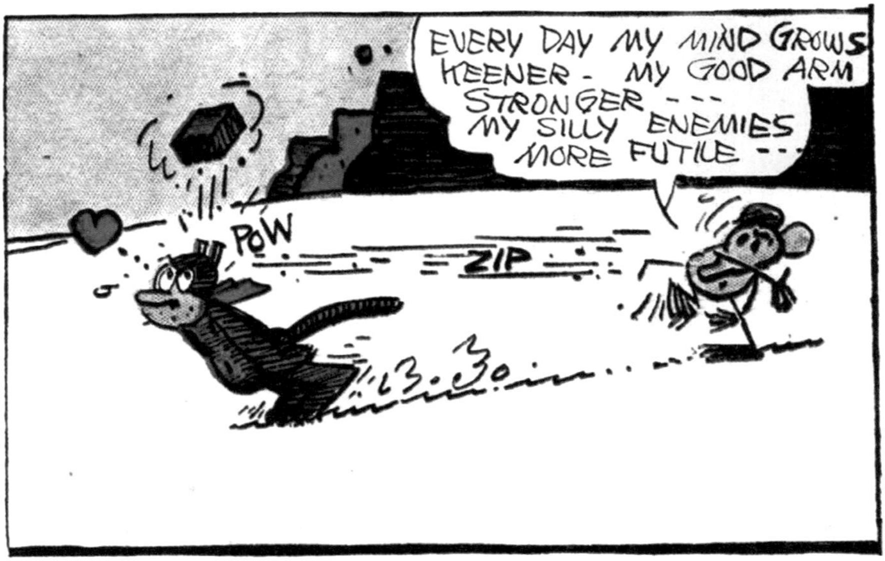

81. George Herriman, *Krazy Kat*, 20 March 1938.

I think the absurdity of Krazy Kat and Ignatz's sadomasochistic romance was appealing to Wojnarowicz precisely because the relationship did not make sense, even as it suggests that love itself can be destructive and obsessive. The cat is "krazy" because she or he—the cat's gender is indeterminate—is in love with the wrong type of animal. In this context, Wojnarowicz's rewrite about the government's being silly and futile might be a comment on the inability of the police to control deviant behavior, such as being in love with the inappropriate gender or, in the larger context of Pier 34, trespassing on city-owned property. But it also might be an early reference to the Reagan administration's shameful lack of response to AIDS, a disease that seemed to be targeting Wojnarowicz's circle of friends.

How weird it must have been to come upon the *Krazy Kat* mural in the empty pier when it was new. I have emphasized how contained it was in comparison to Wojnarowicz's earlier animal paintings. It also contrasts with his later paintings of a huge head and a masturbating figure. But on another level, the comic strip form, with its cells of different sizes that send us on a visual journey through a variety of different spaces, linking water to land, sky to sea, is the perfect metaphor for the pier structure itself. Increasingly, as Wojnarowicz's friends filled the rooms with art, the building became an analogous space, contained and laid out like a grid, yet highly varied and porous. Each room led to another experience and multiple viewpoints that, although seemingly disconnected and even chaotic, became part of a larger message of freedom and survival, a model of how art might "hold it together" amid so much destruction and loss.

The Pier 34 Artists

Sadly, I don't remember ever venturing onto Pier 34 in 1983–84, although I remember hearing rumors of an "art pier" at that time. What I know about that place came some three decades later, through conversations with some of the surviving artists and study of photographs by Javier Domingo, Peter Hujar, Marisa Le Grave, Dona Ann McAdams, Dirk Rowntree, Marion Scemama, and Andreas Sterzing, among others. These photographers had the foresight to document Pier 34 with skill and love. I have been fortunate to become good friends with Sterzing, who approached his subject as a journalist dedicated to recording what he calls simply "The Pier" for posterity. But Sterzing was not just interested in documentation. He sought to understand the scene there, and thus he befriended the artists and earned their trust. The result are portraits of artists and images of art so empathetic and beautiful they stand on their own.

Videographers also documented Pier 34.[15] A short, professionally shot video directed by Ichi Manabe for Japanese Public Television in 1984 focuses on the street artist David Finn, who constructed figures out of trash bags and found materials—what other people might call garbage—and then placed them in urban sites.[16] This footage begins with an aerial shot of the pier and the connecting Holland Tunnel air shaft, then follows Finn onto the pier and up the main staircase. The summer before, Finn had posed some of his bag people sitting on the steps, as if waiting for their friends to arrive by ship, but now the staircase is empty. As Finn walks through the building, he reminisces about that summer: "It was just beginning to get warm, people were very tired of winter. People were also pretty tired of working indoors, I think, and so this was open, lots of space, lots of room. And you could do anything you wanted to, anything you wanted to!" Despite his attempt to conjure up a sense of exhilaration, Finn's narration is nostalgic, and the video's images forlorn. The crunchy sound of his shoes on the rubble of the floor underlines the sense of decay and abandonment. When I learned of this video of Pier 34, I felt I would finally get a sense of what it was really like, but after the initial thrill of getting an overall sense of the building's layout and some of the rooms,

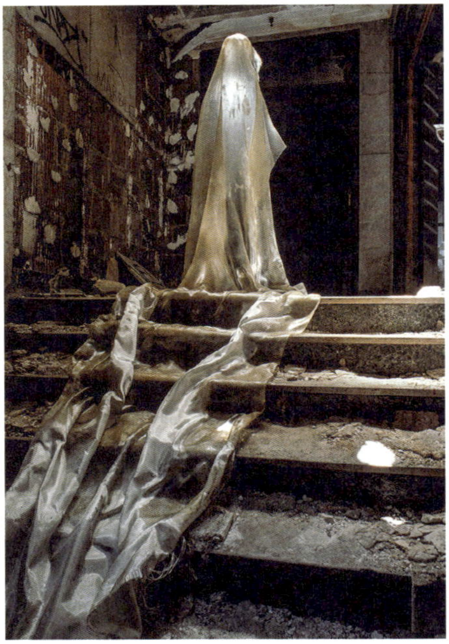

82. Andreas Sterzing, *Robert Jones Shroud*, 1983. © Andreas Sterzing.

I was disappointed by how desolate everything looked compared to Sterzing's vivid photographs, taken when the murals were newly painted. Hardly a year later, the Pier 34 experiment seemed to have become a wasteland.

Although Eric Wolfe's video, made in collaboration with the sculptor Robert Jones, was shot somewhat earlier, perhaps in the late fall of 1983, it is no less dispiriting.[17] Wolfe relied mostly on available light, and much of the footage is very dark. Jones was not part of Bidlo and Wojnarowicz's circle, and he never mentions any of the other pier artists in the interview on the videotape. He claims that he started making work on the piers in 1982, well before most of the other pier artists, and he continued to work there after most of them had left. In contrast to Finn's narration, which emphasizes the piers as a site where dozens of artists work in relative harmony, Jones talks about it as a lonely and frightening place: "the premise of working in this space and in the pier is that you are afraid of it and it's afraid of you, and when you walk in you build it up inside, it builds up." As if to make this feeling of dread tangible, in February 1983 Jones began to make a series of ghostly fiberglass figures molded from cloth draped on a female model (fig. 82). He called these life-size sculptures *Shrouds*. Like Finn's garbage-bag people, he placed these sculptures in dramatic locations—at the top of a stairway, or near a skylight where they would capture the light. Finn's figures were so animated and bodily that when he posed in a mask next to two of them for Sterzing's camera (fig. 83), it is hard to tell which are the sculptures and which is the artist; Jones's figures, by contrast, evoke death. Coming upon them in the middle of the night, he tells Wolfe, was so frightening that it frightened him too.

Leonard Perlson, who showed Jones's work in his gallery, claims that the *Shrouds* were among the first artworks to respond to the AIDS epidemic, which eventually claimed the artist. If so, it is surprising that Jones says

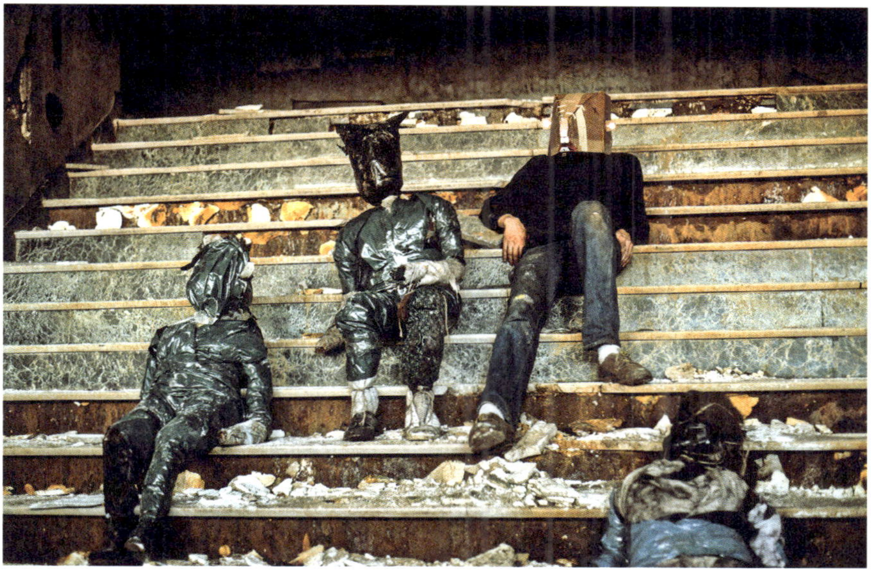

83. Andreas Sterzing, *David Finn, Sculpture, Pier 34*, 1983. © Andreas Sterzing.

nothing about it on the tape. He also repeatedly refers to the shrouds as women, which, given how the disease appeared to be targeting gay men in those early days, mitigates against the specificity of death from AIDS. Jones says that some people saw his figures as spiritual, noting that at night people put lighted candles around them, but he also describes finding one that had been slashed with a knife. Jones's general sense of fearfulness—he keeps trying to get Wolfe and his friends to imagine what it was like for him to hide from the potential attackers he thought lurked everywhere on the pier—is very different from the optimism and utopian sense of community remembered by friends of Bidlo and Wojnarowicz. Following the interview with Jones, Wolfe and his companions tour the rest of the pier, giving glimpses of the works by the other pier artists, whom Jones never mentions. Overall, the video presents the pier as beautiful but inhospitable, an appropriately desolate background for Jones's deathly *Shrouds*.

Fundamentally, both videos are retrospective: they lack the sense of the here and now so tangible in the still pictures taken by photographers lucky enough to be present when the artists were working. Sterzing took pictures of Finn assembling one of his figures out of materials salvaged from the waterfront, and another photograph of the painter Peter White, adding a red

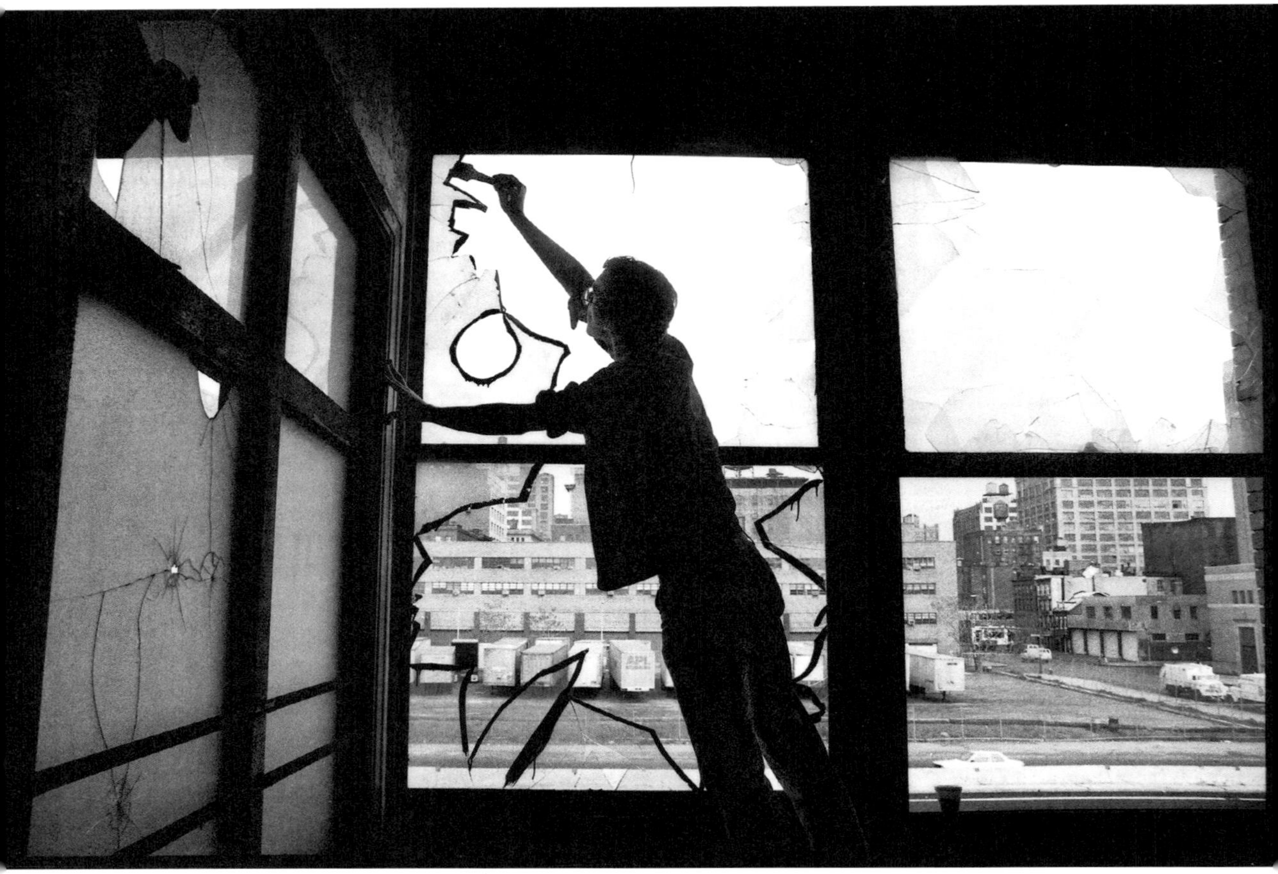

84. Dirk Rowntree, *David Wojnarowicz Painting on Window at Pier 34*, 1983. © Dirk Rowntree. Reproduced with permission of P.P.O.W. Gallery, New York.

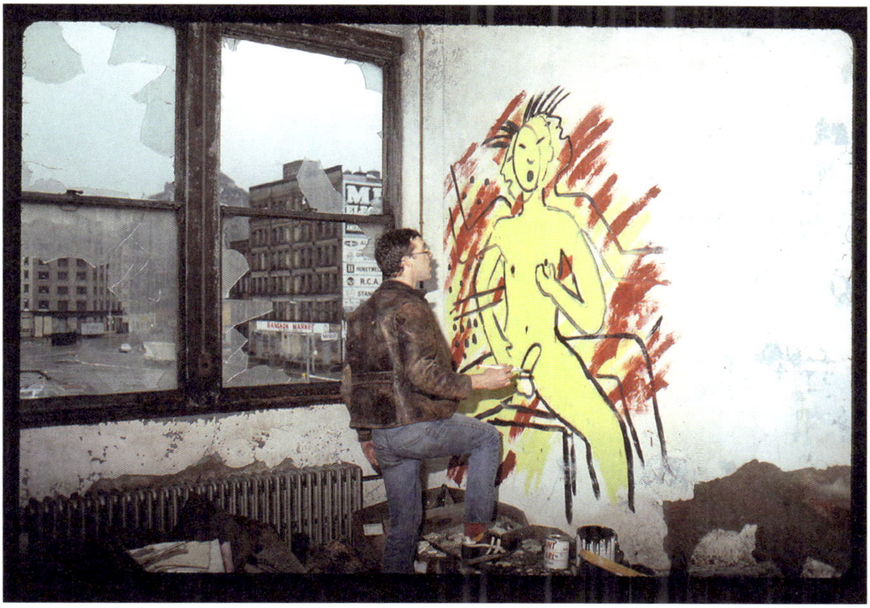

85. Dirk Rowntree, *David Wojnarowicz Painting Nude Yellow Figure at Pier 34*, 1983. © Dirk Rowntree. Reproduced with permission of P.P.O.W. Gallery, New York.

stroke to a head howling in pain or anger. Dirk Rowntree recorded, in black and white, Wojnarowicz painting on a window (fig. 84) and, in full color, making a wall painting of the young Yukio Mishima masturbating (fig. 85). Imagining the queer Japanese novelist as a denizen of the waterfront allowed Wojnarowicz to link the Pier 34 experiment to his earlier masturbating figure in *Arthur Rimbaud in New York*. Rowntree also photographed his wife, Jean Foos, painting one of her exuberant abstract paintings on Pier 34 (fig. 86). Sterzing captured Foos's close friend, the artist and designer Keith Davis, as he was finishing one of his enormous penis paintings (fig. 87). Foos wrote about collaborating with Davis, "We prepared the walls of one room, easily flaking off the industrial green paint with 2 x 4 boards, and revealing smooth white plaster. Keith went exploring for a time, while I got started painting, then he came back and appended a giant penis to my swirling abstract tornado."[18]

Sterzing's photographs of artists on the piers often show them interacting with their work, and they convey feelings of immediacy and, above all, play. The assemblage artist Rhonda Zwillinger is filled with devilish delight as she imitates the pose of Marilyn Monroe featured on the posters that she

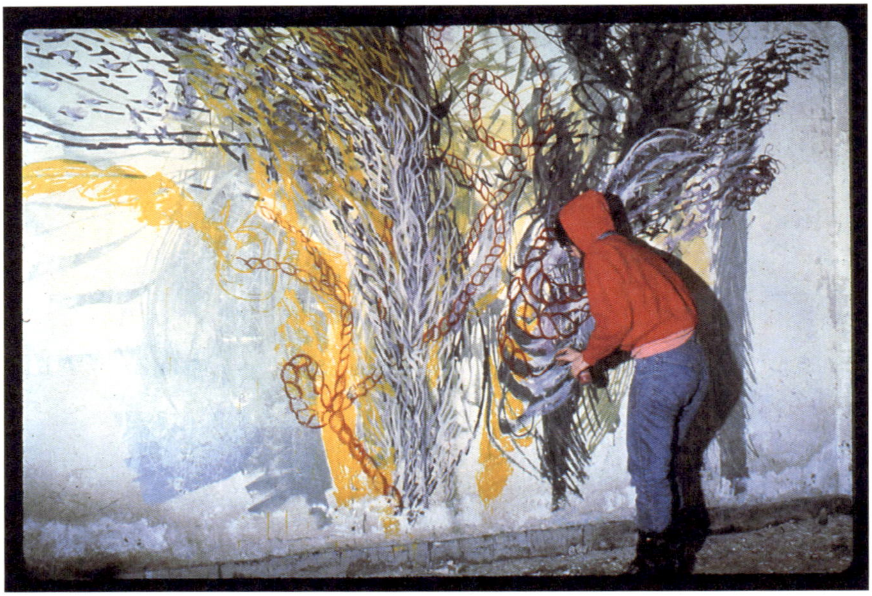

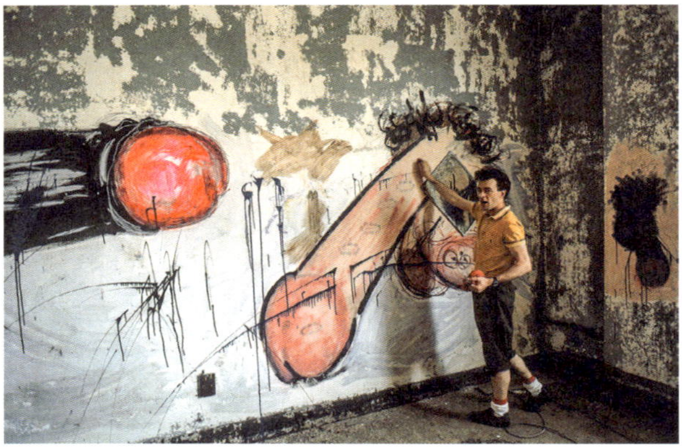

86. Dirk Rowntree, *Jean Foos Painting at Pier 34*, 1983. © Dirk Rowntree.

87. Andreas Sterzing, *Keith Davis, Pier 34*, 1983. © Andreas Sterzing.

repeatedly pasted on the wall, just to the left of White's mural. Sterzing's series of group portraits reinforces this feeling of improvisation and humor. Rather than have the artists pose for the camera in the tradition of yearbook or sports-team pictures, he had them form a line and then reassemble, so that different people would be in front for each shot (figs. 88–89). The images capture both the communal spirit of the place and the ways in which artists competed for attention, all trying to make sure their faces, and by implication their work, would be remembered. In another exuberant Sterzing picture, the painter

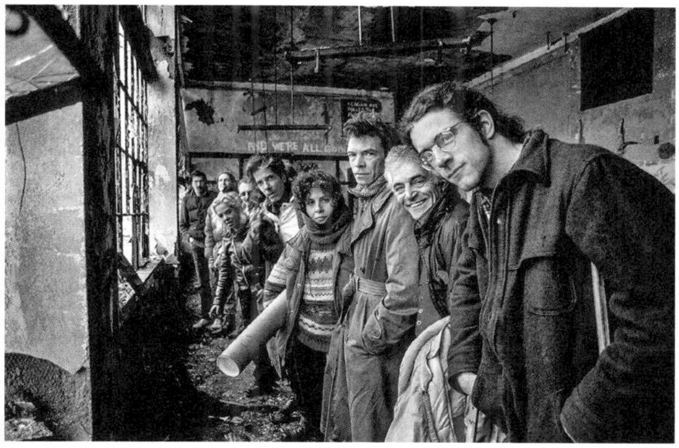

88. Andreas Sterzing, *Group Portrait of Artists, Pier 34*, 1983. © Andreas Sterzing.

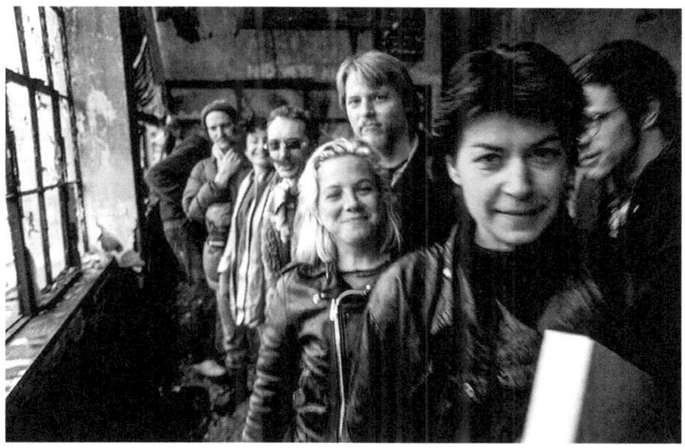

89. Andreas Sterzing, *Group Portrait of Artists, Pier 34*, 1983. © Andreas Sterzing.

Huck Snyder hangs from his feet in a doorway, identifying with the upside-down pink babies he painted all over a men's bathroom (fig. 90). Sterzing's portrait of Snyder in this painted bathroom documents the artist's practice of dating the exact moment of creation, in this case 23–24 May 1983, at different times in the afternoon. But we don't need such precise dating to feel as if we are present at a specific moment: it is built into the vividness of Sterzing's photographs. Despite the challenges of taking pictures in such a setting using only available light, the pictures seem lighthearted and spontaneous.

Not all of Sterzing's pictures of the artists are so optimistic. A portrait of the neoexpressionist Rick Prol juxtaposes the artist's head with the knife depicted in one of his murals so that it seems as if he is being attacked (fig. 91). Whatever Prol's own feelings were, such a picture reminds us that not everyone found the piers a safe place to work. I have already mentioned Jones's

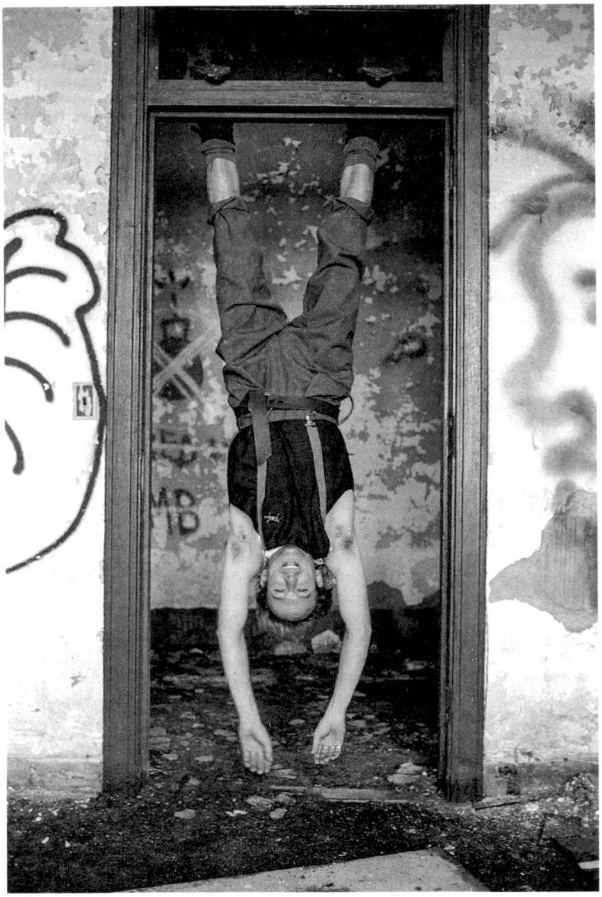

90. Andreas Sterzing, *Huck Snyder, Pier 34*, 1983. © Andreas Sterzing.

feelings of paranoia. Betty Tompkins remembered that she purposely created her image of an "ascending cat" close to where her husband, Bill Mutter, was painting a body builder, both for protection and so the two could get "out of there as fast as we could." Alain Jacquet's widow, Sophie Matisse, wrote to me that her husband went to the pier one night to work on a wall drawing and encountered two men in a heated conversation. He felt that they might turn on him. The next day he learned on the news that someone had been murdered on Pier 34. He told her that "this experience was one of the most terrifying moments of his life as he had real doubts about getting out of there alive. He knew he had walked-in on something pretty bad and he felt a darkness there that reeked of death."[19] Such fears do not negate the less anxious memories of some of the other artists; rather, they remind us of the difficulty of generalizing

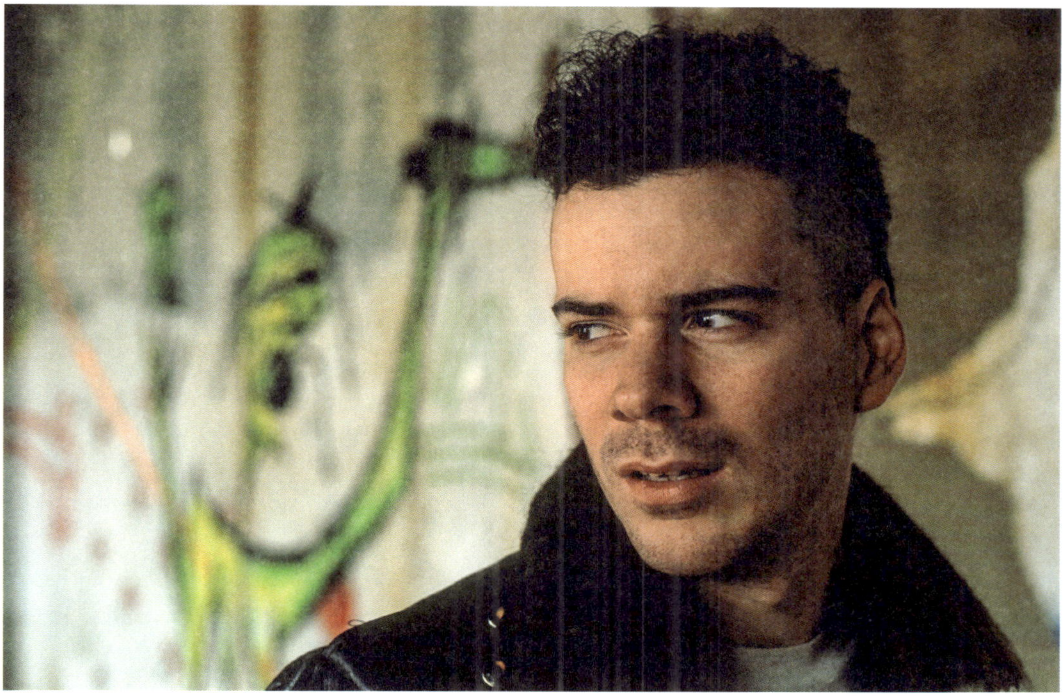

91. Andreas Sterzing, *Rick Prol, Pier 34*, 1983. © Andreas Sterzing.

about the Pier 34 experiment. Whereas artists like Jane Bauman and Foos, both of whom knew Wojnarowicz well, tend to talk about the Pier 34 cohorts as a tightly knit group, David Finn claims that most who ended up working there didn't know one another. While Wojnarowicz and Jones spent years making art on the waterfront, Michael Ottersen, like Tompkins and Mutter, made his pier contributions in a matter of a few hours or a couple of days.

Kiki Smith

Kiki Smith was among the first artists Wojnarowicz brought to the pier in 1981.[20] In one small room she painted small circles on the floor that, for a brief moment each day, aligned with the light streaming through the windows. Smith's use of light relates to Gordon Matta-Clark's pier piece *Day's End*, which he created farther uptown, at Pier 52 near Gansevoort Street. Like Matta-Clark, Smith used the path of the sun as an expressive element. Smith remembers that during these first visits to the waterfront, she and

Wojnarowicz found piles of drawings made by patients from a psychiatric ward, which the artists then used for a collaborative print. The connection they imagined between people marginalized by mental illness and their own sense of alienation from middle-class morality and modes of decorum is a key to much of the art that was made on Pier 34.

Bringing Smith to the pier enabled Wojnarowicz to cement his friendship with her. It also brought a woman artist into the largely male world of the waterfront. Soon thereafter, Wojnarowicz invited Jane Bauman, and the two shared methods of using stencils and spray paint to make pieces, sometimes mingling their images. Other women artists followed, and by the summer of 1983 there were several women working at Pier 34, as Sterzing's group portrait suggests. It is a testament to the spirit of cooperation and comradeship among the core group of Bidlo and Wojnarowicz's circle that, as both Judy Glantzman and Bauman told me, they felt safe working in this derelict location, at least during the day.

The artists who worked on Pier 34 crossed generations, from established figures like Alain Jacquet and Ruth Kligman to emerging artists like Steven Doughton and Zwillinger; they worked in a variety of media and styles, from the performance art of Kim Jones and Paolo Buggiani to the expressionism of Glantzman, Richard Hofmann, and Stephen Lack. I had been researching this project for years before I learned that Georges Rousse, the distinguished French photographer and site-specific artist, made work on Pier 34 that was documented by him, Sterzing, and Hujar. Known for his installations in derelict buildings, Rousse painted naked figures immersed in a network of blue crossing lines all over the toilet partitions of a bathroom and onto the connecting walls. In the spaces created by the crisscrossing lines, he painted the numeral 2. It was as if the doodling that people frequently make on the walls of bathrooms had spread from the toilet stall to the larger public arena. The act of filling the walls with quickly rendered marks, words, and images evokes the release of pent-up emotions. In Sterzing's photographs, the effect of so much visual overload and the collapsing pier itself appears deeply anxious.

If the Pier 34 artists were surprisingly diverse in terms of gender and age, they were less so in terms of race. As far as I know, the only African American artist who worked at Pier 34 was Thom Corn (fig. 92), who was invited onto the scene by Mike Bidlo. Corn directly addressed issues of racial diversity with a mural he titled "New Amero-World Flag," in which bands of color are annotated "red people red, black people black, white people white, yellow people yellow, brown people brown." Around the edges of the flag runs a spikey fringe

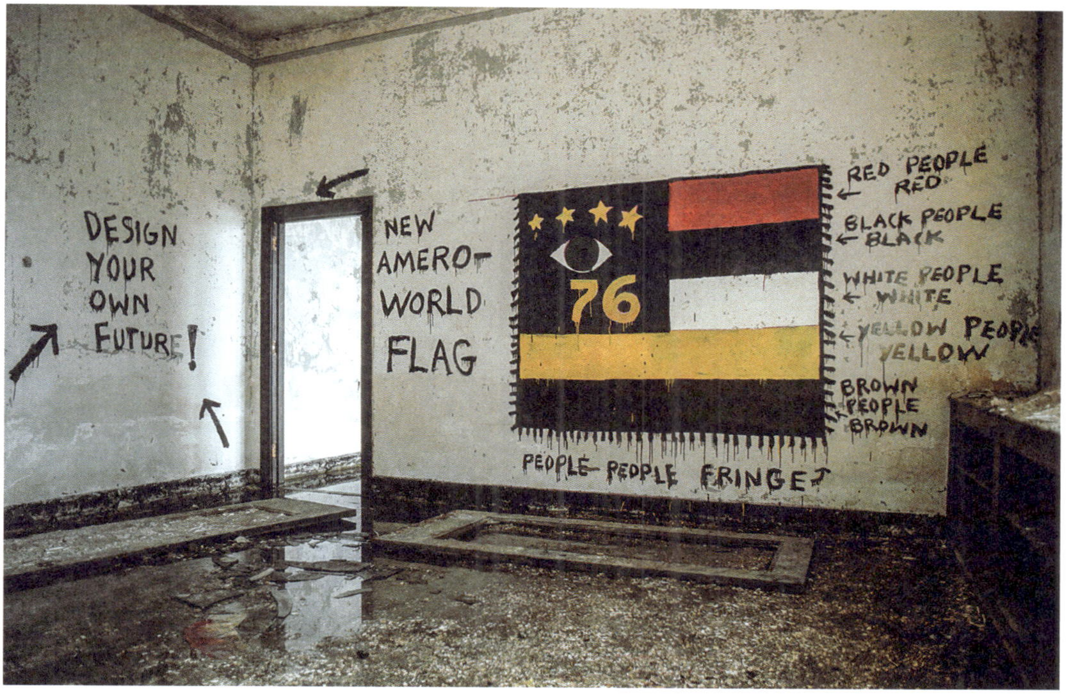

92. Andreas Sterzing, *Thom Corn Mural, Pier 34*, 1983. © Andreas Sterzing.

labeled "people people fringe." Are the pier artists "fringe people" or is everyone potentially "people people"? On an adjoining wall, Corn negated the idea of creating a single flag that could somehow speak for multiculturalism with the imperative "Design your own future!"

Much of the pier art was purposely shocking, testing the boundaries of acceptable behavior and representing life on the edge. Valeriy Gerlovin created a huge painting of a face with syringes for the eyes, linking drug use with ecstatic hallucination—the artist as outcast and seer. Davis's penis paintings, when connected to Foos's tornadolike and more vulvic abstraction, relate artistic and sexual energy. Davis's phallic images might seem puerile, but when joined with Foos's abstraction or related to Frangella's male and female nudes, a polymorphous aesthetic emerges that potentially breaks down the very categories of gay and straight that were, for better or worse, so central to the civil rights movement of the 1970s.

The site specificity of works by Corn, Rousse, John Fekner, and Teres Wydler, among others, challenges the conception of the 1980s art scene as

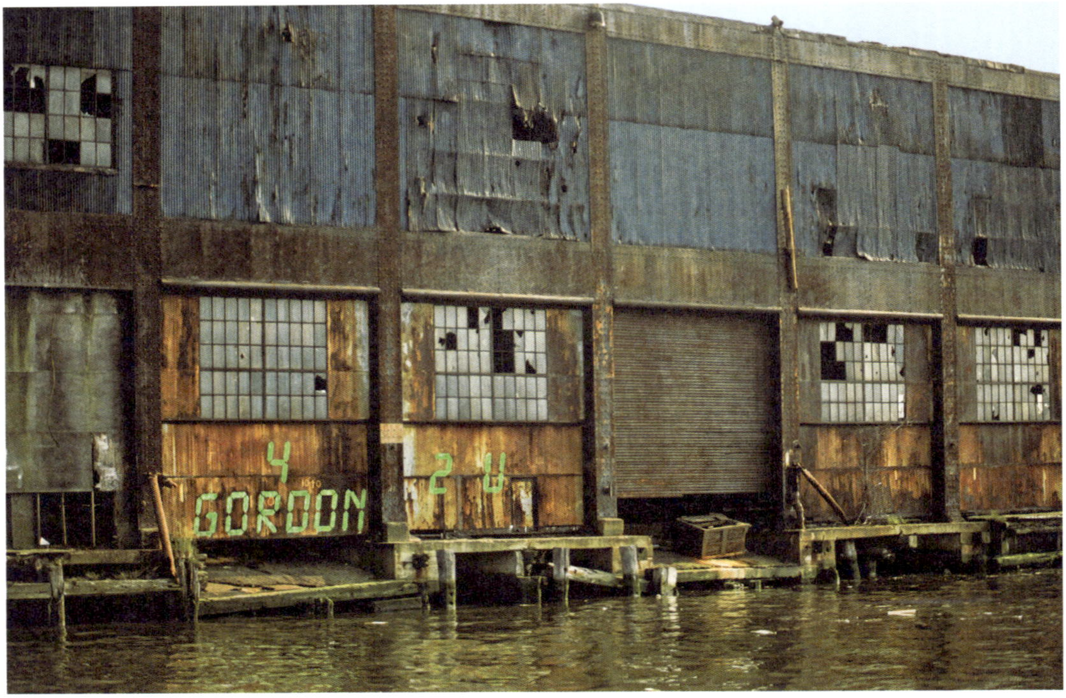

93. Andreas Sterzing, *John Fekner, 4 Gordon 2 U, Pier 34*, 1983. © Andreas Sterzing.

exclusively a turn toward easel painting driven by the market. Fekner's works on Pier 34 looked back to earlier site-specific works. On the exterior of the pier building, he stenciled a moving homage to Gordon Matta-Clark, "4 GORDON 2 U" (fig. 93), and elsewhere he blocked out a window to create a miniature re-creation of Matta-Clark's cat's-eye cut. Matta-Clark was a powerful inspiration for Fekner's transformations of abandoned urban spaces using stenciled letters. Like Matta-Clark's "anarchitecture," Fekner's work is ephemeral and resists commodification; it is always about the site and its historic and communal contexts. Fekner told me that at the time, few of the pier artists in the Bidlo and Wojnarowicz circle had any idea who Matta-Clark was, although *Day's End* was made only eight years before, which is why he felt it was so important to remember Matta-Clark at Pier 34.

Wojnarowicz and his co-conspirator, Bidlo, self-consciously presented the piers as anticommercial. As rumors spread in the spring of 1983 of what was happening on the waterfront, the two artists released a statement to friends in the press that explained their ethos of resisting the gallery system and creating an opportunity for anyone "to explore any image in any material on any surface they chose. This is something no gallery would tolerate." Above all, they claimed that Pier 34 forged a community: "People who lived in this city for years said it was the first time they experienced fulfillment in terms of contact with the art scene and strangers."[21]

Bidlo and Wojnarowicz's statement is poetic. "Drift of water. Drift of thought. Drift of wind," they wrote, and they claimed they chose Pier 34 because "it straddled a tunnel that was a route for things arriving and departing from the city."[22] This feeling of being transported to a place that was neither land nor water—outside time and beyond the reach of societal control—evokes the "other space" of Foucault's "heterotopia." Yet to experience an in-between space in such ruins could also be profoundly disturbing, a reflection not just of the potential to escape outward restraint but also of inward decay and decadence. Above all, Pier 34 was a profoundly lonely place to be. No wonder Wojnarowicz reached out to friends to share his experience. As Carr and others have written, the artist was often torn between longing for solitude and desire for companionship and community. Why not share his discovery with carefully chosen artist friends who could both appreciate the potential of the waterfront and teach Wojnarowicz new techniques and ways to activate such large spaces using paint? Beyond the freedom in having so much space to work in was the generosity of initiation, as artists shared this major source of inspiration with another, short-circuiting the hypercompetitive nature of the art market. Wojnarowicz repeated that initiation, not only by bringing in friends like Smith, Bauman, and Bidlo and urging them to use the pier for their art, but also by starting a chain of communication—Foos told Michael Ottersen, and Glantzman heard about the site from Frangella. "David must have known that the art-for-art's-sake purity of the project could be lost," writes Carr, "but maybe he didn't. He had such an idealistic view of other artists. At least he did then."[23] Inevitably, word spread and artists with no connection to Bidlo and Wojnarowicz or their friends moved in. By the summer of 1983, one could see works by the German painter Rainer Fetting, the Swiss installation artist Teres Wydler, and the Italian performance artist Buggiani. "The place is now international in scope," Bidlo and Wojnarowicz wrote. "Germans, Swedes, Canadians, French, and Americans working side by side. All work is anonymous." Sterzing himself was German-born, and several of his color photographs of the pier were first published in *Stern* magazine in 1984.

One constant of the period was the importance of working within a community of artists that spanned generations and nationalities. Many of the

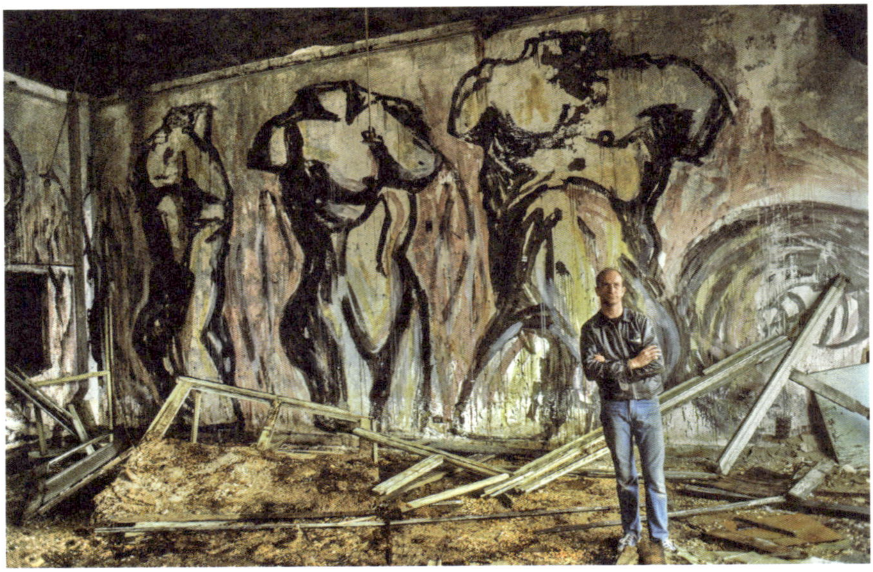

94. Andreas Sterzing, *Luis Frangella, Pier 34*, 1983. © Andreas Sterzing.

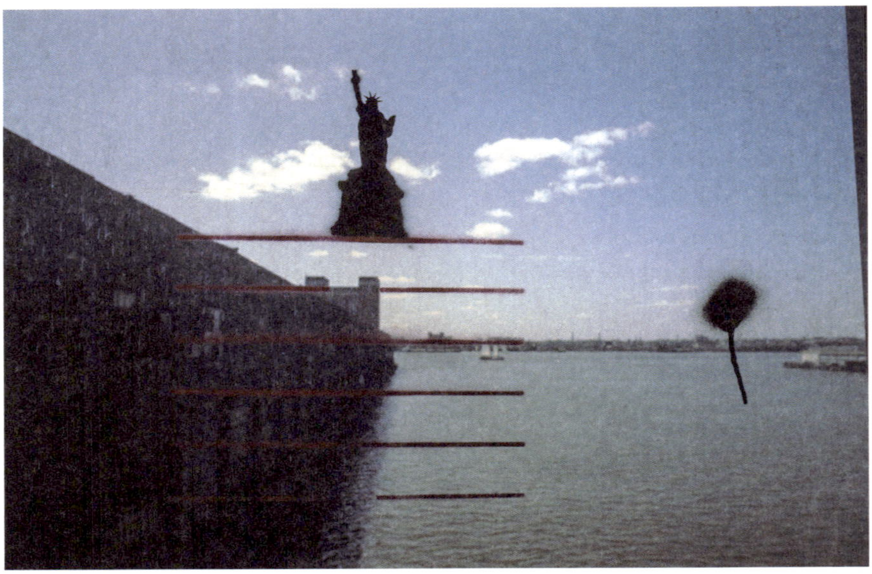

95. Andreas Sterzing, *Jane Bauman Stencil Painting, Pier 34*, 1983. © Andreas Sterzing.

surviving artists recall their friendship with and respect for the Argentinian Frangella, one of the first painters to work on the pier (fig. 94). Frangella's enormous figures and heads, based loosely on classical torsos and busts, not only inspired Wojnarowicz to paint big but also informed the expansive scale of the work of Foos, Glantzman, Hofmann, Lack, Prol, and White, among others. The emotional tenor of this gestural painting worked well with the collapsed state of the pier itself—cracked plaster, broken beams, and rubble echoed the often discordant and violent imagery of the art, creating the justifiable impression that Pier 34 was an extension of East Village neoexpressionism. But on other walls, Kim Jones, a very different kind of artist, painted much more modest images of rats, referencing his performances and his notoriety as the Rat Man. Bauman avoided the walls altogether, spray-painting delicate stencils onto windows to create small bands of color underneath the silhouette of the Statue of Liberty (fig. 95). Best known for lighting himself on fire and driving a motorcycle over the Brooklyn Bridge, Buggiani hung a paper sculpture of Icarus from the ceiling of the main hangar.

Frangella and Bauman often worked alongside Wojnarowicz, and all three influenced one another's work. "The three of us would go down to the pier," Bauman recalled, "and sometimes we'd work on each other's pieces, but in a playful way. That was the most playful I ever, *ever* saw David. He was so comfortable in that milieu, so relaxed. Serious but childlike. Not 'childish' but 'childlike.'"[24] Bauman's distinction between "childish" and "childlike" is critical to much of the art of Pier 34. Sterzing's photographs show Jacquet sucking his thumb, alluding to his mural of a baby's pacifier, and Glantzman proudly blowing a gigantic gum bubble with a big brush in her hand (fig. 96). Snyder's images of babies invoke the Baudelairian notion that the inspired artist sees the world through a child's eyes, as if for the first time.

As Bauman insists, however, the childlike and the serious are not opposites. Fittingly, Wojnarowicz's favorite of his own works on the pier was childlike in its simplicity but sophisticated in its references to Walt Whitman's *Leaves of Grass* and Hans Haacke's *Grass Grows*. "I would buy grass seed," he reminisced, "and throw this grass seed all over. All the disintegrated plaster that had fallen out of the ceiling and all the airborne particles of earth and stuff would actually let this grass grow in the confines of the building, so it would be like an actual meadow inside several rooms that were just so beautiful. . . . Those are some of the gestures that I loved the most and got the least attention because they were the most anonymous—you couldn't sign a blade of grass that says Wojnarowicz."[25] Sterzing's photograph of Bidlo and Wojnarowicz

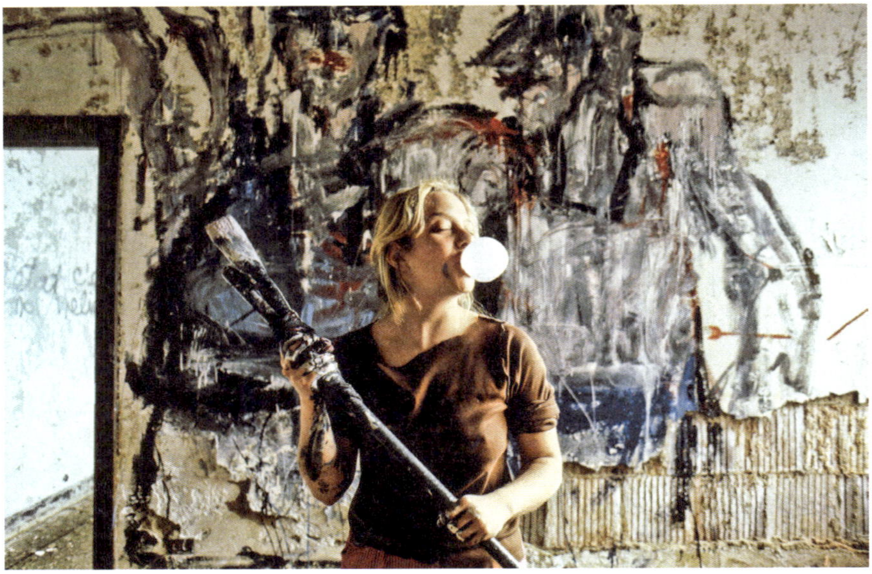

96. Andreas Sterzing, *Judy Glantzman, Pier 34*, 1983. © Andreas Sterzing.

lolling on the grass (fig. 74) commemorates this project, along with the two artists' friendship, which intensified through their work at the pier. Unlike many of the other artists, Bidlo was not interested in making work in situ, but he used the Ward Line terminal as a new setting for his "Not Pollock" drip paintings, which challenged modernist ideas of originality and the authenticity of gestural abstraction. Suddenly, the type of modernist picture that hung in the Museum of Modern Art's pristine white galleries was stretched onto a wall already covered with drips and stains. Disrupting aesthetic hierarchies, the effect recalled the anarchic quality of Pollock's technique and the elemental desire to mark one's territory.

Despite the diversity of the work that was made on Pier 34, one quality separated most of it from the projects discussed in the early chapters of this book: the absence of content that directly referenced the waterfront or directly engaged with the site in terms of its previous history (Fekner's work is an exception). From the beginning, Wojnarowicz and Frangella tended to use the walls of the pier spaces as enormous canvases. For all the differences between the works of Acconci, Whitman, and Matta-Clark, those three artists focused attention on the pier and the waterfront itself. This was true of Wojnarowicz's earlier Rimbaud series, too. Pier 34, by contrast, functioned

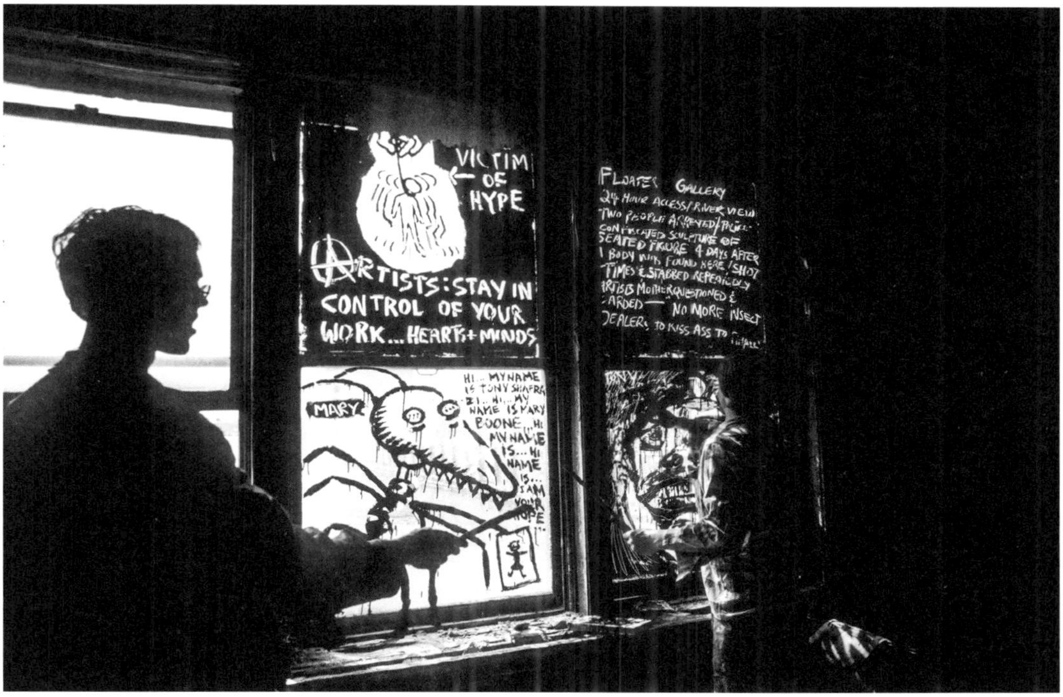

97. Andreas Sterzing, *Mike and David*, 1983. © Andreas Sterzing.

primarily as an exhibition space and a place to make art. Significantly, some of the most interesting work on Pier 34 directly referenced the art world rather than the waterfront. For example, Bidlo and Wojnarowicz collaborated on a window piece that included an image of a hanged artist whom they called a "victim of hype" (fig. 97). Denouncing SoHo art dealers like Mary Boone, it called on artists "to stay in control of your work . . . hearts + minds." Elsewhere, a critic was hanged in effigy and Andy Warhol was laid out in a casket. The anonymity of these last two works reinforced Bidlo and Wojnarowicz's idea that Pier 34 was a site that, resisting commercialism and competition, became a place to see art and be an artist, but where nothing—and no one—would be for sale.

Despite this ideal, however, hype came to Pier 34 quicker than anyone imagined it could. By June 1983, there were so many artists working and competing for territory on the increasingly crowded pier that murals were getting painted over. Publicity followed when the art critic Richard Goldstein wrote the first sustained appraisal of the scene for the *Village Voice*, accompanied by Hujar's photographs of Wojnarowicz's and Frangella's murals and Finn's garbage-bag figures. Goldstein wrote that a visitor "wandering onto the pier . . . might imagine himself stumbling upon the museum of a civilization long ago forgotten—or one that had forgotten about art." Yet the critic's enthusiasm was tempered by the foreboding that any "stylistic innovation is consumed and corrupted in the time between *Voice* deadlines. It took about that long for fashion photographers to discover the pier, and soon it was being used as a background for bathing suit ads."[26] Goldstein also reported that the Anonymous Artists Alliance (a group unrelated to either Wojnarowicz or Bidlo) had distributed leaflets inviting the art world to a wine-and-cheese opening at Pier 34. Unfortunately, the police showed up as well; Sterzing photographed the strange sight of the officers taking one of Bill Downer's sculptural figures into custody, as if they were arresting it. The police shut down the pier, but artists soon cut their way back in and continued to use it until its demolition a year later.

The Pier 34 experiment did not last long—for Wojnarowicz, a couple of years, for others, far less time. Ottersen admits that he was there at most twice, but that was long enough to paint the memorable image of a naked figure cowering under a table in the fetal position, as if to avoid impending Armageddon. Yet no matter how much time the artists spent on the waterfront, a repeated theme in their recollections is the richness and joy of the shared experience. Their memories are also tinged with enormous sadness, however. Keith Davis, Luis Frangella, Robert Jones, Richard Hofmann, Peter Hujar, Huck Snyder, and David Wojnarowicz all succumbed to HIV/AIDS. Bauman recalls Snyder jokingly saying to her, "we're all going to be famous," adding portentously, "I hope it's not going to be after we all die."[27]

One of Sterzing's final images of Pier 34 (fig. 48), a spectacular picture of the demolition of the façade, reveals Wojnarowicz's gagging cow peeking through the rubble. The photograph inevitably fills me with a sense of dread of what was to come. But Wojnarowicz lived for almost a decade after the demolition, and even as we mourn the passing of so many artists before their time, we must be careful not to see in Pier 34 a metaphor for the HIV/AIDS crisis. Above all, we need to resist the reductive and homophobic narratives of the 1980s that see HIV/AIDS as some sort of retribution for the supposed excesses of freedom and experimentation that were so central to the Pier 34 phenomenon and the larger queer waterfront scene. In the end, the power of Bidlo and Wojnarowicz's informal manifesto for Pier 34 lies not in the way it explains or celebrates this particular experiment in creating community, but rather in its encouragement to others to repeat it. Unsanctioned by the authorities and without funding from any museum, university, or other institution, much of the art of Pier 34 was made anonymously and without any intention to sell or exhibit it. To look through Sterzing's and his fellow photographers' remarkable images and to read the recollections of the artists is to sense the exhilaration of this moment of freedom along the waterfront. Bidlo and Wojnarowicz insisted that it could happen again: "This is just a start for all of us. We are all responsible for what it currently is and what it will become. This is something possible anywhere there are abandoned buildings. This is something possible everywhere."[28]

Epilogue

I cover the waterfront
I'm watching the sea
Will the one I love
Be coming back to me?

—"I Cover the Waterfront," music and lyrics by Johnny Green and Edward Heyman

Throughout the 1980s, one by one, the pier buildings on the Hudson waterfront below 14th Street were demolished. The year 1984 saw not only the end of Pier 34 but also the defeat of the multibillion-dollar Westway project, which would have replaced the collapsed elevated highway with an underground freeway topped with green open spaces. The abandonment of the Westway scheme freed up funds and planning resources to move ahead with more modest plans to renovate the existing West Street system. Money was made available to demolish the old terminals, to rebuild a ground-level roadway along West Street and 12th Avenue, and to create a network of parks, promenades, and recreation piers that was largely completed by 2017. With the realization that the area would not be mired in endless construction, money poured into real estate, including a two-bedroom condo designed by Richard Meier that, according to the *New York Times*, was listed in 2012 for $6.75 million In 2009, the first leg of the celebrated High Line opened. It used the old

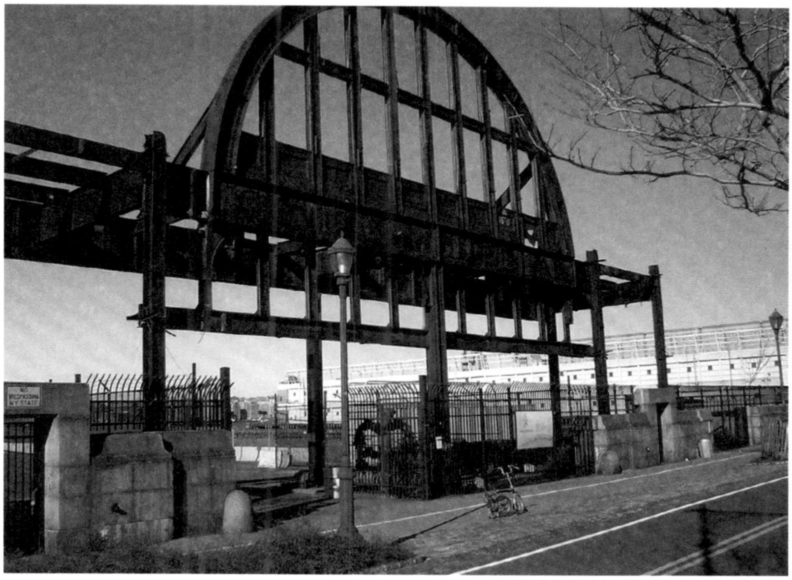

98. Jim Henderson, *Cunard Steel Arch, Pier 54*, 2008. Photo: Wikimedia Commons.

New York Central Railroad spur, which, ironically, was originally designed to assure the viability of shipping in the piers but quickly became obsolete. The finished elevated park runs from Gansevoort Street—three blocks below 14th Street, in the Meatpacking District—through Chelsea to the old Hudson Yards, which is being replaced by a gleaming new city within a city of skyscrapers and shopping malls.

Art still happens on the waterfront, but now it is mostly sanctioned and very expensive, enshrined in Chelsea galleries and the newly relocated Whitney Museum of American Art. Designed by Renzo Piano, the new Whitney vaguely resembles one of the huge passenger steamships that used to dock in the old Cunard terminals a few blocks uptown. All that remains of the beautiful Beaux-Arts façades that lined the Hudson is the metal armature that held up the entrance to Pier 54 (fig. 98), which has been repurposed as the gateway to the pedestrian pier. I appreciate the gesture of saving something from the waterfront's past, but I wonder what it could mean to younger generations. It misleadingly evokes some past conflagration, like the preserved fragments of the World Trade Center, rather than the less glamorous story of how grand places eventually become obsolete.

When the new Whitney opened in 2015, visitors could gaze from its numerous balconies out at the Hudson River and the empty space where

Gordon Matta-Clark's *Day's End* made its debut. This area, once an outpost of the Sanitation Department, was then in the process of being converted into more parkland in consultation with the Whitney, which considered various plans for art projects and programming in partnership with the city. Unlike many critics, I very much like the new museum itself, particularly the way its windowed galleries and balconies look out on the city.[2] Most museums close themselves off physically from their surroundings, but the Whitney has consciously tried to find ways to engage with the neighborhood, in terms of both its educational programming and the way its design opens itself up to the area. Unlike virtually everyone else with an opinion, I hate the High Line. This idiosyncratic response undoubtedly reflects my personal history with the waterfront. Each year it brings more than five million people into a part of the city that I used to feel was my special world. I miss painting on the abandoned West Side Highway on a weekday morning, as if I owned it. Surely, the High Line represents the very opposite of the excitement and danger I felt cruising the waterfront, whether on the abandoned highway, in the labyrinths of Pier 46, or simply walking along West Street. Who knew what I would find?

If cruising the waterfront in the late 1970s had some of the quality of Guy Debord's *dérive*, in which a situation is created where unforeseen things might occur, the High Line today is the perfect example of what Debord called the spectacle—modern life made over into an image. Watching from street level the endless stream of people going back and forth in a predictable pattern, I am reminded of an old *Star Trek* episode in which the *Enterprise* visits a planet that is free of disease but so crowded that there is no room for anyone to do anything but stagger along, pressed against a mass of other bodies.[3] Of course, I am not immune to the High Line's pleasures on a warm spring day, to the lovely and ecologically sound plantings and the splendid vistas, but I hate the way it eliminates all the chaotic aspects of urban life, the flaneur's journeying without destination that Wojnarowicz was so good at describing in his journals. The High Line's path is linear, prescribed, and curated—like an exhibition. All the complications and anxieties of circumventing complex neighborhoods are eliminated—you don't even have to stop for traffic lights. New York becomes something to look at rather than be in.

Of course, even though the waterfront has changed dramatically since the demolition of the piers and the subsequent creation of the High Line, the stories told in this book about the overlapping and adjacencies between subcultures, and the way that art and cruising mixed, did not end all at once. In

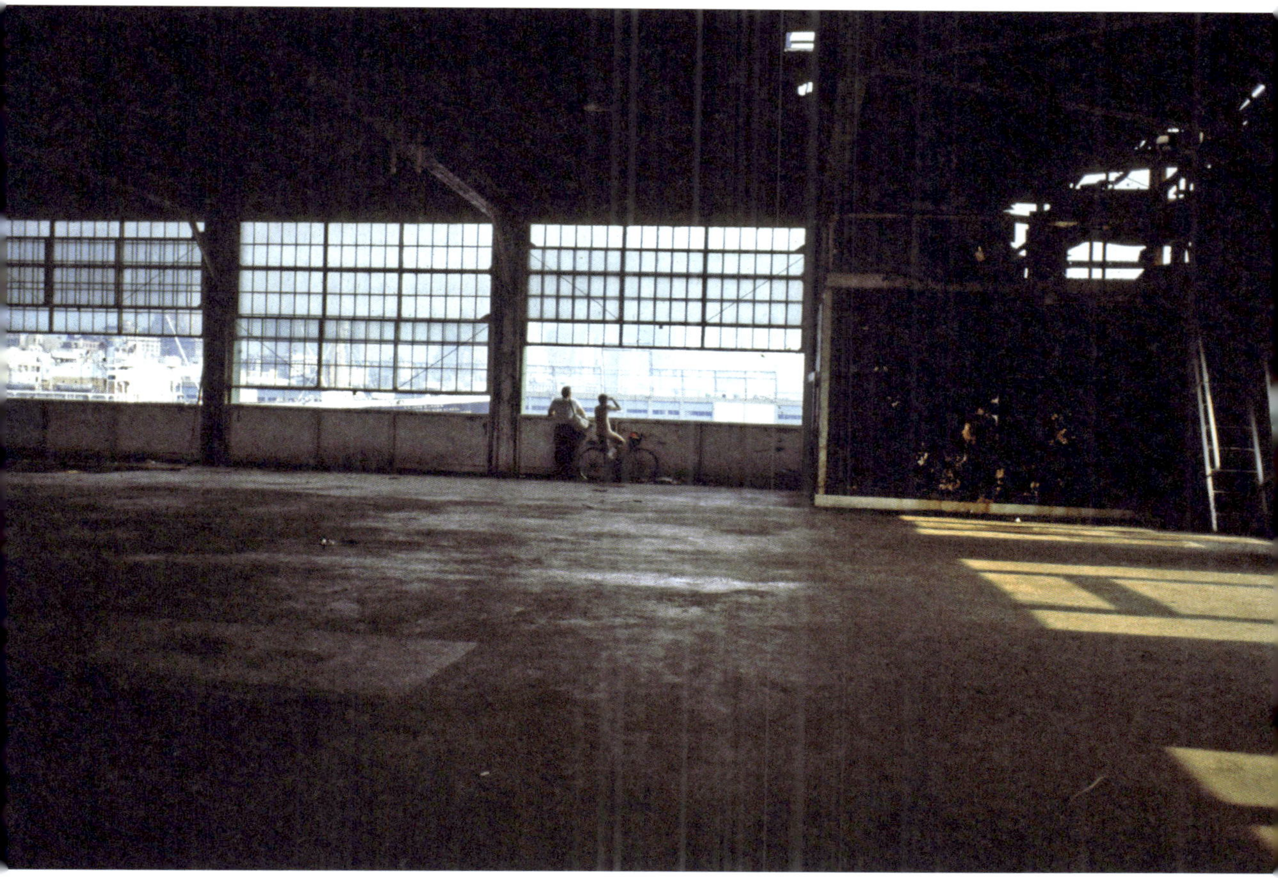

99. Efrain Gonzalez, *Pier 45*, ca. 1985. © Efrain Gonzalez.

the later 1980s, after Pier 46 was destroyed, anonymous sex between men gravitated to Pier 45, but with the death toll from the AIDS epidemic rising, public sex became less popular. The epidemic dampened the optimism of 1970s writing about the liberating and communal role of anonymous sex, which took on an unsavory reputation in the gay community, even though many of its practitioners followed safer sex guidelines.

As the evocative photographs of Efrain Gonzalez suggest, the waterfront continued to be a place of unsanctioned behavior into the 1990s. Gonzalez is probably best known for his photographs of the Meatpacking District's Hellfire Club, which catered to a bisexual leather scene, but he also documented the outdoor night life of the area as it increasingly became a hangout for LGBTQ youth of color in the 1980s and '90s. In terms of the pier scene, Gonzalez took many photographs of Pier 45 (fig. 99). Unlike Pier 46 and Pier 48, it remained in relatively good shape until it too was demolished.[4]

By 1989 I had moved on from the piers, at least physically, to Connecticut. I therefore missed witnessing the struggle by members of the queer community and organizations like FIERCE to resist the redevelopment plans, which ignored the interests of LGBTQ youth.[5] On many levels, FIERCE took up the cause first initiated by Sylvia Rivera, who along with Marsha P. Johnson founded Street Transvestite Action Revolutionaries (STAR) and advocated for homeless and transgender youth until her death in 2002.

Whatever the waterfront below 14th Street has now become, it no longer feels like a margin, a point where the order and coherence of modern life unravel. Throughout the twentieth century, the docks—at their economic height in the 1920s and their nadir in the 1970s—were a place of fascination and danger, desire and violence. Bordering the epicenter of commerce, they were also where capitalism seemed to lose its footing. Now the area has become a major art center. But chances are that it too will fall into decay, as its current pleasures and commodities fall out of style.

When I began this project more than a decade ago, I was most obsessed with relationships between the art and the anonymous sex that took place on the waterfront. But, increasingly, I have become just as fascinated with the buildings themselves. What did the building on Pier 46 actually look like? What would it be like to walk in it again in 1979, when I would be most likely to run into David Wojnarowicz, perhaps as he was spray-painting some phrase on the wall? In the hope of better understanding the layout and structure of Pier 46, I enlisted the expertise of the architect and set designer Alexander McCargar. I asked McCargar to look with me at a group of photographs of Pier 46 by Leonard Fink, Alvin Baltrop, Frank Hallam, and Stanley Stellar. We compared these still images to footage of Pier 46 from the porn film *Non-Stop*, made on location in 1979. We tried to figure out how the rooms in Pier 46 connected, and where the graffiti by Wojnarowicz and Tava were placed in relation to each other. Alex suggested that we ignore the overall look of the room and instead pay attention to things like moldings, or the way in which the paint was chipped on the walls. I was struck by how putting all these photographs of the same rooms together undoes the work of the crop and the close-up, in which the photographer and filmmaker guide our eyes. Suddenly we were free to look around, as it were. Miraculously, one image connected with another and whole rooms opened up to us. For example, there are several Hallam and Fink pictures of the rooms in which Wojnarowicz spray-painted. Hallam's photograph of July 1979 shows the walls largely empty of his graffiti; by 1980, the walls in Fink's photographs are already being covered up by the tags of other artists. Another exciting discovery was that the mural of a giant penis ejaculating into the mouth of a man, before which Hujar posed for Stellar, was the same room with Wojnarowicz's image of a man shooting up heroin.

This process of reconstruction, analogous to archeological digging, gave me the sensation that I was there again. But that feeling was frustrated by the realization that our collection of images was woefully incomplete; we didn't have photographs for all the rooms and walls. Undoubtedly, there is much more evidence out there to find and process. I am not sure whether the incomplete archive that I have collected helps me remember what it was really like to be on the piers, or whether it is creating false memories. And why am I obsessed only with what the pier buildings looked like? What about the smells, and the sounds? What about the beautiful boys I would sometimes see there, distracting me from the graffiti and the views? This study of ruins that you are reading is yet another ruin. Of course, this would have been no surprise to Jacques Derrida, who claimed that experience itself was a ruin and that "scopic pulsion, voyeurism itself, is always on the lookout for the originary ruin. A narcissistic melancholy, a memory—in mourning—of love itself."[6] It was all preordained that fateful day when I first stepped out on the pier.

Notes

Introduction

1. Jacques Derrida, *Memoirs of the Blind: The Self-Portrait and Other Ruins*, translated by Pascale-Anne Brault and Michael Naas (Chicago: University of Chicago Press, 1993), 69.

2. Gordon Matta-Clark, *Gordon Matta-Clark*, edited by Corinne Diserens, with survey by Thomas Crow and essays by Judith Russi Kirshner and Christian Kravagna (London: Phaidon Press, 2003), 12.

3. Matta-Clark, 12–15.

4. George Segal, "On Whitman and Things," *Arts Magazine*, November 1972, 54–55.

5. Walter Benjamin, *The Arcades Project*, translated by Howard Eiland and Kevin McLaughlin (Cambridge, Mass.: Harvard University Press, 1999), 460.

6. Benjamin, 873–74.

7. Dianne Chisholm, *Queer Constellations: Subcultural Space in the Wake of the City* (Minneapolis: University of Minnesota Press, 2004), 47.

8. Walter Benjamin, "A Berlin Chronicle," in *Walter Benjamin: Selected Writings*, vol. 2, edited by Michael W. Jennings, Howard Eiland, and Gary Smith (Cambridge, Mass.: Belknap Press of Harvard University Press, 2001), 600.

9. Michel Foucault and Jay Miskowiec, "Of Other Spaces," *Diacritics* 16, no. 1 (1986): 24, 25, 27.

10. Michel Foucault, "What Is an Author?," *Screen* 20, no. 1 (1979), 28.

11. Guy Hocquenghem, *Homosexual Desire*, translated by Daniella Dangoor (Durham: Duke University Press, 1993), 131–32.

12. Morgan Gwenwald, email to author, 23 August 2017.

13. Christopher Castiglia and Christopher Reed, *If Memory Serves: Gay Men, AIDS, and the Promise of the Queer Past* (Minneapolis: University of Minnesota Press, 2011), 43–44.

Chapter 1

1. See, for example, http://obscuri tyandbeyond.blogspot.com/2010/02 /lost-movie-detective-him-1974.html, accessed 8 November 2017.

2. My source for Tava's statements consists of slides that Frank Hallam took of an article written about Tava's work by Rick Leed in the New York Briefs column of *Blue Boy*, a gay skin magazine. I am not sure of the exact date, however, since he did not photograph the entire article and I have not been able to locate a copy of the original magazine.

3. AA Bronson, interview by Randall Wilcox, posted on the website www.bal-trop.org, accessed 23 January 2009.

4. In his memoir, Delany refers to Kestenbaum by his first name only, but he told me his full name via email in 2013.

5. Samuel R. Delany, *The Motion of Light in Water: Sex and Science Fiction Writing in the East Village, 1957–1965* (New York: New American Library, 1988), 120–21.

6. Delany, 130.

7. Delany, 174.

8. Marco Vassi, "An Evening at the Trucks," *Gay*, 20 December 1971, 5.

9. Charles Shively, "Indiscriminate Promiscuity as an Act of Revolution

(1974)," in *Come Out Fighting: A Century of Essential Writing on Gay and Lesbian Liberation*, edited by Chris Bull (New York: Thunder's Mouth Press/Nation Books, 2001), 138.

10. Shively, 138.

11. Audre Lorde, "The Uses of the Erotic," in *The Lesbian and Gay Studies Reader*, edited by Henry Abelove, Michéle Aina Barale, and David M. Halperin (New York: Routledge, 1993), 340. This landmark essay was originally given as a paper on 25 August 1978 at the Fourth Berkshire Conference on the History of Women, Mount Holyoke College.

12. Pat Califia, *Public Sex: The Culture of Radical Sex* (Pittsburgh: Cleis Press, 1994), 11. Califia later transitioned to Patrick.

13. Quoted in Arthur Bell, "Mayhem on the Gay Waterfront," *Village Voice*, 13 January 1975, 5.

14. Bell, 5.

15. Bell, 5.

16. Andrew Holleran, "Nostalgia for the Mud," in *The Christopher Street Reader*, edited by Michael Denneny, Charles Ortleb, and Thomas Steele (New York: Coward-McCann, 1983), 69. This essay was originally published in the January 1979 issue of *Christopher Street*.

17. Bell, "Mayhem on the Gay Waterfront," 5.

18. *Warehouse Newsletter* 2, no. 1 (5–7 September 1975): 1–2.

19. John S. Turcott, "The Village Piers: A Muggers' Paradise," *Our Town*, 14 November 1975, 1, 12.

20. Frank Hallam, interview by author, 17 May 2009, Manhattan.

21. Robert Whitman, interview by author, 5 February 2009, Greenwich, Connecticut.

22. One frustrating aspect of both Segal's and Whitman's accounts of *Architecture* is the vagueness about the location of the pier where the piece began. Both describe meeting at Chambers and West Streets, directly across from Pier 20 and the Chambers Street Ferry Terminal, but Whitman suggests that this area had already been cleared in preparation for the building of Battery Park City. He speaks of walking a few blocks south. Although no pier number is given, both Segal and Whitman agree that the piece culminated in the waiting room of the Hoboken Ferry Terminal, which was sandwiched between Piers 15 and 16. Segal's description suggests that the group passed through several structures, presumably on either Pier 15 or Pier 16, or perhaps both, before ending up in the ferry terminal.

23. George Segal, "On Whitman and Things," *Arts Magazine*, November 1972, 53–55.

24. Whitman, interview.

25. Segal, "On Whitman and Things," 53.

26. Guy Debord, "Theory of the Dérive," *Les Lèvres Nues* 9 (November 1956), reprinted in *Internationale Situationniste* 2 (December 1958), translated by Ken Knabb, http://www.cddc.vt.edu/sionline/si/theory.html, accessed 20 April 2017.

27. Robert Whitman, interview by Richard Kostelanetz, in *The Theatre of Mixed Means: An Introduction to Happenings, Kinetic Environments, and Other Mixed-Means Presentations* (New York: Dial Press, 1968), 224, quoted in Lynn Cooke, "Robert Whitman: Playback," in *Robert Whitman: Playback*, edited by Lynne Cooke and Karen Kelly, with Bettina Funcke (New York: Dia Art Foundation, 2003), 12.

Chapter 2

1. Vito Acconci, interview by author, 19 April 2009, Brooklyn.

2. Kate Linker, *Vito Acconci* (New York: Rizzoli, 1994), 42.

3. Acconci, interview.

4. Linker, *Vito Acconci*, 42.

5. Michael Kimmelman, "Vito Acconci: From Infamous to Naughty," *New York Times*, 24 March 1991.

6. Willoughby Sharp discusses the project in Luca Lo Pinto, "A Portrait of a Transcontinental Cultural Catalyst: A Dialogue with Willoughby Sharp," *Nero* 14 (June–July 2007): 53–55. He mentions inviting twenty-eight artists, but the 1992 Shunk catalogue lists only twenty-seven (perhaps Sharp meant Shunk-Kender to count as the twenty-eighth). The Pier 18 photographs were originally exhibited at the Museum of Modern Art in 1971. In 1992, the Musée d'art moderne et d'art contemporain in Nice organized an exhibition of the photographs and published a catalogue with an interview with Harry Shunk. In the catalogue, all of the photographs are attributed solely to Shunk. In fact, there is no mention of Kender in the extensive catalogue. See Harry Shunk, *Projects: Pier 18* (Nice: Musée d'Art Moderne et d'Art Contemporain, 1992), quotation on p. 14. The Shunk-Kender archive now is housed at the Getty Research Institute, which has made many of the images of Pier 18 accessible online.

7. Lynne Cooke, "From Site to Non-Site: An Introduction to *Mixed Use, Manhattan*," in *Mixed Use, Manhattan: Photography and Related Practices, 1970s to the Present*, edited by Lynne Cooke and Douglas Crimp, with Kristin Poor (Cambridge , Mass.: MIT Press, 2010), 40.

8. Quoted in Douglas Crimp, *Before Pictures* (Brooklyn: Dancing Foxes Press, 2016), 163.

9. Vito Acconci, *Vito Acconci: Diary of a Body, 1969–1973* (New York: Charta, 2006), 248–49.

10. Lee Jaffe, interview by author, 19 November 2016, Yonkers. Jaffe also discussed with me his piece *Impact*, which involved another collaboration with Acconci. The two artists ran as fast as they could into each other, testing to see who would veer away at the last second. According to Jaffe, this piece recalled for Acconci the game of chicken in the hyper-homoerotic film *Rebel Without a Cause*. It is a parody of the 1960s Clairol hair-color ad, "the closer he gets, the better you look," in which a straight man and woman run in romantic slow motion into each other's arms.

11. For a discussion of the film and its origins, see the 2005 book edition of Malcolm Johnson's original exposés—Johnson, *On the Waterfront* (New York: Chamberlain Bros., 2005)—with an introduction by Budd Schulberg, who wrote the screenplay for *On the Waterfront*.

12. Acconci, interview.

13. Geoffrey Hendricks, phone interview by author, 15 June 2009.

14. Larry Smith, "Participation on a Pier: the Untrustworthy Artist," *The Village Voice*, May 15, 1971, 30, 48.

15. Vito Acconci, phone interview by author, 9 June 2009.

16. Reed wrote this comment on a draft of my book manuscript. For an extended critique of the progressiveness of the avant-garde in relation to queer subcultures, see Christopher Reed, *Art and Homosexuality: A History of Ideas* (Oxford: Oxford University Press, 2011).

17. Acconci, *Diary of a Body*, 259.

Chapter 3

1. Louise Désy and Gwendolyn Owens, "The Gordon Matta-Clark Archive at the Canadian Centre for Architecture," handout given out to researchers by the Canadian Centre for Architecture, 2008. First published in Lorenzo Fusi and Marco Pierini, *Gordon Matta-Clark*, exh. cat. (Siena: SMS Contemporanea and Silvana Editoriale, 2008), 201–8. The misconception that *Office Baroque* was the only major work still standing at Matta-Clark's death may have been allowed to circulate at the time in the hope of saving it.

2. Gordon Matta-Clark, "My Understanding of Art (ca. 1975)," in *Gordon Matta-Clark: Works and Collected Writings*, edited by Gloria Moure (Barcelona: Ediciones Poligrafa, 2006), 204.

3. Quoted in Mary Jane Jacob, *Gordon Matta-Clark: A Retrospective* (Chicago: Museum of Contemporary Art, 1985), 142.

4. Matta-Clark, "Gordon Matta-Clark: Dilemmas; A Radio Interview with Liza Béar, March 1976," in Matta-Clark, *Works and Collected Writings*, 267.

5. Arch Brown, interview by author, 26 February 2009, Palm Springs, California.

6. Gordon Matta-Clark to Wolfgang Becker, 8 September 1975, quoted in Thomas Crow, "Gordon Matta-Clark," in Gordon Matta-Clark, *Gordon Matta-Clark*, edited by Corinne Diserens, with survey by Thomas Crow and essays by Judith Russi Kirshner and Christian Kravagna (London: Phaidon Press, 2003), 8.

7. Gordon Matta-Clark, "Gordon Matta-Clark's Building Dissections: An Interview by Donald Wall," in Matta-Clark, *Works and Collected Writings*, 68.

8. Thomas Crow, *Art in the Common Culture* (New Haven: Yale University Press, 1996), 135.

9. Matta-Clark, "Interview by Donald Wall," 69.

10. Gordon Matta-Clark, "Gordon Matta-Clark's Building Dissections" (undated typescript), in Matta-Clark, *Works and Collected Writings*, 132–33.

11. Matta-Clark, "My Understanding of Art," 204.

12. Matta-Clark, "Interview with Gordon Matta-Clark, Antwerp, 1977," interview by Internationaal Cultureel Centrum, in Matta-Clark, *Works and Collected Writings*, 252–53.

13. Jane Crawford, "Crossover References in the Work of Roberto Matta and Gordon Matta-Clark," transcript of a conference at the Museum of Contemporary Art, Chicago, October 2002, reprinted in Matta-Clark, *Gordon Matta-Clark*, 217.

14. Quoted in Crow, "Gordon Matta-Clark," 11.

15. Quoted in Jacob, *Matta-Clark: A Retrospective*, 142.

16. Matta-Clark, "Gordon Matta-Clark: The Making of Pier 52, an Interview with Liza Béar, March 11, 1976," in Matta-Clark, *Works and Collected Writings*, 215.

17. Tina Kukielski, "In the Spirit of the Vegetable: The Early Works of Gordon Matta-Clark (1969–71)," in *Gordon Matta-Clark: You Are the Measure*, exh. cat., edited by Elisabeth Sussman (New York: Whitney Museum of American Art, 2007), 42.

18. Crow, "Gordon Matta-Clark," 28.

19. Carl Jung, *The Archetypes and the Collective Unconscious*, translated by R. F. C. Hull (Princeton: Princeton University Press, 1990), 21; see also 38.

20. Matta-Clark, "Interview by Donald Wall," 57.

21. William Rubin, *Matta*, exh. cat. (New York: Museum of Modern Art, 1957), 4.

22. As far as I know, Matta-Clark never mentioned his father's painting or Roberto Matta's fantasy about the Hanged Man inhabiting his wife's pregnant body. And yet it is inconceivable to me that Matta-Clark would not have read William Rubin's catalogue for the MOMA's retrospective of his father's work and spent time contemplating the import of the drawing of his own mother's womb.

23. The connection between Gordon Matta-Clark and Yves Klein has been explored in a physical and satirical way by the performance artist Danny Devos in his 2009 work *A Bastard Meeting Between Yves Klein and Gordon Matta-Clark on the Gold-Plated Corpse of James Lee Byars*.

24. Roger W. McAdam, *Floating Palaces: New England to New York on the Old Fall River Line* (Lincoln, R.I.: Andrew Mowbray, 1972).

25. Matta-Clark, "Work with Abandoned Structures, ca. 1975" (typescript), in Matta-Clark, *Works and Collected Writings*, 141.

26. Gordon Matta-Clark, "Matta-Clark's Childhood Influences," interview by Donald Wall, *Architecture New Jersey* (July–August–September 1979), 24.

27. Pamela M. Lee, *Object to Be Destroyed: The Work of Gordon Matta-Clark* (Cambridge, Mass.: MIT Press, 2000), 123.

28. Matta-Clark, "Making of Pier 52," 216.

29. I would like to thank my colleague at Yale University, the mathematician Roger Howe, for his help in finding the right term to describe the shape.

30. Quoted in Jacob, *Matta-Clark: A Retrospective*, 25.

31. Matta-Clark, "Making of Pier 52," 219.

Chapter 4

1. David Wojnarowicz, *In the Shadow of the American Dream: The Diaries of David Wojnarowicz*, edited by Amy Scholder (New York: Grove Press, 1999), 148 (undated entry).

2. Wojnarowicz, 146 (entry dated 6 March 1980).

3. See Tony Kushner, "Introduction," in David Wojnarowicz, *The Waterfront Journals*, edited by Amy Scholder (New York: Grove Press, 1996), xi–xv.

4. Sylvère Lotringer and Giancarlo Ambrosino, *David Wojnarowicz: A Definitive History of Five or Six Years on the Lower East Side* (Cambridge, Mass.: Semiotext[e], 2006), 159.

5. Lotringer and Ambrosino, 168.

6. Michel Foucault, "Sexual Choice, Sexual Act: An Interview with Michel Foucault," interview by James O'Higgins, *Salamagundi* 58–59 (Fall 1982–Winter 1983): 19.

7. Wojnarowicz, *Shadow of the American Dream*, 169 (undated entry).

8. Wojnarowicz, 138 (entry dated 21 February 1980).

9. In 1983 our paintings were in *The Saint Show* at the Harm Bouckaert Gallery in New York City, but I have no memory of being introduced to Wojnarowicz, nor do I know whether he was even at the opening.

10. In 1990, on the occasion of the first gallery exhibition of the *Arthur Rimbaud* series, Wojnarowicz told David Hirsch, "it was the first series or body of work that I was able to accomplish." David Hirsch, "New York Adventure: David Wojnarowicz, P.P.O.W.," *New York Native*, 3 December 1990, 48.

11. There have been some discrepancies about the dates of the *Arthur Rimbaud* series. In the exhibition catalogue *David Wojnarowicz: Tongues of Flame*, edited by Barry Blinderman (Normal, Ill.: University Galleries of Illinois State University, 1990), perhaps with Wojnarowicz's approval, it is given the date 1978–79. However, Wojnarowicz's biographer Cynthia Carr insists that he did not start posing figures with the Rimbaud mask until 1979. The discrepancy may be due to the fact that Wojnarowicz made drawings of Rimbaud masturbating in 1978 that became a kind of template for the 1979 photograph on the same theme.

12. See Jim Lewis and Andrew Roth, *David Wojnarowicz: Rimbaud in New York, 1978–79* (New York: Roth Horowitz, 2004) for the most extensive publication of the photographs in the series that were both printed by Wojnarowicz and his estate.

13. These scripts are now in the David Wojnarowicz Papers at the Fales Library, New York University (NYU).

14. Sylvia Falcon, "Twenty Artists: David Wojnarowicz," *East Village Eye*, October 1983, 17.

15. Quoted in Mysoon Rizk, "Nature, Death, and Spirituality in the Work of David Wojnarowicz" (PhD diss., University of Illinois at Urbana-Champaign, 1997), 25.

16. Hirsch, "New York Adventure," 48.

17. Blinderman, *Tongues of Flame*, 118.

18. Quoted in Rizk, "Nature, Death, and Spirituality," 25.

19. Cynthia Carr, *Fire in the Belly: The Life and Times of David Wojnarowicz* (New York: Bloomsbury, 2012), 133. See also Donald Kuspit, "The Last Rimbaud," in *The Rebirth of Painting in the Late Twentieth Century* (New York: Cambridge University Press, 2000).

20. Arthur Rimbaud, *Rimbaud: Complete Works, Selected Letters*, translated by Wallace Fowlie (Chicago: University of Chicago Press, 1966), 303–5.

21. This unpublished, unsent letter is in the David Wojnarowicz Papers, Fales Library, NYU.

22. Craig Owens, "The Allegorical Impulse: Toward a Theory of Post-Modernism, Part 2," *October* 13 (Spring 1980): 76.

23. Rosalind Krauss, *Cindy Sherman, 1975–1993* (New York: Rizzoli, 1993), 17.

24. Louise Lawler, "Prominence Given, Authority Taken: An Interview with Louise Lawler," interview by Douglas Crimp, *Grey Room* 4 (Summer 2001): 80.

25. Douglas Crimp, *Before Pictures* (Brooklyn: Dancing Foxes Press, 2016), 181.

26. David Wojnarowicz, journal entries, 8 May 1978, David Wojnarowicz Papers, Fales Library, NYU.

27. Patti Smith, *Just Kids* (New York: HarperCollins, 2010), 23.

28. Edmund White, *Rimbaud: The Double Life of a Rebel* (New York: Atlas & Co., 2008), 1.

29. Dennis Cooper, "Introduction," *Little Caesar* 5 (1977): 3.

30. The image of Wojnarowicz and the Eiffel Tower appears in Wojnarowicz's 1978 Paris journal in the David Wojnarowicz Papers, Fales Library, NYU.

31. Enid Starkie, *Arthur Rimbaud* (New York: New Directions, 1961), 144.

Chapter 5

1. Frank Hallam, interview by author, 17 May 2009, Manhattan.

2. Hallam, interview.

3. Joseph Lovett, unpublished transcript of the film *Gay Sex in the 70s* (2005).

4. Alvin Baltrop, "Ashes from a Flame: Photographs by Alvin Baltrop," manuscript, edited by Randall Wilcox, quoted in Douglas Crimp, *Before Pictures* (Brooklyn: Dancing Foxes Press, 2016), 171.

5. Shelley Seccombe, *Lost Waterfront: The Decline and Rebirth of Manhattan's Western Shore* (New York: Fordham University Press and Friends of Hudson River Park, 2007), 13–14.

6. Seccombe, 57.

7. Frank Hallam's journals are housed in the LGBT Community Center National History Archive in New York.

8. Frank Holland [Frank Hallam], *Debut: Chicago, 1952* (Bloomington, Ind.: Xlibris, 2008), 9–11. This novel was self-published.

9. See Douglas Crimp, "Alvin Baltrop: Pier Photographs, 1975–1986," *Artforum*, February 2008, 262–73. See also Alvin Baltrop, *Alvin Baltrop: The Piers*, edited by James Reid and Tom Watt (Madrid: TF Editores, 2015).

10. Baltrop, "Ashes from a Flame," quoted in Crimp, *Before Pictures*, 171.

11. Unless otherwise noted, the details about Fink's working method and life come from speaking to Leonard Fink's close friend James-John Joseph (Jim) Gigliello, whom I interviewed by phone on 15 May 2014. Gigliello, a psychologist, met Fink through a mutual friend in the leather community in 1980. Jim modeled for Fink and spent time with him both in the darkroom and out photographing in the city.

12. Gigliello insists that the photographs were never exhibited in his lifetime. Fink's cousin Susan Caplan, however, believes that they may have been in some sort of exhibition, although she herself did not see it. I interviewed Susan Caplan on 13 May 2014 in Manhattan.

13. Gigliello, interview.

14. Guy Hocquenghem, *Homosexual Desire*, translated by Daniella Dangoor (Durham: Duke University Press, 1993), 103.

15. Stanley Stellar, interview by author and Darren Jones, 22 November 2011, Manhattan.

16. Hallam told me that when he was volunteering at the Gay and Lesbian Center, he saw pictures of himself taken by Fink, but I have not located them.

17. Arthur Tress, interview by author, 26 December 2002, Cambria, California.

18. Hocquenghem, *Homosexual Desire*, 131–32.

19. Stellar, interview.

Chapter 6

This chapter is based on the research I did for the exhibition and catalogue *Something Possible Everywhere: Pier 34, NYC, 1983–84*, which I curated at the 205 Hudson Gallery of Hunter College of the City University of New York in 2016. The exhibition featured the photographs of Andreas Sterzing and works from the period by many of the artists discussed in this chapter. I thank the staff of the gallery, especially Susan Breyer, Mikey Estes, Tim Laun, Joachim Pissarro, Jocelyn Spaar, Sarah Watson, and Annie Wischmeyer, for their support and guidance.

1. See U.S. Army Corps of Engineers, *The Port of New York: In Three Parts*, part 2, *Piers, Wharves, and Docks* (Washington, D.C.: Government Printing Office, 1932), 334.

2. Barry Blinderman, ed., *David Wojnarowicz: Tongues of Flame*, exh. cat. (Normal, Ill.: University Galleries of Illinois State University, 1990), 54.

3. David Wojnarowicz, *In the Shadow of Forward Motion*, exh. cat. (New York: P.P.O.W., 1989), 18.

4. James Romberger, email to author, 18 March 2017. Romberger and his wife, Marguerite Van Cook, generously shared their thoughts and memories about Wojnarowicz and his work.

5. Stan Lee, Roy Thomas, and Neal Adams, *X-Men: In the Shadow of Sauron*, no. 60 of *X-Men*, September 1969, 17.

6. *Krazy Kat*, 15 October 1934, reprinted in Michael Tisserand, *Krazy: George Herriman, a Life in Black and White* (New York: HarperCollins, 2016).

7. In the end, *Life* chose a different picture of Wojnarowicz in which he is not holding the machine gun.

8. James Romberger and Marguerite Van Cook confirmed that Wojnarowicz was a fan of Pee-Wee Herman, or at least of the later children's show, and that he always had dinosaur toys around.

9. Mysoon Rizk, "Nature, Death, and Spirituality in the Work of David Wojnarowicz" (PhD diss., University of Illinois at Urbana-Champaign, 1997), 85.

10. Blinderman, *Tongues of Flame*, 54.

11. Significantly, in this regard, Wojnarowicz's first serious experiment in collage is the 1978 *Bill Burroughs' Recurring Dream*.

12. Cynthia Carr, *Fire in the Belly: The Life and Times of David Wojnarowicz* (New York: Bloomsbury, 2012), 224.

13. The image of Pat swimming appears in the weekly strip of *Terry and the Pirates* of 15 May 1935. See Milton Caniff, *The Complete Terry and the Pirates*, vol. 1 (San Diego: Library of American Comics, IDW Publishing, 2007). Wojnarowicz's lover Tom Rauffenbart, in the introduction to the 1996 edition of the collaborative graphic novel *7 Miles a Second*, mentions that Wojnarowicz's murals on the piers "were based" on *Terry and the Pirates* and *Krazy Kat*, although as far as I know, I am the first to try to locate the original strips. Tim Rauffenbart, "Introduction," in James Romberger, David Wojnarowicz, and Marguerite Van Cook, *7 Miles a Second* (New York: DC Comics, 1996), 2.

14. Blinderman, *Tongues of Flame*, 115. Cynthia Carr told me that Wojnarowicz recounted stories of these bus trips to

a lake, as did James Romberger, who drew an image of the young Wojnarowicz swimming in the second edition of *7 Miles a Second.* See James Romberger, David Wojnarowicz, and Marquerite Van Cook, *7 Miles a Second*, 2nd ed. (Seattle: Fantagraphics Books, 2012), 42.

15. In addition to the two videos discussed here, Marion Scemama shot footage of the piers for a film she discusses in an interview, in Sylvère Lotringer and Giancarlo Ambrosino, *David Wojnarowicz: A Definitive History of Five or Six Years on the Lower East Side* (Cambridge, Mass.: Semiotext[e], 2006).

16. I want to thank David Finn for making a video copy of this film available to me. In the run-up to the Hunter College Art Galleries Pier 34 exhibition, the graduate fellow Susan Breyer reached out to Japanese Public Television to see if they could locate the original raw footage for this video, but they were unable to locate it.

17. I want to thank Margaret Winslow, curator at the Delaware Art Museum, who brought to my attention this video, a copy of which was in Robert Jones's estate. Unfortunately, neither she nor his estate has been able to locate Eric Wolfe, and so we know nothing about the intended purpose of the video or whether it was ever shown publicly.

18. Quoted in Jonathan Weinberg and with Annie Wischmeyer, eds., *Something Possible Everywere: Pier 34, NYC, 1983–84*, exh. cat. (New York: Hunter College Art Galleries, 2016), 27.

19. Sophie Matisse, email to author, 10 August 2017.

20. Smith discusses Wojnarowicz's bringing her to the pier soon after meeting him in 1981, in Lotringer and Ambrosino, *Wojnarowicz: A Definitive History*, 83. She discusses the work she made in *Something Possible Everywere*, 63. Although I have no doubt that she was one of the first people Wojnarowicz took to the piers, her reminiscences seem to compress later visits into her initial tour, since in the Hunter College Art Galleries catalogue she talks about seeing Finn's sculpture, which wasn't created until 1983.

21. Mike Bidlo and David Wojnarowicz, "Statement," David Wojnarowicz Papers, Fales Library, New York University. The text was published in *Benzene* (Fall–Winter 1983–84), unpaginated.

22. Bidlo and Wojnarowicz.

23. Carr, *Fire in the Belly*, 224.

24. Quoted in Carr, 204.

25. Blinderman, *Tongues of Flame*, 54–56.

26. Richard Goldstein, "Post-Graffiti: The Pier Group Makes Its Mark," *Village Voice*, 21 June 1983, 41.

27. Sterzing told me of this conversation.

28. Bidlo and Wojnarowicz, "Statement."

Epilogue

1. C. J. Hughes, "On the Waterfront, Minus the Stevedores," *New York Times*, 21 September 2012.

2. See my review "Cruising the Waterfront," *Art in America* (May 2015): 128–35.

3. "The Mark of Gideon," episode 71 of *Star Trek*, first broadcast on 17 January 1969.

4. One of the best ways to get a sense of the beauty of Pier 45 before it fell into decay is to watch the 1978 film *The Eyes of Laura Mars*, which focuses on the story of a female fashion photographer (played by Faye Dunaway) stalked by a serial killer. Improbably, Mars's photo studio is located at the end of Pier 45. In a scene in which she is driven to her studio, and another in which she is chased by her stalker, we get a sense of the building's vast central hangar and its spectacular vistas of the adjacent piers.

5. For a discussion of the struggle against the redevelopment and gentrification of the waterfront and the rights

of LGBTQ youth of color, see Benjamin Shepard and Greg Smithsimon, *The Beach Beneath the Streets: Contesting New York City's Public Spaces* (Albany: State University of New York Press, 2011). FIERCE, "a membership-based organization building the leadership and power of lesbian, gay, bisexual, transgender, and queer (LGBTQ) youth of color in New York City," has produced, in collaboration with Paper Tiger Television and the Neutral Zone, *Fenced OUT*, a documentary that focuses on the waterfront and the organization's role in resisting gentrification and "raising awareness about the increasing displacement, violence, and criminalization experienced by LGBTSTQ youth of color." See the FIERCE website, http://www.fiercenyc.org/fenced-out-fierces-youth-produced-documentary, accessed 24 April 2017.

6. Jacques Derrida, *Memoirs of the Blind: The Self-Portrait and Other Ruins*, translated by Pascale-Anne Brault and Michael Naas (Chicago: University of Chicago Press, 1993), 68.

Index

Italicized page references indicate illustrations. Endnotes are indicated with "n" followed by the endnote number(s).